DEEPER ROOTS

ABOUT THE AUTHOR

Katherine Butler Jones' articles on African American family history have been published in *Orion, American Visions* and *Copia* magazines and in the anthology *The Harlem Reader,* edited by Herb Boyd (Crown 2003). Katherine was named the New England PEN Writers "Discovery" author in 1996 for non-fiction and in 2007, her play, *409 Edgecombe Avenue: The House on Sugar Hill* was produced at The Boston Center for the Arts. Katherine received her B.A. from Mount Holyoke College, her M.S. from Simmons College, her doctorate in Education from Harvard University and was a Fellow in the New York Public Library's Scholars-in-Residence Program at the Schomburg Center for Research in Black Culture. Katherine taught African American History at Boston University and Urban Education at Simmons and Wheelock Colleges. Katherine lives in Massachusetts with her husband. They have eight children and nine grandchildren.

DEEPER ROOTS:

AN AMERICAN ODYSSEY

Katherine Butler Jones

ISBN-13: 978-1490451411
ISBN-10: 1490451412

Printed in the United States
Cover Design by Vivian Ng

For my grandchildren: Alexander, Shannon, Julia, Khari,

Sophia, Nicholas, Malik, Micah and Xan

May you always remember the stories of the ancestors

and

Della Richards

A native of Costa Rica with Jamaican ancestry, Della made it

possible for me to be involved in the many activities that have

been a part of my life. She was a marvelous human being, a

second mother to our children, an amazing chef and a talented

seamstress. She was an integral part of our household for

eighteen years.

Rest in Peace

Contents

Acknowledgments

Special thanks to my husband Hubey and to our children: Karen, Lauren, Harlan, Renee, Lisa, Hamilton, Cheryl and Tanya who have inspired me by their example to keep moving down the road of life with hope, strength and confidence. Their spouses, John, Michael, Ken, Abim, Noland and Ibrahim have enriched my life.

Ann Aceves, Tim Ferguson and Shirley Stewart brought the publication of *Deeper Roots: An American Odyssey* from dream to reality. Barbara Beckwith, Vera Barad, Marie Brown, Bernice Buresh, Stephanie Friedman, Nadja Gould, Robert Hayden, Emily Heisted, Barbara Hindley, Julian Houston, Phebe Hoss, Willard Johnson, Gloria Powell, Diana Korzenik, Diana Lachatanere, Hylan Lewis, William McFeeley, Arnold Rampersad, Alice Shabekoff, Mable Smythe, Barbara Schwartz, Laverne Williams, Bennett Windheim, Vivian Ng and Thelma Wilson helped in so many ways to bring this project to fruition.

Left to Right: Lisa, Renee, Lauren, Karen,
Hubey, Harlan, Hamilton, Kathy holding
Cheryl - 1972

Tanya circa 1981

Introduction

Many years ago the Jones family, all ten of us—my husband Hubey and our eight children—gathered in the living room of our home in Newton, Massachusetts. Rays of sunshine streamed through the windows as our children Karen, Lauren, Harlan, Renee, Lisa, Hamilton, Cheryl and Tanya (ranging in age from seven to twenty at the time) sat on the gray sofa and slipcovered chairs ready to present their individual research on African American history. Our three invited judges, friends of the family and experts in the field, were there to offer their critiques. A prize of ten dollars would be awarded to the first-place winner; lesser amounts to the runners-up. Anxiety mixed with anticipation charged the air.

The idea for this contest came to me years before. As an educator, administrator and parent, I was confronting the need for African American history in the curriculum at all levels—preschool through graduate school. The event took hold as an annual family tradition. Each year the young people would write or recite a poem, present a report or select a person to tell us about. During this particular presentation Tanya, our youngest, has chosen to find out about Alex Haley. The miniseries based on his 1976 best-selling book, *Roots*, had captured her imagination. As part of Tanya's project she wrote to Haley, asking him questions and

Deeper Roots

requesting an autographed photograph. The long-awaited photograph and letter from Haley arrived one day before her presentation.

Tanya stands up. Her voice sings with joy as she tells the story of Haley's family saga that she has so carefully researched. Her two braids bounce on her shoulders and her face is radiant as she passes around the six-by-four envelope containing the precious letter and photo for all to see. On the brown envelope Haley has typed what he could decipher from Tanya's handwriting and has added this comment, "Postman, Please Help. Tanya, 7, wrote me giving this attached return address." The address, clipped from the bottom of her letter and taped to the large brown envelope, included her first name only and an incomplete home address.

Alex Haley began his letter by gently admonishing Tanya for omitting the important details of her family name and address. Then he told her, "I clearly remember when I was eight. In fact that was about the time that I was hearing from my grandmother the old family stories that stored away in my head and years and years later stirred my curiosity into starting a long research that finally led me into writing the book *Roots*."

When I told this story to my African American Studies class at Boston University, I offered it as a metaphor for the larger history of African Americans—many of whom, during slavery functioned without last names, address unknown. What country did you say you were from? To which group did you belong? The information was incomplete and often hard to come by. But, just as the mail carrier served as a link that enabled Alex Haley to reach Tanya Jones, this African American family history celebration in our living room was an attempt to fill in the gaps, create a link and make our connection with the past. I asked my students to interview their grandparents to understand the impact of world events on

Introduction

the lives of another generation by connecting to the larger world through personal histories and, more importantly, to solidify a generational bond.

The need to know who we are and where we came from can release an irresistible energy linking the past to the present. Today, increasing numbers of people are spending countless hours researching genealogy and traveling to areas of the world from which their forebears came. The use of DNA to connect with previous generations in distant places has become a reality.

Our daughter Renee, a senior in high school, gets up from the couch with her typewritten notes held in her slender brown hands. "I was born nine months after Mom and Dad took my brother and sisters on a trip to Jamaica, West Indies to meet Mom's family who lived there. I feel a special attachment to that country where my life began, so I called my grandmother in New York City to find out more about her birthplace."

Renee's distinctively low voice carries me back to that trip—to the quaint sleepy seaport town of Falmouth, Jamaica, where the blue-green waters of the Caribbean lap against the fine white sand. Just a stone's throw from the ocean was the small house where my Aunt Mae warmly greeted us at the door. When I crossed the living room and saw our wedding picture prominently displayed on the table, I knew we were truly an honored part of our Jamaican family.

"The sleepy town was too quiet for my grandmother," Renee reports. "She told me that some of the Falmouth women still carry bundles on their heads. My grandmother, Meme Clark, left on a boat bound for Manhattan in 1921. She came on vacation to see her sister and brothers who had moved to this country. It was the height of the Harlem Renaissance and Meme Clark never left." Renee continues, "My maternal grandfather died when Mom was fifteen years

Deeper Roots

old. To learn the story of my grandfather's family I telephoned Cousin Sue in Connecticut. She told me that Edward and Hannah Weeks, two of my great-great grandparents, lived near Canada in Keeseville, in the northernmost section of New York State. Cousin Sue said she thought they were involved with assisting escaped slaves, but later their daughter moved to Boston where my grandfather was born in 1882. By 1890 the family came to the 'promised land' of New York City where my grandparents later courted."

Our children, who are now adults in their thirties, forties and fifties, tell me that the information they learned from their annual research projects and their exposure to their history and culture were the most important gifts I ever gave them. I believe that this knowledge has subtly directed their life choices. Our children are artists, curators, teachers, psychologists, political and social organizers, law professors, international project managers, documentary film editors and researchers, news reporters, news researchers and news editors. I also believe that they have less fear of the things outside of their comfort zone for they have travelled all over the world for their cultural and educational enrichment, professional experience and for philanthropic purposes.

But right now I am curled up on the sofa watching television, wrapped in an Obama blanket from the last campaign. Hubey is settled in his favorite chair as we await the beginning of the second presidential debate between Mitt Romney and President Obama on this October evening in 2012. As the commentators drone on about what points need to be made by each of the opponents my thoughts bring me back to my introduction to Barack Obama and the inauguration of the first African American President of the United States of America.

Introduction

My daughter, Lisa, gave me an autographed copy of Obama's 1995 book, *Dreams From My Father* with the notation:

> *To Katherine Jones--*
> *I can't wait to read more about your own family's remarkable journey! All the best to you, and may our paths cross someday soon.*
> *Barack Obama*

The President was embarking on his political career after teaching and practicing civil rights law, and working as a community organizer in Chicago. Obama and my son-in-law were classmates at Harvard Law School and both were considered for the position of president of the *Harvard Law Review*. Obama would become the first African American to be elected to the position. They were friends and remained so after graduation. Ken and Lisa were early supporters and as I read his book and followed his progress—I became a fan as well.

By 2004 Obama's political star was starting to shine brightly and drawing the attention of the populace and the powerful. In the summer of 2007 during Obama's first presidential campaign I attended one of his fundraising events. I brought the signed copy of his book with me in the hopes that he would once again autograph it. After a brief conversation, he looked at my book and wrote:

> *To Katherine –*
> *I'm glad we met, and now look forward to seeing you in the White House!*
> *Barack Obama*

I was thrilled when he won and I could not wait to attend the inaugural ceremony.

Deeper Roots

Hubey and I left Boston on an early morning flight to Washington, D.C. on the bitter cold morning of Tuesday, January 20, 2009. We arrived at the ceremony as Vice President Joe Biden was addressing the multitude of people gathered on the mall. Long johns, woolen slacks, knee high boots, hat, gloves, scarfs and a fur coat my mother had given me was not enough to fend off what felt like sub-zero winds. Under all that clothing I also wore the cameo brooch handed down through generations of daughters from my great-grandmother. This was a perfect time to wear a brooch that symbolized a link between the past and the present because this inauguration symbolized the future.

The emotional excitement of this historic occasion shared with people from all over the country and the world was both joyous and sobering. I was close enough to the podium to see the oath-taking without the aid of binoculars. Our children, six of whom were in attendance stood further back in the crowd, and two others watched at home on television. Later that day, we cheered the President and First Lady as they paraded down Pennsylvania Avenue.

After the ceremony we ducked into Legal Seafood to warm our insides with lobster bisque. As we talked with people around the table we realized we had close mutual friends in common. We all rode the MTA with fellow Americans of all stripes, including farmers from Iowa, using passes specially printed for the occasion with the President's picture. Oh were those trains and buses filled to overflowing, yet not a word of complaint was uttered among the passengers.

We rested at the home of family members and changed clothes in preparation for the Inaugural Ball. Our great nieces helped me get ready by watching me apply makeup for the New England Ball—the last ball of many that the President and First Lady would attend. The Obamas arrived around

Introduction

midnight and danced as though this was their first event of the evening. That was a lovely time but it did not totally erase from my memory the nastiness of the campaign that preceded the ceremony and the balls. Now we were in the midst of another campaign.

There is no doubt that history was made when we elected Barack Obama in 2008. However, there was controversy during the campaign and after the election regarding President Obama's background. His opponents argued that he was not born in the United States and, therefore, did not meet the criteria to be President of the United States. But the President's maternal lineage was undeniably American (and white) and there was ample documentation to verify this. Opponents then suggested that hospital and birth records were altered/forged or just did not exist; that although his mother and grandparents were born in the United States, he was not.

Their focus also turned to the President's paternal lineage, which is based in Africa. A false link was then made to an African birth. Although there is no evidence to support any of these claims, the controversy continues against a standing President of the United States and that is appalling. There has never been a case in the history of the United States when a candidate's ancestry was called into question because those candidates have all been white.

It is no secret that those of the African diaspora were treated as chattel and in the vast majority of instances their existence was only recorded on a line of a slave owner's inventory list. But our President, strictly speaking, is not of the African diaspora. His mother was white and his father came to the United States to study and then returned to Africa. If President Obama's maternal background had been different, opponents might have been able to "muddy" his lineage enough to plant doubt as to his citizenship and his right to be President. How sad it would have been had our

Deeper Roots

President been uninformed regarding his lineage. This knowledge allowed him to inform (and correct when necessary) the inaccurate information spread by his detractors. Make no mistake, the forty-fourth President of the United States is a born and bred American through and through like previous presidents—but he does not look like them because he is of African descent. This confused a great many people and those who stood against the President capitalized on that ignorance and seeded doubt among the electorate.

It is sad that political opponents seized on what we lack as a race—our history. The fact is when you do not know your history, people can (and will) say anything. The President made a concerted effort to know his roots and, therefore, to know himself. Our lack of historical self-knowledge is a liability that we must correct as soon as possible.

I also believe that activism remains a necessary aspect not only in terms of reclaiming our history but in fighting for our community and ensuring our future. I came to activism like so many black women—in response to policies and actions perpetrated against my community and my family. Agitating and 'politicking' was not in my life plan but the social context dictated a change in that plan. As a black woman born in the first half of the twentieth century, I received what most of my sex and race did not—an excellent education—and I used that skill to agitate. While I was growing up, W.E.B. DuBois publicized the term, "talented tenth" in his 1903 essay, *The Negro Problem.* Loosely defined, it referred to the ten percent of educated Negroes who would raise the standards of the race. How ironic that the term, "talented tenth" could not be used to describe me because these educators and activists were also called "exceptional men." This omission of black women by black men was accepted within the social context

Introduction

of that time and space. But in the end it did not matter and it probably never did outside the realm of social rhetoric.

The fact is that change in the black community always involved the black woman—and in many instances was instigated by us. The classic example is, of course, the Civil Rights Movement. The Movement, like most movements of this size was nationally mobilized by the many grassroots organizations across the nation. What is now acknowledged through the plethora of texts chronicling the era is that those organizations were overwhelmingly run by women while the figureheads were overwhelmingly men (unless it was a "woman's" organization).

Given the social mores of the day, it was my parents' intention to obtain the best education for me so that I could, at least, earn a relatively decent wage whether or not I was married or had a family. The fact that we lived in Harlem, a community rich with cultural, educational and philosophical choices made my parents' intentions possible. It was a tremendous stroke of luck that my education also prepared me to contribute on behalf of my people during the struggle for civil rights.

My life is not a blueprint but a testimony to those who came before me. This book chronicles my journey (with all its twists and turns) back to my history and my ancestors. It also charts my journey within the context of the larger history since we cannot operate in a vacuum. Our actions are often reactions in response to circumstances developing around us.

I argue that it is imperative that we reclaim that which was taken from us—our history. No matter what we might learn about our ancestors, nothing can be worse than not knowing who we owe for our existence.

P.S. I use the terms "Negro," "colored," "black" and "African American" throughout the book. They all refer to

Deeper Roots

people of African descent. The usage is within the social context of the time I am writing about and means nothing more than that.

Alex Haley

March 22, 1982

Dear Tanya,

So much thanks for your letter, which you
sent to my publisher in New York, who sent it
along to me, and it arrived today. Now, if we
have any kind of luck, this letter from me will
also reach you. But, little honey, always
remember that when you write someone a letter,
you should tell them your <u>last</u> name, too. And
be sure that you carefully spell out your address.

Anyway, of course I'm flattered that you've
chosen me as a person you'd like to learn more
about, as your letter says, and I'm glad to
send you the picture that you request.

Congratulations that in another four months
you'll reach eight whole years of age. I can
clearly remember when I was eight. In fact, it
was just about that time that I was hearing from
my Grandmother the old family stories that somehow
stored away in my head and years and years later
stirred my curiousity into starting a long research
that finally led me into writing the book <u>Roots</u>.

Take good care of Tanya, study hard, and be good!

FIND THE GOOD — AND PRAISE IT   Alex Hiley

DREAMS FROM MY FATHER

To Katherine Jones —

I can't wait to read more
about your own family's remarkable
journey! All the best to you,
and may our paths cross someday
soon.

Barack Obama

To Katherine —

I'm glad we met, and now
look forward to seeing you in the
White House! *Barack Obama*

Kathy, Hubey and Senator Barack Obama at a Presidential fundraiser
Summer 2007

Chapter One: Meme Clark

An "English" Woman Invents a New Life in Harlem

My mother, Meme Elgitha Clark, was British to the bone. She had proper clipped English diction and a melodic voice. I can hear it still rippling with laughter. For most of my life, I assumed her precise grammar and award-winning penmanship had been honed at Oxford University where, as she told me, she had matriculated before moving to New York City in 1921. In my mind's eye, I could see my mother standing on the faraway Oxford campus, dressed all in white, just as she is in a photograph from the 1920's. My mother's chocolate brown skin contrasts vividly with her white dress, white stockings and shoes. She is five feet five inches tall and slender, wearing a watch band that dangles just below her wrist bone. The brim of her white hat nearly meets her arched eyebrows. Her dark eyes are focused defiantly on the camera.

Meme (pronounced Maime) was a loyal colonial British subject, and like others of the petite bourgeoisie in Jamaica, she identified deeply with the traditions and glory of the

Deeper Roots

British Empire upon which, she was quick to mention, "the sun never set." She was ninety-nine years old before the sun set on her life, and her voice still comes to me clearly, calling me to reflect on her life and to measure the vast influence she had on me, her only child.

Although the formal, reserved manner of the British aristocracy was emulated in Meme's Jamaican household, her rebelliousness shimmered just beneath the surface. I can hear her mimicking the bass voice of her stern father, Sergeant Major Robert Clark of the Constabulary Force of Falmouth, Jamaica, addressing his wife: "Mrs. Clark, why can't you manage that young lady?" "He was talking," my mother explained, "about the time I was expelled from school for refusing to apologize to my teacher for referring to her as a baboon from Jamaica."

The wonder was that my mother was enrolled in the school to begin with. I marvel at the foresight and resourcefulness of my grandmother, who convinced the headmaster of the all-male school her sons attended to admit my mother and her younger sister, Mae. The academic standards at the school were rigorous and successful performance was expected in preparation for the Oxford and Cambridge University equivalency examinations.

In those days penmanship was still an important art and my mother excelled in the art, winning first prize in a competition sponsored by the British Crown. Mom learned of her achievement, she told me proudly, when a formally-attired courier bearing a ribboned certificate on a silver platter stepped out of a horse-drawn carriage in front of her house and asked for M. Clark. The headmaster had been clever and kind; he avoided using Meme, a telltale girl's name, so the judges could not discern her gender and would consider the submission without prejudice.

At the age of fifteen, this outstanding student was commanded by the King of England to study telegraphy in the

2

Chapter One: Meme Clark

capital city of Kingston, located on the south coast of the island, ninety miles from her north coast Falmouth home. My mother had to learn to operate the electric telegraph machine invented by Samuel Morse and the code he developed—a series of long and short signals sent by cable to instantaneously communicate messages across land and sea. After passing the examination for this prestigious position filled by young women, my mother was assigned to various parishes all over the island. She enjoyed the new places and people she met in her work but in 1921 Meme decided to visit her older sister, Maud, and her brothers, Bert and Oscar, who had lived in New York City for many years. Harlem was her destination. "I had heard so much about America. I had to see it for myself. I liked what I saw and so I just stayed," she told me.

The story of her travel to America was one I heard many times throughout my childhood. It was a story that my mother told me while we sat together in Dad's lounging chair in the bedroom next to the window, intermingled with the stories she read to me from beautifully illustrated volumes displaying colored plates of *Hans Brinker* and the *Silver Skates* and *Heidi*.

"The boat left from Kingston," my mother said. "My brother Willie was a customs officer there so he arranged for my passage. I was a young woman then. Thin as a rail. I could dash up a flight of stairs, two at a time. I traveled with a friend, Daisy, from our home in Falmouth. We planned to visit for a month. She and I shared a cabin on the boat. It took us three or four days to get here from Jamaica. I was seasick the whole time and never left the cabin. Daisy went out on deck for breakfast, lunch and dinner. Oscar met me at the boat. Daisy's people weren't at the dock so she had to go to Ellis Island first."

"My brothers, Oscar and Bert and my sister, Maud, rented rooms in a building called the Pinkney Court on 140th

3

Deeper Roots

Street between Seventh and Lenox Avenue. When they took me there I wondered, 'What is this? Flowers in the lobby? Ring a bell and an elevator comes?' I had never seen a place like this. Then Bert introduced me to the landlady, and she too was from Jamaica."

"Oscar and Bert bunked up together to give me a space of my own. The boys were out to sea a lot of the time. Bert was a waiter on a cruise line to Alaska, and Oscar worked as a steward on the Cunard cruise ship line."

"Soon after I got settled in Harlem, my brothers would take me around the city. People were out in the streets at all hours of the night. I couldn't believe my eyes. We went to cabarets to see Josephine Baker and Lena Horne perform. We would eat in the restaurants on Seventh Avenue. I remember seeing Florence Mills in the musical Shuffle Along. I could never have imagined anything like it."

"Each month I packed my bags to go home," Mom said of her early years in New York City, "and each time I decided to stay for just one more month. Since jobs 'for colored' were plentiful and my visit was extending, Bert asked me one day, 'Meme, what do you want to do for work?' 'Telegraphy, of course' I responded. Bert fell on the bed laughing. 'They don't hire any jigaboos for that work here,' he said."

The adjustment to the strange ways of Americans was difficult for Mom. In Jamaica the Clark family had employed servants to perform household tasks but in New York the only work my mother could find was domestic service in the homes of white families. Mom's sister Maud held a job as a maid for many years with the Chronheimer family, owners of Wildroot hair products, but my mother could not easily accept that role reversal for herself. On her first job as a domestic the conflict between her previous life, her self-concept and her status as a maid struck a bitter cord.

"At noontime the Czechoslovakian maid called me," my mother remembered. "She said, 'Meme, lunch is ready.' I

4

came into the kitchen and offered to set the table. 'We don't set the table for us.' Greta said. 'No tablecloth? You eat off of a bare table?'" My mother remembers that she went into the servants' room and cried like a baby.

"Next I got a job working as a governess taking care of a toddler," she recalled. "It was Maud's job, but she gave it to me since she had been there for a while and could easily get another. The family lived on Central Park West. One day we were getting ready to go out. The baby was just learning to walk, so I had to take a stroller out too, so she could rest when she got tired. You know how these mothers are, crazy about the child getting out in the sun. I had the baby ready, and went to ring the elevator bell when I heard the mother say to hurry me up, 'The best part of the day is going.' Well, I went back into the apartment, packed my bag, then strode to the door and declared, 'Good-bye, Mrs. Watkins.' I wasn't used to anyone talking to me like that. Then came another job as a governess for Johnnie, but I was getting bored taking him to the park and picking him up from school. One day his mother asked me to set the table. That's the maid's job, and I am *not* your maid. That was my last day on that job. I quit."

My mother's independent spirit, pride and unwillingness to be treated as a subordinate conveyed an impression of strength and aloofness to those around her. Indeed, West Indians as a group were noted for their thrift, certain pushiness and a refusal to play an inferior role to anyone. As a result, for example, the Pullman Company did not willingly hire West Indians for jobs as porters, chefs or waiters on railroad cars. "If a West Indian gets one step from a beggar, he's ready to start a business," people said. The new immigrants also stirred up resentment among those African Americans already living in Harlem. In the book, *Harlem, Making of a Ghetto*, Gilbert Osofsky quotes a ditty of the 1920s that aptly expresses those sentiments:

Deeper Roots

When a monkey chaser dies,
don't call the undertaker,
Just throw him in the Hudson,
and he'll float back to Jamaica.

"Monkey chaser" was a derogatory term for West Indians.

My mother soon found the perfect profession for her independent spirit in a new hair-growing technique that had begun gaining acceptance in the early 1900s in "Harlems" throughout the hemisphere. It was this technique that inspired Mom to become a beautician. This process of hair styling, which helped women of African heritage resemble Euro-American women, not only transformed the appearance of hair but made fortunes for some women who went into the beauty culture business. Sarah Breedlove, known at the turn of the twentieth century as Madame C.J. Walker, was the fabled entrepreneur who made this revolution possible.

A protégé of hairdresser Annie Pope-Turnbo, Sarah Breedlove became a Pope-Turnbo agent and sold her mentor's products, which had worked successfully in growing her own hair. Soon Breedlove concocted a new hair-growth formula, claiming that the process came to her in a dream (Pope-Turnbo claimed theft). From her "dream" formula Breedlove developed an international business of beauty products and, as Madame Walker, she established schools in major cities to train Negro women in her method of hair care. Meme first learned of the process from her landlady.

"My landlady came back from the hairdresser one day, and she looked so different," Mom recalled. "I asked her, 'What did you do to your hair, Mrs. Vaughn?'"

"'Girl,' she said, 'I went over to Seventh Avenue at a beauty shop called Frankie's. They sat me down in this chair and washed my hair real good. Then after the hair was dry, they put some grease in it and messaged the scalp well. Next thing I know, this lady takes out a thick metal comb with a wooden handle. I said 'Mable, watcha gonna do with that?' She said, 'Mrs. Vaughn, don't you worry 'bout a thing, I'm going to take care of you just fine.' She heated this comb over a low flame, and then she ran it through my hair while the comb was still good and hot. Now she takes each piece of hair up in a way so she don't burn my head. The hot comb takes out all the kinks. Meme, it was like magic. You can see how long my hair is now."

"I knew that I wanted to try this out for myself," my mother said. "So the next day I went over to Frankie's on 137ᵗʰ Street and Seventh Avenue. You had to go down a set of stairs to enter the shop. I can remember this warm gust of air that hit me in the face when I opened the door. The sweet pungent aroma of hot grease on pressed hair filled my nostrils. As I glanced around the room I noticed that each of the four operators had her own booth with a chair and stool to sit on, and a counter for the combs, grease and pressing irons. The sink was on one side; you had to walk across the room to get your hair washed."

"The shop was filled with girls from the show at the Cotton Club. They had finished rehearsal for the morning and were all there to get their hair 'fried' and styled by Frankie before curtain time. The place was jumping with laughter and talk. The beauticians were the source of knowledge—giving advice to troubled souls, ministering to wounded spirits, sharing the joys and sorrows of daily life. And there was Frankie in his corner, standing over a customer and doing her hair. You should have seen the way he handled those curling irons. Clip, clip, the two metal prongs snapped together, lodging the strand of hair in their grip. He knew just how many seconds to hold the hot iron in the hair to make the wave that he wanted so the hair wouldn't burn. I just stood there in awe. 'What can I do for you madam?' he said. 'Oh, I think I'll have my hair washed

Deeper Roots

today.' 'Very well, someone will be with you in a few minutes,' he replied. When they finished with me I looked like a new woman. My hair was down below my shoulders. It was beautiful. Right then and there I knew that I wanted to be a beautician."

"I asked Frankie to teach me the hairdressing trade and he agreed," Mom recalled. "Soon I was managing the shop for him when he would go to watch the chorus girls rehearse for these musical shows that brought the white people to Harlem. Many of Frankie's customers would get tired of waiting for him and asked me to do their hair. I was always efficient and aloof and my appointments would be met on time. 'No waiting on Miss Clark.' For some reason the other operators were called by their first names, but I was always Miss Clark." "You remember Frankie, don't you?" Mom asked me. "He did your hair when you graduated from high school and when you got married. He didn't charge you, either. 'That's for old times, Meme,' he said."

Beauty and style were intrinsic to the Harlem culture back then and it remains so to this day. As mom recalled, "when I worked for Frankie he used to dress up these feminine men. They would have a dance each year to show off these gorgeous gowns—the Fairies' Ball, they called it." The annual grand event was at Rockland Palace Ballroom on 155th Street and Eighth Avenue. Langston Hughes, poet and social critic, described this ball as "the strangest and gaudiest of all Harlem spectacles."

"How these men could get their big feet into these high-heeled shoes!" was my mother's laughing memory. "I would stay to watch them get fixed up. I used to stand there with my mouth wide open."

Jane Jackson, another hairdresser and Mom's close friend, was a member of the Cosmopolitan social club. Cosmopolitan also held a masquerade ball at the Rockland Palace each year. As a little girl I used to go to Miss Jackson's apartment

Chapter One: Meme Clark

to watch the preparation of hors d'oeuvres for her table guests and ogle her fancy furniture (which in later years I recognized as Louis XIV). Each year Miss Jackson appeared at the masquerade ball as George Washington, complete with white powdered wig and Colonial-style costume. These publicly validated reality-altering events brought momentary escape from the harsh stings the world imposed on Negro life. For one night in the year, a Negro woman could be the first president of the United States, and a man could be a glamorous woman if he wished to be.

"When Frankie and Jennie got married (she was a showgirl and he was the salon owner), I was asked to manage the shop for fifteen dollars for the week that they went on a honeymoon. Things ran like clockwork then. One day I decided to work at home," Mom said, "and my newly-acquired customers came with me. That way I avoided all of the nonsense in the shop—cigarette smoke, loud talk, gossip, hot goods dealers always coming in and out to sell you what they just stole, number runners at the door to collect bets and then to stop in the afternoon to tell what number came out and pay off the ones that hit that day. You know, everyone's business was in the street, boyfriends treating their lady friends badly. And all of the gossip: 'Meme, did you hear, so and so . . . What do you think I should do about . . . .' So hair straightening became my livelihood. Customers of all descriptions came to my apartment to have their hair done. Teachers, maids, nurses and lawyers crossed my threshold and when they left, they were transformed. Many of those customers became my close friends and we shared many laughs together!"

My mother's good friends were like an extended family for me growing up. One summer, a customer, Mrs. Woodland, set up a Christmas club account for me at the Seamens Bank near her office. I put away fifty cents a week and Mrs. Woodland collected and deposited the money for

Deeper Roots

me and brought back the account book so I could watch the coins accumulate to twenty-five dollars—which I used for Christmas shopping. Years later when I was in college, Mrs. Woodland also let me substitute for her at her work when she went on a week-long summer vacation. Another customer, Maudester Newton, a career counselor at the Harlem Branch YWCA, advised me to work as a counselor at a camp in New Hampshire run by Church of the Master, a Presbyterian Church in Harlem. Hilda French took me to Saturday matinees of Broadway shows and paid to have my nails manicured so I wouldn't pick the skin around my cuticles. When I was away at college, Tillie Cochrane, who held a sales position at Lord & Taylor Department Store, brought ice cream and cake to celebrate my mother's birthday after she had her hair done.

So popular were hairdressers that there were three in our building: Miss Jackson, Miss Smith and my mother—and there was never competition among them. Each woman had her own clientele, and "Jackson" was one of my mother's closest friends. I learned about politics, religion, human relations and the pleasures of gossip from overhearing the conversations in the kitchen while my mother worked.

"Meme, what do you think about Congressman Adam Clayton Powell, marrying Hazel Scott, a divorced cabaret singer?"

"I hear he locked the church doors one Sunday and told the congregation they better like it or else," my mother replied. The gossip did not end at Frankie's shop.

My mother recalled, "I made good money what with tips and all. I charged two dollars and fifty cents a head. Six people a day. You could really do something with that kind of money. I saved up and bought myself a baby grand piano. I shared my new apartment on Washington Heights' elite Sugar Hill with my sister Maud. I would call down to Andrew Geller, a prestigious shoe store, and have them

Chapter One: Meme Clark

bring the shoes up to the apartment for me to select what I wanted. I dressed in the latest styles, and I could even afford fur coats paid for on the installment plan. I bought Oriental rugs and had my draperies custom made by Mr. Bionder. I really lived high on the hog. Where but in America could a person start with nothing and build a new life?"

Meme was not alone in her feelings of untethered possibilities. In the early twentieth century immigrants came to America from all of the Caribbean Islands without quota limitations. Adam Clayton Powell Sr., then minister of the Abyssinian Baptist Church, described Harlem as "the symbol of liberty and the Promised Land to Negroes everywhere." Within this rich world, West Indian immigrants clustered with arrivals from the various islands, each group considering themselves superior to the others. Jamaican, Trinidadian or Barbadian—the islanders referred to the places from which they came as "home," and they formed societies to assist newcomers in adjusting to the new environment while maintaining their cultural traditions. "They were just too clannish," Mom observed. Yet these close family and island connections served them (and Meme) well.

Another Jamaican immigrant who thought he could accomplish great things in the United States was Marcus Garvey. He would become the most famous Jamaican man in the early 1920s by utilizing community connections across the country. He had left his homeland in 1917 after failing to gain support there for a nationalistic scheme to relocate all black people to Africa. Finding a more responsive reception in Harlem, Garvey developed an organization, the Universal Negro Improvement Association (UNIA), which eventually numbered two million people. The UNIA purchased ships for its Black Star Line to carry people of the African diaspora back to Africa where Garvey envisioned they would live permanently.

11

Deeper Roots

Its members dressed in military-style uniforms; a nurse corps of white-uniformed black women paraded on Seventh Avenue in Harlem to the beat of drums, while Garvey (a short, dark-skinned, stocky man with a plumed hat cocked at an angle on his broad head) rode in a convertible limousine. These powerful visual images marking the success of Garvey's movement attracted many followers. The UNIA built pride in the working-class people who made up its membership while the organization was castigated by members of the Negro elite (such as James Weldon Johnson and Dr. W. E. B. Du Bois) and by some of the West Indian immigrant groups. By 1925 Marcus Garvey had been tried in Federal Court for using the federal mail for fraudulent purposes, found guilty, and deported back to Jamaica. Although he was a hero to many blacks, he was a threat to both the black and white establishments. I often wish that I had been alive when Marcus Garvey captured the imagination and galvanized people around the world to idolize him or hate him. His programs, newspapers, ship purchases, and bold ideas gave inspiration and a renewed sense of pride in one's African heritage.

My mother, on the other hand, was not impressed by Garvey, to put it mildly. "I would never associate with him. He was a lower-class, uneducated man," Meme remarked. The elements of social class and skin color always remained distinguishing criteria for acceptability in my mother's world. "Most of the Jamaican men came to America because they were in trouble at home," Meme said. "Marcus Garvey was an example. He could not make a success of his movement in his native Jamaica, so he came here. But the American men I met in Harlem seemed no better than the Jamaican men who had immigrated here." That assessment, however, soon changed for Mom.

"One summer I rented a chauffeured limousine and took my vacation at a resort in Pawling, New York, about an hour

Chapter One: Meme Clark

north of New York City. After a few days, I noticed this man paying special attention to me. He would draw my chair out at meal time, and would walk to the center of town with me. He was different from the other American men that I had met—very soft spoken and courteous. I was Miss Clark to him, and he introduced himself as Mr. Butler. I later learned he was a postal clerk at Station K on East 87th Street. Curiosity had motivated him to find out who I was, driving up to the resort in a fancy car. When the week was over, he rode with me to the city and offered to take me back to my apartment. He carried those bags up the four flights to my door without a complaint. Then he invited me to go to hear Paul Robeson sing at Town Hall. I accepted the invitation and on the designated night I got dressed and presented myself when the doorbell rang. There he was, dressed in a tuxedo. I said, 'Come in, and make yourself comfortable. I will be with you in a minute.' I went back to my room, changed into a long gown, put on my elbow-length white kid gloves and sashayed back to the living room to make my second appearance. Now we were ready to do the town. When we got downstairs, I just stood still on the sidewalk. Mr. Butler got the message. He hailed a cab, and we were on our way."

At the time of my mother's arrival in Harlem in 1921, my dad was one of twenty members of the Knickerbocker Whist club, a card-playing group of men that aimed to "cultivate within our circle that mutual respect and fraternal feeling that will conduce to our greatest success—treat each other always with candor but in a spirit of moderate and friendly consideration." Those characteristics, embodied by my dad, probably attracted my mother to him.

The romance between Meme Clark and Theodore Butler is recorded in the exquisite greeting cards and hand-painted note cards that my mother sent to my father that he saved throughout his life, carefully tucked on the bottom shelf of

Deeper Roots

his bookcase. Although my mother presented herself to me as the object of my father's pursuit, in truth she made it quite clear in her communication to him that she was very much interested in his attention. I can only surmise from this letter that my Dad had apprehensions about remarrying after a divorce, and my mother tried to allay his anxiety in these words of wisdom:

> *Your experience and viewpoints are of the miserable past.*
>
> *This is a new era and a different woman and if you let me be Captain!!!! I'll guarantee you a very joyous sail. Although I have had no previous experience in this line, my knowledge is great and I have learnt that life is just what you make it....*
>
> *You can change any condition in your life to a better one if you keep poised. In time of unusual circumstance, quietly seek the "inner self" and trustingly look for guidance. In time of stress "be still and know" there is no occasion for worry anxiety or fear for there is a Power within you mightier than any other outer condition on which we can depend to guide us straight through our greatest good--if we invoke its aid and follow its direction.*
>
> *If you nourish the love and interest you profess to have, there shall be nothing to fear...*

Her love for my father was, I believe, a shock even to her. When Mom arrived from Jamaica, she was a self-described bachelor girl. Eleven years later, when my dad proposed, she hesitated and answered demurely, "I'll think about it." But in

14

Chapter One: Meme Clark

response to his next question, "Where do you want to go for our honeymoon?" she quickly replied, "Niagara Falls, of course." And so the wedding date was set for August 21, 1932.

Motherhood was not in Meme's plan either. She was forty-one years old, and she wanted no interruptions in the independent lifestyle and the thriving hairdressing business she had developed. Three years after their marriage, however, Rhoda Smith, my mother's customer and friend, squinted her eyes at Mom's pouting mouth and enlarging figure and said, "Meme, you won't be the first woman to have a baby and it won't be the end of the world." My parents' union lasted for nineteen years and ended all too soon when my father died in 1951 at the age of sixty-seven.

Mom's home was her castle—a castle in which she presided in regal style. With three steps through the foyer you entered the living room where Dad liked to sit in the winged chair near the French door, reading newspapers into the night. Slipcovered sofas graced the two corniced windows that framed the New Jersey skyline and where neon lights nightly illuminated the roller coaster and Ferris wheel at the Palisades Amusement Park. Farther north, you could see the massive yet delicate structure of the George Washington Bridge majestically spanning the Hudson River between New Jersey and New York. A Chinese lamp matched the red-draped windows and the black Hardman & Peck grand piano dominated the rest of the room.

Through the double French doors was my parents' bedroom. I would sit on my mother's lap in the aluminum-framed chair by the bedroom window while she read to me for hours from *The Patchwork Quilt*, a lavishly illustrated book of children's stories. I loved to hear *Goldilocks and the Three Bears*, *Hansel and Gretel*, and my favorite, *The Three Little*

Deeper Roots

Pigs. "I read to you until my throat was dry," my mother told me.

For a break in routine, we would climb up two flights of stairs to the roof, where I rode my red and white tricycle and jumped rope on the red-tiled clay surface. We could walk around the entire perimeter of the roof, stepping over the foot high ridges—like seams of the building. On the west side of the house the surface changed to tar. The huge barrel-shaped water tower with its large domed top loomed over the area. Sometimes Mom would bring a basket of clothes to hang on the clothesline while I played. I liked to watch the homing pigeons flying over the pink geraniums in the green window boxes of the five penthouse apartments. I could hear the flapping of the birds' iridescent blue-gray wings as they swooped down to their rooftop roosts. They were tended by a teenager we called "Birdie" who lived on the tenth floor and raced the birds between Brooklyn and Manhattan with messages clamped to their legs.

In my room, Mom watered the row of plants on each of the two windowsills every other day. Around each stem she placed crushed raw egg shells and on occasion brushed the leaves with milk so that they glistened. A long rectangular painted kitchen cabinet was where I put my school papers, my *Unity Wee Wisdom* magazines and two maroon Schrafft's candy boxes. Dad would bring Mom five-pound candy selections of chocolates for her birthday, Valentine's Day and Easter. In those emptied boxes I kept my scissors, paste and Audubon bird cards and the Coca-Cola sets of species of animals, butterflies, fish and flowers. My junior-size bed with its cherry headboard stood in the corner of the room, next to the brown mahogany bureau with attached mirror. Our neighbor and friend Robert Harris had picked up each of the pieces of furniture in my room at auction. I kept my blackboard easel collapsed behind the bed when I was not using it to save space. When I got older I decorated the walls

Chapter One: Meme Clark

with pictures of male movie stars cut from the front page of the magazine section of the Sunday New York *Daily News*. Dana Andrews was my favorite but Cary Grant, Alan Ladd and Gregory Peck also met my enraptured gaze. On my bureau I kept my Fada radio which was encased in yellow plastic. That radio is now a collector's item; I saw one like it displayed in a shop on Fifth Avenue for $500 and I now wish that I had kept mine. That radio was a birthday gift from an important man in my life, Elmer, my cousin and my father's favorite nephew. Elmer often came to visit us, and always spared time to play with me. He had a ready smile and a warm temperament like my Dad and he had a medical condition which made him ineligible for the draft. One day he brought his new fiancé, Ethel, to introduce her to the family. After they all spent an hour or so chatting, I approached this woman whom I considered to be an intruder and said, "you can leave now." I realized Ethel would get most of Elmer's attention and I was jealous.

My mother's world revolved around our home. There was no need for me to have a key to the house because she was always there to welcome me home from school. Mom did not visit family or friends; they had to come and visit her—and they did. Her ventures away from home were walks in the neighborhood, bus and subway rides to Macy's and to Radio City Music Hall (though never in the rain.) My mother took me to the splendor of Radio City Music Hall for the morning show where we glided across the thick rug carpeting to see the Rockettes' synchronized steps and watch the orchestra magically emerge from the pit to accompany the stage production of the Easter or Christmas shows. Mom also took me on shopping trips to Macy's Department Store. On the fourth floor, next to the escalator and across from the children's shoe department, I would buy a container of chocolate milk from the refrigerated compartment at the back of a wooden replica of Elsie the Cow wearing a garland of daisies around her neck. Elsie remains the trademark of Borden, Inc. which dispatched a uniformed milkman to deliver milk to our apartment every day. Despite the busy nature of Macy's, I felt at ease there. One day my mother and I became separated. When she came to claim me from the Lost and Found Department I remarked, "Oh, Mother, you got lost."

Mom's love of her home did not, however, prevent her from travelling when the need arose. After I went away to college, Mom would ride by car with other parents to visit me at college and when I married soon after graduation from college and moved to Massachusetts, Mom would come to visit Hubey and me by train or bus. She joined us for Christmas and came to help out after the birth of each of our children as our family grew. She helped enormously when we went on vacation by keeping a few children with her while we traveled with the other children.

◆　◆　◆　◆　◆

I very much wanted to visit Jamaica on vacation, and Mom often urged me to go there to see for myself the source of the innumerable stories she told me about her family, their customs and beliefs—her roots. Now that I was married and had children of my own, I yearned for them to share the journey with me. At last the time came when I, as an American-born member of the Clark family, could pay a visit to my mother's homeland.

Our family deplaned at Montego Bay on a March afternoon in 1964. We were met by a warm gust of tropical air and a driver who knew our family well and had been sent by my Aunt Mae. "Welcome to Jamaica," Mr. Clark (no relation) said in a lilting Jamaican cadence, tipping his hat and opening the rear door of a well-used gray four-door sedan. Hubey

Chapter One: Meme Clark

sat in the front seat with Mr. Clark. My little girls, Karen, aged five, and Lauren, three, wearing the yellow, orange and white striped dresses my mother had made especially for the occasion, settled next to me in the back seat. Harlan, our one and a half-year-old son, nestled comfortably on my lap during the twenty-minute ride to Falmouth. As we bumped along the narrow curving road outside of Montego Bay, we passed meandering goats and graceful women carrying bundles on their heads.

Mr. Clark narrated the scene: "Here is the circle in the center of Falmouth where market women come every morning to set up stalls and sell their produce. Saturday is the busiest day," he continued while navigating through traffic. "That is where the women come down from the countryside on the bus. Now we are on Duke Street. Do you see the gray stone building? That is the Anglican Church where your family, the Clarks, belong. And the cemetery next to it is where your grandparents are buried."

As Mr. Clark spoke, the places and routines that my mother had told me about for so many years began to come to life. At the same time, the images in my mind's eye underwent radical revision as I saw the reality of modern-day Jamaica, which in the 1960s was undergoing severe economic hardships. These hardships were brought on by foreign debt and the devaluation of currency in conformance with demands made by the International Monetary Fund and the World Bank, organizations on which the country depended. Although Jamaica was technically independent of colonial rule, the export and import regulations and foreign currency exchange rates imposed by former colonial nations economically crippled the country.

Mr. Clark knew the nooks and crannies of his homeland, but I wondered if he knew about the English Moulton-Barrett family who had owned 30,000 acres of this land as early as the 1600s. The poet Elizabeth Barrett Browning had

Deeper Roots

Afro-Jamaican blood in her veins and the Moulton-Barrett descendants still live in Jamaica as members of the social elite—their financial fortunes having declined with the demise of the slave-based plantation system. Founded by Edward Moulton Barrett (Elizabeth's grandfather), Falmouth is located in Jamaica's northern coastal parish of Trelawny. Barrett sold off sections of the land to his friends who, in turn, established plantations. Falmouth would become a major port in the Atlantic Triangular Slave Trade route. Jamaica became the leading sugar producer of the era and Falmouth was home to eighty-eight plantations and almost 30,000 slaves. The plots, planted in cane, dotted the land as far as the eye could see and the machete-wielding slaves who chopped the cane eventually turned their tools to other uses. Their organized revolts periodically (yet predictably) filled the air with billowing black smoke and the acrid smell of burning cane until 1838, when the British ended slavery. Down at Falmouth Harbour, a few blocks from my ancestral home, we passed the large black cannon pointed at the sea, and at the ghosts of enemy ships that once plied the waters under the flag of Spain. The cast-iron artillery, like the wealth of the Moulten-Barrett family, represented a source of power now invisible, yet still wielding its influence on the island.

No visible evidence remained of the once comfortable and influential status of the Clark family among the African-Jamaican middle class in Falmouth. The house that we pulled up in front of, described by my mother as having a winding circular driveway, resembled the bunkhouses I had lived in at summer camp. It had a thatched wooden roof and wooden plank siding which bore witness to the effects of many hurricanes.

The door opened. A woman with sharp-boned ebony features resembling those of my mother's sister Maud

Chapter One: Meme Clark

greeted us. "You are finally home," Aunt Mae said, embracing each of us. The last Clark of the ten-member family, Mae had never left Jamaica or even this house where she was born. She was the daughter who stayed to take care of her mother and sister until their deaths. My generous grandmother made certain that her daughters would be protected by passing on her property to them exclusively. Eventually, my mother inherited the property.

We entered a sparsely-furnished living room with wide wooden floorboards, hand-rubbed with coconut oil to a lustrous shine. Against the wall stood the prized black upright piano where Aunt Mae, ruler in hand, had once taught music for a halfpenny a lesson to the neighborhood children. Of course, all of the Clark daughters took piano lessons when they were young. And on the living-room table, positioned on a white crocheted table scarf, was a picture of Hubey and me on our wedding day. The only photograph in the room, it had stood on that table for the past nine years. I knew it had been there for years, thanks to the layer of accumulated dust on the cardboard frame. I realized at that moment that we had a special place in our Jamaican family, and I did feel that we—Hubey and I, Karen, Lauren and Harlan had come home.

After a few days with Aunt Mae, I learned my first lesson in the strict separation of classes that dominated Jamaican life and culture. When we were planning a visit to my cousin Methlin, in Mona Heights (a suburb of the capital city of Kingston), Aunt Mae told us that we should hire a driver and ride comfortably in a passenger car. But I wanted to see how people traveled so we decided to journey by public transport, in a vehicle comparable to a rusted-out school bus. This choice drew strong protest from my aunt, who despite her meager circumstances would never mingle with the "lower class" and other travelers. But mingle we did, jammed into the old bus, packed in like subway riders in New York

Deeper Roots

City. The bus traversed the mountainous regions of the country along a single dangerous dirt road stopping in villages along the way, maneuvering precipitous curves with the horn blaring a warning to oncoming traffic. Rural poverty was evident everywhere—and yet the terrain was magnificent.

Four hours later, we arrived in the capital city where swarms of people move about the busy and congested streets. Rastafarians add to the clamor, playing reggae on steel drums. As the bus pulls into the Kingston depot, Methlin is waiting for us. My cousin is a short, middle-aged woman, wearing a well-filled starched white short-sleeved shirt with a navy blue ribbon tie at the neck and a matching navy blue skirt. Her thin dark brown hair is swept back away from her round face which lights up with a radiant smile. Her slanted eyes remind me that a great mixture of people make up the Jamaican population. "Out of many, one people" is the national motto. Methlin is delighted to meet our children for the first time.

Methlin and I had met before when she visited Aunt Maud in New York, before our children were born. Hubey and I took her to the Empire State Building and to Horn & Hardarts, the food automat for lunch where, like so many other visitors, Methlin was intrigued with putting coins into a slot and opening the door of the sandwich or dessert compartment. A pharmacist like her father before her in Falmouth, Methlin worked at the pharmacy of Geddis and Grant, a large Kingston Department Store. There she received shipments and supervised dispensation of dangerous drugs ordered from Canada. Her advanced education, critical to her life goals, was paid for by Aunt Maud, who sent money from the United States. As a young girl, Methlin had boarded with her Aunt Meme for a few weeks at the telegraphy post in Port Antonio, Jamaica, where she observed her aunt at work.

Chapter One: Meme Clark

Now, we push our way through the crowded street to Methlin's four-door sedan. Soon we are out of the city limits passing manicured lawns, the landscaped gardens of the University of the West Indies and brilliant displays of beautiful tropical flowers with shiny red and yellow petals. However, I notice that the houses are fenced in with locked gates. Methlin's home is quite nice though not elaborate with modern conveniences and ample guest rooms. Our dinner had been prepared and is served to us by the cook and maid. Hubey asks, "Where will the maid sit at the table?" Methlin is aghast. "She'll eat in the kitchen," is her curt response. After cleaning up the dishes, the maid departs for her home. A bit later, Methlin takes us to meet a friend of the family. It is beginning to rain, and we see the maid walking home in the pouring rain without an umbrella. "Aren't you going to stop and give her a ride? I ask. "No, we don't do that here," Methlin responds. I learn another lesson and began to grasp the basis of my mother's belief system which attributed value to class and appearance as reliable measures of social status and personal worth.

In 1973, Methlin moved to New York City like her aunts and uncles before her. And, like her Aunt Meme, has never returned to Jamaica and has no intention of going back even for a visit. Later, Methlin was joined in Harlem by her sisters Ouida and Phyllis (who moved into her apartment building on Broadway at 135th Street.) Each sister had her own apartment in the huge complex, and the three of them gathered faithfully for Sunday dinner together—peas and rice, oxtail, greens and gravy. My mother never prepared Jamaica's traditional cuisine, so this was a special treat for me. Whenever I was in New York City and could arrange it, I would join them. The conversation around the table on these Sunday afternoons in Harlem inevitably turned to the antics of the British royal family. "Isn't it a shame," Phyllis laments, "how this generation have disgraced the name of the King

Deeper Roots

and Queen by their behavior. They act just like common people." The identification with the Royal family and self-worth based on class that was so evident in my mother's worldview has been passed on to the next generation—a generation that is now dying out without passing on the flawed belief system regarding social status and class. Phyllis now lives in Florida, Ouida passed away a few years ago and I buried Methlin in the summer of 2012.

After one trip to Jamaica that Hubey and I made without our children, Mom and I examined the photos that we had taken of her home in Falmouth and its environs. "Those women are still carrying bundles on their heads!" she exclaimed. "Now you know why I wanted to see something else and came here. New York was a real adventure." I realized once again the stark contrast between the two places. Falmouth seemed to be caught in a bygone era, and I could understand why my mother found the staid social customs of the 1920s in Jamaica too restrictive for her adventurous spirit.

My mother had complicated feelings about her place of birth that I have never fully understood, even to this day. "Why don't you go for a visit to Jamaica?" I asked her. Oh, the past is past," she said. Nearly five decades had slipped by since she abandoned her lush mountainous Caribbean Island, a long separation and yet she always referred to Jamaica as home, even though in fact, America was her home now.

Mom, to my surprise applied for citizenship soon after Dad died so that my living parent would be an American. She also faithfully fulfilled the responsibilities of citizenship by voting in every election. When Karen was born on Election Day, November 3, 1959, Mom said she would take the train to Boston right after voting at her local polling place.

Chapter One: Meme Clark

Meme Clark Butler displayed flexibility in some aspects of her life, but held firmly to her death her beliefs about the appropriate appearance of Negro females. My daughter Lauren recently reminded me of her experience as a young girl. "When I was five years old, Karen and I went to stay with Ba for a week in New York. My grandmother washed my hair, straightened it with a hot comb, and curled it. But when I returned home, you immediately washed my hair again, and combed it back to the braided style that I always wore," she explained. The struggle between my mother and me about appropriate hairstyles and their symbolic importance was evident.

My mother would always come and help when a new grandchild arrived. That was the reason for her visit in 1969, the year Hamilton, our youngest son, was born. When I came home with the new baby she took one look at my hair, now cut in a 1960s Afro, removed herself to her bedroom, and laughed hysterically for ten minutes. She was laughing to keep from crying. All of her working life, she had tried to make African Americans appear to have hair like white women—a route to social acceptability. And all that effort was now devalued. Her own daughter had chosen to wear her hair like the African "natives" my mother had been taught to hold in disdain. The work that she had done to pay for my piano lessons, art lessons, clothes, summer camps, education and cultural experiences had literally, in her eyes, gone up in the smoke of the hot comb. I never concurred with my mother's emphasis on outward appearances, and certainly found the ease of caring for a natural hair style advantageous, but it was more than a disagreement over appearance—it was much deeper than that. Meme's narrative of her own life contained no references to her African ancestors. However, Jamaica was built on the backs of those

Deeper Roots

forebears and so it is part of our family's history—acknowledged or not.

My mother was born in Jamaica and lived in America, but England was always her reference point. Her pinkie formed a graceful arc when she sipped her tea and she gave me many lessons in the value of the English currency in relation to American denominations. "A pence is a penny, a farthing is equivalent to your quarter, a pound is worth five dollars of your money," she would explain. And during her thirty years in Jamaica, my mother was steeped in British history, but not one word about the history of the Maroons, the West Africans who were brought as slaves to the island, retreated to the hills, armed themselves, and refused to be dominated by British forces. Nor did she learn about the Arawak Indians, who were destroyed by diseases brought by the European colonists, and by the violence of the colonists' military attacks upon them. To the world, Meme reflected British mores and customs in the way she carried herself and her personal appearance.

However, the inner aspects of Meme's life reflected the African traditions and culture of our ancestors. Meme's independent spirit, and her choices based on her own sense of agency, was uncompromising and reminiscent of the countless Africans who systematically rebelled against the Jamaican plantocracy that enslaved them. Her decision to start her own beauty business was also evocative of the free West African women of the fifteenth century who traveled in caravans to trade with the Berbers of North Africa. Once bonded, African women created their own marketplaces to barter and sell among themselves in order to augment the meager provisions provided to them by plantations owners.

Meme generally rejected European religious institutions and rituals stating, "I've spent more time in churches than the law allows." She worshipped in her own way in her own home by meditating and reading the Daily Word, which she

26

ordered from the Unity School of Christianity in St. Louis, Missouri.

She also bypassed European medicine. Mom never went to the doctor, except to have her eyes examined—her belief in self-healing was comparable to the faith of a Christian Scientist but what she practiced was based in African tradition. "My body is the temple of the living God, and no illness is to be found there," she repeated, trying to will any sickness away. Each time I caught a cold, Mom climbed up on the stepstool and brought down a green metal box filled with herbs that she kept on the top shelf of the kitchen cabinet; then she went to work mixing an herbal brew that would either cure you or kill you. Those herbs were periodically replenished by friends visiting from Jamaica who brought the fresh "medicine" to Mom. When I was ill, in addition to the herbs, she rubbed my chest with Vicks VapoRub. It is not surprising that Mom used Vicks. It was the closest thing to preparing a homemade salve that contained healing essential oils like castor, camphor, eucalyptus and peppermint. Mom would spread some of the smelly ointment on my throat and wrap my neck with a towel pinned in place. I could feel the warmth of the salve penetrating through my skin. When she was at her weakest, Meme relied on the African traditions passed down through the generations.

There has been much written about the power of maintaining African culture on the plantations in the Caribbean and the Americas and about the power of those traditions in surviving the brutal plantation system. Mom utilized what was familiar to her and she was illustrative of the lingering power of those traditions.

The dichotomy between us and within herself was never resolved and I can only speculate at this point as to the reasons these contradictions existed in the first place. Perhaps the answer lies in her upbringing and the belief system of her parents as opposed to her own personal experience.

Deeper Roots

Locating documents attesting to the life and times of my grandparents was a challenge, and the old family bible disappeared years ago. However, there are oral remembrances —remembrances that cast more shadow than light on our family history.

During those Sunday dinners with my cousins Methlin, Phyllis and Oida in Harlem, I learned that my grandmother, Catherine Simpson, prepared meals for the prisoners and her daughters took those meals to the jailhouse every day. My daughter, Cheryl, in an interview with Meme for a school project, discovered that her great-grandmother was born in Duncan, Jamaica in the 1870s. Catherine's mother died when Catherine was very young and her father married again. Her stepmother did not treat her well and she had to care for her four siblings. Catherine married at the age of fifteen and began a family of her own. By all accounts she was a kind and generous woman whom people referred to as "lady bountiful," never refusing requests for money, food or clothing from neighbors. She passed away at the age of eighty-seven at the family homestead in Falmouth.

Her husband, Robert Clark, was quite the opposite—firm and autocratic. Grandfather Clark chose not to share any information about himself before his appearance in Trelawny Parish and marriage to Catherine Simpson. They would have eight children together, Flo, Maude, Mae, Meme, Oscar, Bert, Willie and Fred. It came as a shock to me to learn that one son (I believe it might have been the youngest child, Fred) was killed by a rock thrown at him while he was riding on horseback in the water in Jamaica. Another son, Bert (one of the two brothers who helped Mom settle in Harlem) worked on a cruise liner and disappeared somewhere in Alaska never to be seen or heard from again. My mother never spoke about either tragedy.

Mom's father was a member of Jamaica's Constabulary Force (JCF). I found the silver chalice presented to him in-

Chapter One: Meme Clark

scribed with the date of his retirement from the JCF, May 8, 1897. During Sergeant Major Clarke's tenure and rank within the JCF, he would have been one of an extremely small minority within the majority population of those of African descent in Jamaica. This may explain the Clark family's sense of social superiority.

In terms of Meme's loyalty to Britain, the history of the JCF is quite illuminating and provides some answers to Meme's and her family's preference for all things British. Essentially, the creation and growth of the JCF developed as a result of Jamaica's tumultuous social and political environment. Moreover, the JCF was conceived by the British government and its growth was nurtured under England's tutelage.

African bondsmen and bondswomen rebelled against the chains of slavery from the time they were brought to the Jamaican plantations. In 1655, Spain surrendered Jamaica to Britain leaving the enslaved behind with the hope that they would fight the English. The now-free slaves fled into the interior mountains. These Africans, called the Maroons, wreaked havoc on English-owned plantations and accepted runaway slaves into their mountainous communities, thereby multiplying their numbers. This continued until the Maroon Wars of 1738 when the British signed treaties with the various insurgent groups. During this time, the British military was the only formal armed force in Jamaica. The only thing close to a local police force was formed in 1716 when individuals were stationed as night watchmen on the plantations to guard against raids—especially by the Maroons. These night watchmen were the predecessors of the JCF.

In 1831, the Jamaican Slave Rebellion destabilized part of the island and in 1832 the British authorities attempted to establish a permanent police force in addition to the British military. This force would be comprised of local citizenry.

Deeper Roots

One can speculate that the British hoped that the local force would have an ear closer to the ground than the British authorities in order to allay more uprisings. That was not to be the case.

In 1838 Jamaicans of African descent were granted full emancipation. They could now vote and choose where—and for whom—they worked. However, the vast majority of them could not find employment and an exorbitant poll tax prevented them from participating in the political process. This unstable state of affairs continued for over twenty-five years. During the 1864 elections less than 2,000 black Jamaicans (out of a total population of 436,000) were eligible to vote. Rumors began to circulate that slavery would be restored. Black Jamaicans in St. Ann's Parish (located next to Trelawny Parish where Falmouth is located) petitioned Queen Victoria in England. They asked for land that had been abandoned in order to cultivate it and provide employment. Jamaica's British governor advised the Queen against the idea and the Queen declined the request; she advised them to work harder.

In 1865 a protest by freed Africans resulted in a volunteer militia group shooting and killing the protestors in front of the Morant Bay Courthouse in the eastern parish of St. Thomas. Rioting ensued and Britain dispatched troops who shot, executed and flogged over 300 Jamaican men, women and children. After the Morant Bay Rebellion, the Jamaican Assembly was dissolved and Jamaica became a crown colony of the United Kingdom. So, although Britain did not re-institute slavery it did tighten its socio-economic hold on the island and its people. It was at this point that the British authorities improved the ragtag local police force that would become the JCF of today.

During the latter half of the nineteenth century, Britain established pension criteria for its civil servants and those standards would have applied to the British colonies as well.

Chapter One: Meme Clark

Therefore, working backwards from the date of my grand-father's official retirement from the JCF (1897), and assuming he worked for approximately thirty years and retired between the ages of sixty and sixty-five (according to the aforementioned pension criteria), he would have been in his mid-twenties to early thirties during the Morant Bay Rebellion—in the prime of his life and profession. He was also a member of the JCF during the strongest push Britain had ever made to bring the black citizens to heel in a region of Jamaica that was a hotbed of rebellion.

Why my grandfather decided to go to Falmouth is a matter of speculation as well. Falmouth, before emancipation had almost ninety plantations and was, therefore, home to a large number of Jamaicans of African descent who were now free but dissatisfied and unemployed. Falmouth also re-mained a major port and region of commerce—a place where indentured servants from India and China were now doing the work of former slaves (indentured servants were cheaper than free men and women). If, like most black Jamaicans, he was looking for work, Falmouth was not the ideal place to find it. However, Robert Clark found a place in a now-focused local police force whose mandate was to observe and report, not serve and protect.

The JCF, therefore, was a force that was formed (and developed) by the British in response to the rebellions, up-risings and protests of people of African descent on the island. It is not surprising then that, as a result of his profession, Sergeant Major Clark's loyalty would lie with the British and his household (Meme included) reflected that loyalty.

Also, unlike many Jamaicans of African descent, Meme was a ferocious reader and the popular reading subject of the era revolved around the adventures of missionaries and travel writers and their journeys into darkest Africa. Although the most famous writer was sympathizer and anti-

Deeper Roots

slavery crusader David Livingstone, the vast majority of material written by others depicted Africans as an ignorant and brutal lot—a lot most people would not want to be aligned with. I can only imagine the mental images my mother must have formed about the African savages.

Despite our differences, however, we always encouraged my mother to come and live with us but she declined our invitation for years. After all, Methlin did her shopping, and called her every night, and neighbors came to check in on her—especially Mrs. Wilkins, across the hall in 12B, who arranged for Meals on Wheels and got assistance for Mom's bathing and grooming.

Finally, in 1986, my mother decided she was ready to give up the responsibilities of living alone. As many West Indian women do, Meme had always kept her birth date a secret. After she moved in with us, she reluctantly claimed that she was born in 1900. But when Mom came home from an extended stay in the hospital, the visiting nurse came to interview her. The two of them were seated in the living room, and I was in the nearby dining room within earshot of their conversation. "Mrs. Butler," the nurse began, "I have to ask you a few questions. First, what is your place of birth and birth date?"

"I was born in 1891 in Falmouth, Jamaica, but I changed my age when I came to this country so that I could get a job more easily. People preferred to hire younger women. I told them I was born in 1900; it was an easy year to calculate from. My husband didn't even know my real age," she laughingly confided. I couldn't believe my ears. I wrote 1891 on a piece of paper—almost as if I were pinching myself to make sure I was not dreaming and to make this surprising information seem real. If I had known my mother was now in her mid-90s, I would never have allowed her to stay in New York in an apartment by herself.

Chapter One: Meme Clark

I had another surprise many years before. One day in 1979, as I was interviewing Mom about her life for a psychology course I was taking. She said, "I left Jamaica for the very first time when I came to America."

"What about your studies at Oxford in England?" I asked. "Oh, I made that story up to impress the admissions officer at the Ethical Culture School," she said mischievously. And after a short pause, she followed up with, "You got in, didn't you?"

My mother had astutely assessed the American system and knew that a British accent, etiquette and education were highly valued. She gauged correctly that the admissions officers at an exclusive private school in New York would be mightily impressed by an Oxford matriculate. She put her accent and manners to work on my behalf and created a variation on her identity—an image that not only the admissions officer but I and all of my friends and my children believed. I was proud of my Oxford-educated mother, never questioning for one moment the authenticity of her chosen identity. And I am proud of her now—proud of her inventiveness, spunk, and style.

Chapter Two: Theodore "Thede" Butler

A Man for All Seasons

He always wore a hat. Grey or brown felt in the fall and winter, a firm straw- brimmed hat in the summer which he tipped to the ladies passing by—it was the polite thing to do. My father's honey brown face, calm and composed was punctuated by bushy dark eyebrows. His five-foot five-inch height and warm complexion reminded some of the Harlem spiritual leader, Father Divine. But my dad was a postal clerk in New York City, one of the few 'clean' secure jobs colored men could attain. He was quite a catch.

However, my father's first marriage in 1914 at the age of thirty-two produced no children and ended badly. After the divorce my father, by all accounts, embraced his status as an

Deeper Roots

attractive single man—until he met Meme, my mother. Neither his mother, Elizabeth, nor his sister, Jessie, approved of a second marriage, but they didn't approve of his single life either. In a letter Jessie wrote to him, she expressed concern that he was catnip to many women whose intentions were less than honorable. This situation was complicated by the fact that his mother moved in with my father after a fire destroyed the home she shared with Jessie, Jessie's husband and six children in Windsor, Connecticut. Despite the wishes of his family, Thede married Meme on August 21, 1932.

When my Mom's sister Maude asked, "What are you going to name the baby?" My dad, puffing out his fifty-two-year-old chest and holding his balding head high replied, "Theodore Jr." As his first and only child and daughter, I was indeed a surprise and my dad, Theodore Harold Butler, was my pal.

When I was old enough he took me to the playground and pushed me in the swings. Together we saw the Ringling Brothers and Barnum & Bailey Circus at Madison Square Garden. Every year we went to the Macy's Thanksgiving Day Parade with the giant helium gassed balloons of Donald Duck and Superman floating above our heads. But the most memorable adventures with my Dad took place much closer to home. We lived within walking distance of two parks: the Polo Grounds and Yankee Stadium, where Joe DiMaggio played. I grew up loving baseball.

Our kitchen window overlooked the Polo Grounds. Built in the 1890s, it was the home of the New York Giants baseball team before they moved to San Francisco in 1957. The Polo Grounds was also shared with the New York Yankees until 1923, when Yankee Stadium, "the house that Ruth Built," was designed to accommodate the increasing number of fans who came to see George Herman Ruth, the King of Swat. Before baseball was desegregated in 1947, the Polo Grounds was also the home of the Negro League's Cuban

Chapter Two: Thede Butler

Giants. I noticed that the only time large numbers of white people came into our neighborhood was to attend sporting events held at the two ball parks.

From the window I could see the colorful clothing of the fans seated in the left field stands and hear the booming sound of the announcer's voice: "Number 15—first baseman—Johnny Mize, at bat." Sometimes I would see the white ball rise into the upper deck of the left field stands for a home run. The roar from the crowd was almost deafening. I would listen to the game on the radio while watching the Polo Grounds to see the pop-up fly balls. Finally, when I was eight years old, Dad began taking me to the Polo Grounds and Yankee Stadium to watch the games.

As my dad and I walk hand in hand across the street and up the Harlem River Drive to the Polo Grounds, we join the throngs of people swarming from the subway at 155th Street. I take double steps to keep pace with my dad as the rapidly moving crowd carries us toward the admissions gate. "I'll pay the extra money so we can sit in box seats." I hand him money saved from my allowance and money my mother's customers had given me. "That's fine with me," Dad says. He plunks down seven dollars on the counter to pay for both of our tickets.

My heart beats faster as the usher escorts us down the aisle steps near the first base line, pulls out his dust mitt and brushes off our green slatted seats. Dad inconspicuously places a quarter in the usher's hand as I sit down. I try to record the game on the scorecard with Dad's help but the action on the field distracts me as do the calls of "getcha hot dogs, beer and Cracker Jack," from the barker carting his offerings up and down the aisle steps.

The stadium is always full when the Brooklyn Dodgers play their arch-rivals, the New York Giants. The Dodger fans live only an hour's subway ride away, so they come in large numbers to support their team—but I am a Giants fan. My

Deeper Roots

Dad roots for the Dodgers, and even more avidly after Jackie Robinson joined the team in 1947, the first Negro to play in the major leagues. Despite the fact that I am a Giants fan, I always root for Jackie when he comes up to bat. When Robinson hits a single, I watch him tease the pitcher by dancing back and forth along the baseline with his arms outstretched like an eagle. Then he makes a sudden dash and safely slides into second base, adding one more stolen base to his major league record.

Many times during Robinson's major league career, players from opposing teams deliberately slid into second base, Jackie's field position, with their spiked shoes aimed not at the bag but at his legs in an attempt to injure him. These men did not want to play baseball with "niggers." Even on his own team, shortstop Pee Wee Reese was one of the few players who befriended Jackie when he joined the Dodgers. On occasion a black cat would emerge from the dugout of the opposing team when Robinson was at bat. Nevertheless, Robinson's entry into the major leagues gave African Americans renewed hope that the walls of segregation were breaking down. What we didn't realize so long ago was that those walls would have to be dismantled brick-by-brick.

Ten years earlier, in 1937, African Americans thought anything was possible in sports for Negroes after Joe Louis decked the Irish fighter James Braddock. Louis became the heavyweight champion of the world, a title he retained during my childhood. The "Brown Bomber," as Louis was called, still holds the record for the most fights won in his division.

I was allowed to stay up late whenever Joe Louis fought. Dad and I sit next to the Stromberg-Carlson console radio in the living room listening intently to the bout, cringing with each blow that Louis absorbs. My mother goes to bed and covers her head with a pillow. "What's happening to him?"

Chapter Two: Thede Butler

she asks us each time the announcer raises his voice. Finally, the fight is over and Mom comes to join us in the living room cheering, "Hip, hip, hooray, he's won again!"

All of Harlem rooted for Louis, because in a way he was fighting a battle for racial equality for each one of us. "The boxing ring is the only place that a Negro man can beat up a white man and get away with it," my father said. However, when Louis knocked out Max Schmeling in the first round of their second bout at Yankee Stadium in 1938, he scored a symbolic blow for the United States against Nazi Germany before America entered World War II. When Joe Louis was drafted into the Army, I knitted a beige scarf for him and sent it to his training camp at Elton, New York, because I wanted him to be warm. That year I asked Santa Claus for boxing gloves to emulate my hero and each night took my father on in mock contests. I wore one glove, he wore the other. When Dad fell down from one of my "blows" and named me heavyweight champion, my mother laughed.

♦ ♦ ♦ ♦ ♦

As a child, my father's beloved black-varnished bookcase seemed to dominate the foyer of our apartment, and it still did on the autumn day in 1990 when I took the key from the foyer closet to open its glass doors. On top of the bookcase was the German-made mantle clock that strikes every fifteen minutes, adding a measure until it chimes the hour. The clock reminds me of time passing and the contents of the bookcase draw me back to bygone years. The front door of our apartment opened into a small foyer, and with three steps you entered the living room where Dad often sat in his winged chair near the French doors leading to my parents' bedroom reading newspapers into the night. He was always reading newspapers. Each day when he came home from work, he would bring a magazine or comic book for me

Deeper Roots

folded in his newspaper. He read the New York *Times*, the New York *Daily News*, the *Daily Mirror*, and the *World Telegram and Sun* every day. I can see him now, reading by the bedroom window, leaning back in his chair, puffing on his pipe with *Half and Half Tobacco.*

I sat cross-legged on the floor on that rainy afternoon to explore the bookcase's bottom shelf, the one below the shelves containing a gold-tooled set of the complete works of Charles Dickens, Edgar Allan Poe and Louis Stevenson. This bottom shelf was the place where my father saved the important fragments of his life. There was a letter from Dad's third grade teacher, Miss Boyle written in 1890 (it must have had special meaning since Dad saved it all these years). There were membership cards to the YMCA and to the Mount Olivet Baptist Church, tintypes of family members, the 1843 wedding certificate of his grandparents, and a packet of a dozen letters from his lifelong friend, Kenneth Spottswood, written in 1900. I pulled out a teal blue folder containing handwritten speeches Dad made as a young adult. As I rummaged through the sheaves of papers, one of the speeches drew my attention—it was the argument Dad presented for the Debating Society at the New York Colored Men's Branch of the YMCA in 1907. The heading of the paper written in my father's strong flowing hand, reads, "Booker T. Washington is a Detriment to the Negro People." I would subsequently discover that there was a substantial personal and community history associated with this speech. As I unfolded the cream-colored lined paper the four decades since my father's death collapsed into yesterday.

My father died when I was fifteen years old, an age well before I knew enough or cared enough about his early life to ask him the questions that I now yearned to ask. However, there were enough clues in his bookcase to help me piece together some of the history of our forefathers. I traced that history back to 1775 pre-Revolutionary America in

Chapter Two: Thede Butler

Rensselaer County, New York, where my paternal great-grandmother was born. I discovered that our family members were free blacks when slavery was still a part of life in New York State (it did not end until 1827). Those ancestors were church founders, farm owners and activists in the Underground Railroad. I also discovered the beginnings of my Dad's life—a life that was just like the lives of countless other ordinary African Americans who lived in Manhattan in the early years of the twentieth century.

My father grew up in New York City at a time when poor, shabbily-dressed African Americans were pouring into the city fleeing a rash of lynchings in the South. In the late 1800s, the newcomers contrasted sharply with the black aristocracy of New York—ladies who rode in carriages and employed Irish immigrants as their domestic servants and gentlemen who sported waistcoats and spats, owned homes and businesses and sent their daughters to Oberlin College and educated their sons at Harvard University. Proud of their Dutch ancestry and their connection with the founding colonists of seventeenth-century New Netherlands (located on the southern tip of Manhattan), the men formed an exclusive club of black elite, the Society of the Sons of New York, based on their long-standing generational origins.

Dad was not one of the Sons of New York by birth or social status. He was born in Boston on December 6, 1882 to John and Elizabeth Butler in their home at the back of Beacon Hill where Massachusetts General Hospital now stands. The colored neighborhood consisting of rows of wooden houses has now been replaced by the hospital and elegant townhouses.

On the same back slope of Beacon Hill stands the African Meeting House built by free black men in 1806. People of different races met there to speak out against slavery as the abolitionist movement gained strength in the city. Frederick Douglass, escaped slave and famous abolitionist, made his voice heard from this pulpit. The building, located in the heart of the then-black community, housed a school for black children in its basement, and the surrounding area was a place where escaped slaves could find safety and refuge from slave catchers in "safe" houses in the neighborhood.

The African Meeting House stands a few blocks from the Massachusetts gold-domed State House, where the first African American Governor of the Commonwealth, Deval Patrick, was sworn in on its steps in 2007. Across the street from the State House is the bas relief of the 54th Regiment of the Civil War, the first regiment of northern black men who volunteered to fight to end slavery. The Meeting House became a Jewish synagogue as the neighborhood population changed, but in 1987 a week of celebration was observed when the building was restored as the Meeting House and became a National Historic Landmark. It was to this site, part of the Black Heritage Trail, that I brought teachers to learn about this area and the part that it played in our national history.

Although my grandparents lived in—and my father was born in—this historic community, my grandmother, Elizabeth, was actually born in Keeseville, New York, where her parents were involved in helping escaped slaves find freedom in Canada. My grandfather, John Butler, according to family oral history, was an escaped slave from Richmond, Virginia. Sadly, by 1900 Elizabeth was a widow living with her brother and her three children in New York City, according to the Federal Census.

The New York City building where the Butler family settled, 230 West 62nd Street, was a tenement—a vast structure of 400 rooms that offered neither light nor ventilation. Social worker Mary Ovington, who was instrumental in having these unfit tenements replaced by suitable housing, described the buildings in her book, *Half a Man,* as "human hives honeycombed with little rooms thick with human beings."

One day in 1991, as a blustery wind blew swirls of snow across my path, I walked down 62nd Street to find the site where these airless rows of tenements once stood. In the shadow of Lincoln Center, the pink five-story Amsterdam Apartment houses are numbered in the same way as the previous housing, making it easy for me to find the exact place where my father once lived. How close I felt to my father—walking the same street that I knew he had walked as a boy. Although I attended elementary school only a few blocks from here, I wondered why Dad never told me that he once lived so close to my school. Perhaps because the area where they lived, between 60th and 66th Streets and between Tenth and Eleventh Avenues, was called San Juan Hill, an area where veterans returning from the Spanish American War came to live. It was, in fact, a hill and a battleground in the turf wars that flared between Irish residents and their black neighbors. To the west was the Hudson River. To the east were the enormous New York stockyards, a grain elevator, and the Eastman Dressed Beef warehouse. The freight cars of the New York and Hartford railroad lines crossed the area at a diagonal on unprotected tracks when my father was a child. This part of Manhattan is laid out like a grid with the avenues running north to south and the streets running east to west. Eleventh Avenue was called "Death Avenue," because so many children playing there were stuck by trains. As I walked along Eleventh Avenue in 1991 I saw remnants of track, sparkling shards of steel still embedded in the black asphalt of the street.

Between 1890 and 1900, 25,000 black people migrated to New York City from the South, in part because of the 590 lynchings of black men and women that took place in the South between 1890 and 1895. By the end of 1900, 36,246 blacks lived in Manhattan (mostly in the San Juan Hill area

Deeper Roots

where Dad lived and the "Terrible Tenderloin" section between 20th and 53rd Streets on the west side of Manhattan), 18,367 blacks resided in Brooklyn, and the remaining 6,053 lived in the other boroughs of Queens, the Bronx, and Richmond (Staten Island). Although it was a great increase, these people of color still made up less than five per cent of the city's population.

As the northern migration continued, Booker T. Washington, a former slave, founder and principal of Tuskegee Institute and the most influential African American of the day, urged his followers to stay in the South and contribute the labor necessary to rebuild the agricultural economy. His strategy implied that racial equality was not presently the goal of the Negro population.

"Cast down your buckets where you are," Washington admonished blacks in his famous Atlanta Compromise speech of 1895. This political stance guaranteed him the continued financial support of Northern industrialists like Andrew Carnegie, William Baldwin and Robert Ogden, all of whom served on Tuskegee's Board of Trustees. Washington's message was what men like these wanted to hear, and they generously filled Tuskegee's coffers. A strong opposing voice from black leadership had not yet emerged, although in 1901 Monroe Trotter, a Harvard-educated black Bostonian of radical persuasion launched *The Guardian,* a newspaper that would consistently champion racial equality. Despite Booker T. Washington's plea, hundreds of men, women, and children continued to flee the dangerous Southern region arriving in New York City by boat and train each day.

I can imagine my father at age seventeen, in June 1900, riding his bike from his tenement building along Eighth Avenue to 53rd Street. As Thede turns onto 53rd Street, he passes the steps leading up to the recently-constructed elevated train (informally called the "el") station. Only a few years earlier, the clattering noise of the el caused white-owned businesses and churches to relocate farther uptown. As they moved, they sold their properties to African American buyers. In those days the trains co-existed with horses, whose clop-clop on the cobblestone streets would sound in Thede's ears as he maneuvered his way between horse-drawn carriages. The cuffs on his knickers and ribbed socks separated with each pump of the pedals. His collarless white shirt, slightly damp, strained to hike its way up from his belt. His brown brimmed cap tilted jauntily to the left and rested just behind his hairline—exactly the way he wore it in a photograph I cherish.

By 1900, West 53rd Street had become a Mecca of black life—culturally, spiritually and intellectually. This section of Manhattan was the cultural predecessor to Harlem and the renaissance it is known for. Restaurants, social clubs and hotels had opened on the street in addition to Saint Mark's Methodist Episcopal Church, Saint Benedict the Moor Roman Catholic Church and Mount Olivet Baptist (my father's church). They had all moved there from downtown, as did the Colored Men's Association of the YMCA, where Thede was a member. The transformed area remained so, well into the 1920s. The *Evening Telegram* stated that "53rd Street is to the Negro colonies what Fifth Avenue is to white society." Jimmy Marshall's famous hotel and restaurant at 127-129 West 53rd Street catered to artists and theatrical people. Benjamin Thomas Maceo's exclusive restaurant at 213 West 53rd Street served the clergy, the literati and the aristocrats, including the Society of the Sons of New York. At a time when businesses were just beginning to install telephones, Maceo's was one of the few African American establishments listed in the telephone directory in 1900. To make a reservation, the operator connected you to Columbus 800.

I can see Thede pull his bicycle up at the door of Maceo's to rest a minute, catch his breath and then continue on past the building that the aforementioned Society of the Sons of New York had purchased for $20,000. This was the place members met to discuss the crisis of the hordes of Southern Negroes invading the city. The club members were clergy and successful businessmen—mainly caterers and shop owners—whose cultured and refined lifestyle was accessible to only a few of their race. Some members were sons of well-known abolitionists. The second generation of merchants had amassed considerable sums of money and relocated to Brooklyn, where they socialized with one another exclusively.

Every year the Society held an elaborate April ball. The major social event of the season, it was attended by the elite 400 and catered by the best chefs. Not to be outdone, the Society of the Daughters of New York formed their own organization in 1886, two years after their male counterparts, and later the Sons of the South, made up of the accomplished newcomers, founded their own social club. All of these distinct groups formed the higher echelons of the African American elite.

The tinkle of ragtime piano and the sounds of a live four-piece orchestra permeate the air as Thede continues his journey past Jimmy Marshall's hotel and restaurant where people to flock for good food and good conversation. James Weldon Johnson and his brother Rosamond Johnson have taken summer residence from their work in Florida at Marshall's twin brick row houses to further pursue a career as a song-writing team. The Johnson Brothers had recently composed *Lift Every Voice and Sing* performed by 500 schoolchildren as part of a celebration for Abraham Lincoln's birthday in 1900. That song later became known as the Negro National Anthem.

Meanwhile, white actors were entertaining audiences by "corking" up in blackface, painting their lips red, and representing Negroes in derogatory ways. George Walker and Bert Williams (also residents of Marshall's hotel) launched their famed vaudeville act, *Two Real Coons*, in which they brilliantly spoofed white actors caricaturing "darkies." For years such satire was the only form of entertainment by blacks that was acceptable to the white clientele. But in 1900 Williams and Walker brought their vaudeville production of *Sons of Ham* to Broadway, at the same time that the Johnson brothers were composing songs for musical productions using all-black casts. The Johnson brothers' compositions were moving away from the minstrel tradition by writing popular hits in Broadway musicals, sung by noted white performers. The thriving entertainment industry began to draw deeply and profoundly from the artistic talents of the African American community, a community largely located at that time along 53rd Street.

My father would have ended his bike ride at the newly-rented space of the Colored Men's Branch of the Young Men's Christian Association at 132 West 53rd Street. Thede was one of the first members (and its Corresponding Secretary) of the Branch, joining immediately after it opened its doors in 1900. Its creation was the culmination of Mount Olivet Baptist Church's mission to expand its ministry and the national YMCA's mandate to increase membership in urban communities. The application submitted by the Colored Men's Association for branch affiliation was granted by the YMCA with one proviso—that attendance and activities by the colored membership be restricted to that branch. This restriction insured that it would be the only branch of the YMCA in New York where Negro men could attend lectures, classes, listen to music or rent rooms. My father's membership was so important to him that he kept his annual membership cards carefully stored in a black leather cardholder on the bottom shelf of that bookcase.

Deeper Roots

When I was doing research in the YMCA archives I asked to see the records of the Harlem Branch, momentarily forgetting (until I saw the group's photograph) that in 1900 Harlem was a white community. Sadly, the YMCA archives hold no records for the historic beginnings of the Colored Men's Branch, but my dad saved carbon copies of his communications representing his branch as Corresponding Secretary. The bookcase, therefore, held the only records for that branch. From these artifacts I learned something particularly valuable to me—that the Colored Men's Branch had a YMCA baseball team and that Thede not only played on the team but he wrote the team's constitution. My love of baseball was apparently inherited.

At the Y, Thede would find his boyhood neighbor and lifelong friend, Kenneth Spottswood, waiting for him. Ken, a tall and lanky young man, lived with his family in the same tenement as Thede and his family. In 1900 Thede informed Ken that, "I just got a job for the summer in Brielle, New Jersey, not too far from Asbury Park. I'll be leaving next week. Will you let me know what's going on at the Y and at church?" Ken responded, "You lucky guy. Sure, I'll keep you informed. I'll write to you." Ken did write, and my father kept the letters in their envelopes, each bearing a pink one-cent stamp, dating from June to September. The correspondence with Ken revealed the feelings, interests, activities, political and social issues that captured these two young men in particular—and the black community in general—at the turn of the twentieth century.

Of personal interest, Ken wrote in July, 1900 of a significant event in Thede's life that captured Ken's attention:

> *Congratulations -- Uncle Thede, it can't come much nearer to 'pop.' Why man you ought to be tickled to death. I envy you Thede, leaving all jokes aside I presume you wear a larger sized hat now.*

48

Chapter Two: Thede Butler

Well! Well!! who would have thought __Uncle__ Thede. __Mamma__ Jessie, and __Grandma__ Butler. Give Mrs.   White   and   Mrs.   Butler   my compliments....__Unclehood__: Young man, remember you are no longer the frivolous light-hearted boy you used to be; not the belittled, insulted and despised nobody of bygone days. You have secured that unchanging, unalterable dignity, ordained by the Almighty— uncleship. Yes, you are an uncle, hold up your head and throw back your shoulders to a greater extent than you used to when you and I marched down 76th Street from your work at 7PM evenings years ago.

Thede indeed took his role as uncle seriously. Both Thede's father and brother had passed away, leaving Thede as the only surviving male in the immediate family. After Jessie's husband abandoned her and their six children, Thede supported them and his widowed mother for at least fifteen years after the fire in Connecticut that destroyed the family homestead.

In addition to the good news about Thede's new family status, the summer of 1900 was also particularly hot—not only in the heat that enveloped the city but politically and socially as well. That same July, Thede writes to Ken from Brielle, New Jersey, "It's about as pretty a place as you could care to lay your eyes on. There is a horse, a row boat, a pretty cottage and plenty of fruit trees, excellent fishing, but no woods that I have discovered as yet." In turn, Ken writes of the oppressive summer heat and the employment issues that he and others in the African American community were experiencing. Ken's envy cannot be masked:

I know you will have wonderfully developed muscles carrying water from the well every day.

Deeper Roots

Oh, the Country the Country! If you like the country so well, you can stand the ocean breezes that would freeze a brass monkey at night..and 'Old Sol' who would melt the heart of coldest ice. ..the bumpy roads, and muddy ground./././ I certainly wish I was down there with you./././ I dread the summer when I think of the sultry days and dreadful nights down our way. I am sorry to disappoint you, but I cannot go down to the YWCA entertainment as I need a pair of shoes and that would leave me broke. I was copying a letter for the boss yesterday when he said, 'Kenneth, if you don't mind I think I'll raise your wages to $3.00.' I tell you Thede my blood boils in my veins when I think of it.

Kenneth often wrote to Thede on his employer's stationary, and obviously resented his present status and he fantasizes about a day when the firm will be called Diller and Spottswood.

In New York City, access to jobs with adequate pay is a chronic problem for the working-class blacks of New York City, who are largely relegated to menial jobs and often exploited. On September 9, 1900, The *New York Times* made this suggestion: "Let the Negro learn to clean stables, care for horses./././run lawn mowers./././" Needless to say, neither Ken's father or my father were willing to follow this advice. Ken describes his situation:

You know father isn't working now and how that makes things. I am completely handicapped. I give him all my earnings save a quarter and that is soon gone by the time my laundry bill is paid. And there's so many things I really need and want to get. But I hope he'll get something soon." [Ken

Chapter Two: Thede Butler

subsequently lost his job as well.] *"I have received no word from Altman yet. I think that's a mild way of putting 'Niggers not wanted here.' .. . Say Thede; Are you thinking of taking a Civil Service examination this fall? If you are, write and let me know which exam and for what you are going to take and I will file an application with you as soon as possible. I know a lad named Percy Green, he took the examination three times for P.O. clerk and failed, passed was appointed about a month ago. Is now in the General P.O. getting $12.50 a week and he gets raised every certain length of time.*

Thede did take the civil service exam, and he began work as a clerk in that same General Post Office in 1903. His job was boxing mail to be routed to different parts of Brooklyn. Since there were no zip codes at that time, he had to memorize the location of the streets on the "scheme" in which the mail for that area should be placed. Among his papers, Dad saved most of his rankings on his annual postal tests on which he routinely scored one hundred percent, or in the high nineties. Promotions in the U.S. Postal Service were supposedly based on test performance, but although my father's performance was impeccable, many whites were promoted above him... and then needed to be trained for their job by my dad. Even so, work in the postal service was considered a good job for blacks at the time, offering regular pay, raises, vacation time, sick leave and medical coverage, and no heavy lifting. My dad told me how angry he was when President Woodrow Wilson re-segregated federal offices and lunch areas for employees in Washington, D.C.

The Colored Men's Branch of the Y did, however, allow Thede and Ken to dream of a life beyond the post office. The

Deeper Roots

branch offered courses in history, advanced math, bookkeeping, debate and rhetoric. Ken writes:

> One of my fondest dreams was that I would become an author loved and adored. Here, portraying the shameful abuse which we of the unfortunate race bear so uncomplainingly. Gaining the sympathy of the general public with stories with themes portraying the injustice of our lot. ...Oh Thede! I dream of so many things I scarce dare tell you or you might think me a greater fool than I really am.

Such idyllic dreams and aspirations are abruptly interrupted by evidence of the injustice of the real world. The stifling heat of August 1900 exacerbated racial tension between Irish and black communities in the city. As Ken reported to Thede that summer:

> I was riding up home on a fellow's wheel about 10:30 Tuesday night on 8th Avenue when two colored fellows said, 'Say fellow if you want that wheel you better get out of here.' I rode up hitting up faster thinking it was some bad coons who wanted to steal the wheel. When I got to 37th Street two white fellows came up to me and told me to go through the block quickly if I didn't want to get in trouble...I thought they were alluding to the colored lads who had spoken to me at 35th./././I got on again and flew uptown.

Upon researching Ken's odd encounters that night, I discovered the fascinating circumstances that led up to that day's events. On August 15, 1900, the most violent attack on Negroes in New York City took place since the Draft Riots of

Chapter Two: Thede Butler

1863. Two days earlier one Arthur Harris had emerged from a store on 41st Street and Broadway, where he had purchased a cigar, and saw his lady friend, May Enoch, in the grip of an unknown man. This man, unbeknownst to Harris, was a plainclothes policeman, Robert Thorpe, who was in the process of arresting Enoch on charges of solicitation. As Harris tried to release his companion from the grip of this stranger, Thorpe hit him several times with his nightstick. In the ensuing struggle, Harris knifed Thorpe in the stomach, fatally wounding him. Harris fled New York City to Washington, D.C., where he was later apprehended. May Enoch was arrested.

On the Tuesday evening crowds gathered near Thorpe sister's home, where the body was being waked in traditional Irish fashion. An interracial scuffle broke out, which escalated into a riot in which white citizens and some policemen attacked African Americans. That night, ruffians took control of the streets between Broadway and Seventh Avenue from 34th to 42nd Streets, beating African Americans indiscriminately while the police stood by and watched or, in some instances, participated. Rocks were thrown through the windows of rooms where African Americans lived. Groups of men invaded public places in search of blacks to beat up. Fifty years earlier, "For Colored Only" signs had hung over the sides of Jim Crow street signs in New York City. Now those signs were gone, but black people were dragged from trolley cars and attacked.

As the rioting unfolded, James and Rosamond Johnson were in their studio at Marshall's, working late on a production with Billy Johnson. Rosamond had arranged to meet a friend, Barry Carter, another theatrical colleague, later that night for a social engagement. At the conclusion of their rehearsal, the Johnson brothers escorted Johnson to the car stop. They waited for an hour and no car passed. Johnson finally hailed a hansom cab. Since the cars were not running

53

on schedule, Rosamond decided not to meet Carter as planned and the Johnson brothers went home, only to be awakened in the early morning and notified that Carter had been beaten in the head with a lead pipe and taken to jail after he and his lady companions had walked unknowingly and with tragic consequences into the troubled area. According to James Weldon Johnson, Carter never fully recovered from his severe head injuries. Chants echoed through the street that terrible night urging the mob to get the Johnson brothers, George Walker and Bert Williams — names that the hoodlums knew because of the fame of these popular artists and performers. According to many reports, the assault had been planned in advance as retaliation for Robert Thorpe's death.

The August 16, 1900 New York *Times* reported the riot on the front page: "Fully 1,000 people gathered and started to clean off the side streets of Negroes." Only a sudden thunderstorm quelled the violence which sent hundreds of people to the hospitals. The New York *Tribune* characterized the treatment of African Americans as being as bad as in the South and said that the incident had "disgraced" the city.

On the following evening, against the advice of his father and friends, Kenneth ventured down to the place where the disturbances occurred.

> *I walked down 8th Avenue to 40th Street. Little kids called me nigger. I ain't noticed them...I went up B'way to 49th Street where the Old Guard new building./././ and the Brewster carriage are, well it's kind of dark there and as I go to walk past, out jump a crowd of men./././ I hate to run, especially from such curs as those so far below me. Someone came up like a flash and knocked me down in the gutter./././ kicked me in the face till I was unconscious. When I found myself, I was at a*

Chapter Two: Thede Butler

party's house who bathed my face....I only got
bruised by the eye./././ It is simply outrageous
and terrible the way innocent blacks were treated
by mob violence during the past week.

The riot was a wake-up call. New Yorkers got the biggest jolt, but the mistreatment of blacks throughout the country had been intensifying as the Reconstruction period ended. The New York African American community mobilized to form a Citizens' Protective League and hired attorney Frank Moss to secure affidavits from victims of the riot. T. Thomas Fortune, editor of the African American newspaper, the New York *Age* served as an officer of the League. The Reverend Dr. William Brooks, pastor of St. Mark's Church on 53rd Street and the League's president was the most influential of African American clergy in New York City. "We ask for no money consideration, only conviction and removal from the force of those officers whom we are able to prove guilty." Dr. Brooks wrote to New York City Mayor Robert Van Wyck.

The League organized a public meeting in Carnegie Hall on September 12, 1900, to raise money for legal expenses. Kenneth wrote Thede about the event which drew 3,500 people. "About that meeting, Thede, at Carnegie Hall, I hardly know how to begin. It was a rattling, great, stupendous success. Such a demonstration Carnegie Hall has never had."

Among the many speakers who came to the podium that night were religious leaders such as Bishop William Derrick, Bishop of the New York Diocese of the African Methodist Episcopalian church, Republican Party activist, and supporter of Booker T. Washington. One person who particularly impressed Kenneth was Marchita Lyons of Brooklyn. Miss Lyons's prominent New York family had moved to Rhode Island and petitioned the governor to admit her to high school. The first black to attend high school in

Rhode Island, she had graduated with honors. At the time of the rally, Lyons was a teacher in the Brooklyn schools, and later she became a principal. Kenneth wrote:

> *She is the finest woman orator I ever heard. Perfect in her grammar, irreproachable in her delivery, she held her audience and swayed it as she pleased by a gesture, a nod, a word./ ././ .*

> *A collection of $1,000 was taken up and Bishop Derrick said he wanted 100 men to band together under a captain./././ each man pledged himself to give five dollars within the next 30 days./././ It was an orderly and well dressed audience. The League means business. It means to fight through every court in the land until it obtains justice.*

A police review board was established to hear the testimony of the complainants. But according to an account by Frank Moss in *Story of a Riot*, the victims were treated as though they were the instigators of the attacks they suffered. Despite requests for review by the mayor and letters of appeal to Governor Theodore Roosevelt, the efforts of the Citizens' Protective League resulted only in a whitewash.

Ninety-nine years after this ugly injustice, little had changed In New York City's police relationships with blacks. In 2000, New York City policemen were exonerated by the jury after firing forty-eight bullets and killing innocent Amadou Diallo as he stood on the stoop of his building. Diallo was an African immigrant and son of wealthy, educated parents who immediately traveled to the city from abroad. They were shocked, dazed, and horrified by the reckless behavior of the police. The trial of the officers involved in the shooting was held 150 miles away from the crime in Albany, New York, to avoid mass demonstrations in

Chapter Two: Thede Butler

New York City in the event the perpetrators were acquitted, which they were.

In a letter two weeks after his ordeal with the mob of 1900, Kenneth counters Booker T. Washington's assertion that political involvement was not necessary for Southern Negroes.

> *As to the disenfranchisement question, let me say this....It is shamefully illegal because it is unconstitutional. ... If any state can ignore any part of [the] constitution when it so desires, of what importance is that document...?*
>
> *Therefore the disenfranchisement question is not only one of vital importance to the blacks, but if anything a graver one for the better element of the whites to carefully consider.*

My father would have agreed. Usually Thede spoke softly; I knew him as a quiet and gentle man. But I imagine the veins on my father's neck pulsed on the warm autumn evening, the seventh day of October, 1907 (seven years after the riot) when he addressed the audience at the New York City Colored Men's Branch of the YMCA. Twenty-four-year-old Thede rose and approached the podium as a member of the debating team, to declare loudly and clearly that "Booker T. Washington is a detriment to the Negro people."

The assembled audience at the Colored Men's Branch is listening attentively as Thede continues:

> *Washington's policy is the policy of peace at any price. Passive submissiveness to any wrongs that may be visited upon us. A peace which seals our lips for fear of offending someone when an*

Deeper Roots

innocent member of our race is lynched or burned
at the stake.

That speech, written in my father's strong, flowing hand on the cream colored paper—made me think about the horrendous postcards I saw on exhibition at the New York Historical Society in the Spring of 2000—postcards printed with photographs of black men hanged from trees, their limp bodies mutilated, souvenirs made of body parts. The gleeful onlookers of the lynchings which included children and women stared defiantly into the camera lens. More than 428 lynchings occurred in the United States from 1900 to 1905, most of them were based on unfounded charges of black men raping white women. The formation of the principle agent of the lynchings, the Ku Klux Klan, was given impetus by Ben Tillman, a Governor of South Carolina, and for twenty years a United States Senator who lectured extensively around the country spreading his message of hate and violence.

In his speech my father asks:

> *Must we stand by and hear Ben Tillman and his*
> *follower Thomas Dixon assert that there is no*
> *virtue in our women and for those reasons we can*
> *never equal our Anglo Saxon brothers?   Who*
> *among you who was loved by mother, sister, or*
> *sweetheart feels that such can pass unchallenged?*

> *A peace that must be bought with the priceless*
> *heritage of our franchise, a peace that brings*
> *injustice and discrimination, peace which exacts*
> *our manhood, I say is too dear a price to*
> *pay....Progress (and) aggressiveness must go hand*
> *in hand in the upward movement of any people.*

Chapter Two: Thede Butler

These we must have at any cost even to the extent
of opposing Dr. Washington.

Right on—I say, more than a century later. I wish I was at the YMCA that evening because I never heard Dad speak in public. How proud I am of my dad. I framed the original three-page text written in his beautiful penmanship, and signed "Theodore H. Butler, October 23, 1907," and hung it on the dining room wall of my own home where my children and friends and guests can see my father's words. I count my blessings to have the legacy of his words and the tangible mementos of his life.

Over forty years after he gave his speech, I remember Dad singing to my mother and me, "Darling, I am growing old…Silver threads among the gold."

His kind and loving spirit dwells within me.

Chapter Three:

Home to Harlem and 409

It is April 1936. Meme and Thede Butler and I ride home in a cab from nearby Columbia Presbyterian Hospital, where I was born two weeks earlier—two weeks was a normal stay for mother and baby back then. My father carries me under the green awning emblazoned with the white numerals, "409" where the uniformed, white-gloved doorman tips his hat and opens the wrought-iron-framed glass door. We ascend the four marble steps into the lobby. White and black rectangular tiles set in a herringbone pattern edge the Oriental carpets. The rugs muffle the sound of footsteps as my parents walk past the columns embellished with gold leaf toward the elevator at the right end of the T-shaped lobby. The hall man is announcing a visitor on the intercom and directs the guest to the other manned elevator at the opposite end of the lobby. Flower arrangements adorn the tables alongside the Jacobean benches next to the elevators. "Blessed bundle," buxom Mrs. Dial comments in her sonorous voice as she rides on the elevator with us to her ninth floor apartment. We continue up to the twelfth floor. Our apartment is the first one on the left when we get off the elevator.

We enter our home and Dad puts me down in a bassinet mounted on wooden wheels, designed and constructed by the resident handyman, the cigar-smoking Milton Hinks. The bassinet was draped with a peaked canopy of white organdy hand sewn by my mother's friend, Jane Jackson, a hairdresser who lived in apartment 7C. Twenty-three years later, my mother resurrected the bassinet and set it up for my daughter's first visit to this same apartment. Both Mr. Hinks and Ms. Jackson were invited to see and welcome Karen.

Everyone who was anyone in New York City's African American community knew of "409." Just hail a cab in Harlem and say "409" and the driver would know where to take you. Walter White, W. E. B. Du Bois, Roy Wilkins, Thurgood Marshall, leaders of the NAACP, and other black elite lived at 409 during the 1920s, 1930s and through World War II.

This thirteen-story red brick apartment house on Edgecombe Avenue and 153rd Street dwarfs the other buildings on Sugar Hill. Sited on Coogan's Bluff, high above the Harlem River, the E-shaped structure commands a view of the Bronx and lower Manhattan as well as the Palisades of northern New Jersey. Neighbors sit and chat on a series of green-slatted wooden benches directly across the street from the entrance to 409. Behind the benches iron grillwork extends ten blocks along an uninterrupted promenade where maple trees shade the avenue. Cool water bubbles up from the pebbly stone fountain where you may quench your thirst

Chapter Three: Home to Harlem and 409

after climbing the seemingly endless concrete steps from Eighth Avenue to the Hill.

Harlem and 409 both figure prominently in American and African American history. From our kitchen window I can also see a white brick house, the oldest colonial residence left standing in New York City. From this mansion General George Washington commanded his troops during the Battle of Harlem Heights during the Revolutionary War, scoring a decisive victory against the British for the control of Manhattan. However, two weeks later, the colonists defeated the rebels, won back the island and held it until 1783. This house, the Morris-Jumel Mansion at Edgecombe Avenue at 160th Street, was advertised in the pages of the *Post Boy* newspaper of May 6, 1765 as part of "a 100 acre farm lying between two rivers, convenient for fishing, clamming and oystering." The mansion, on its grassy sloping grounds looks oddly out of place in the midst of the concrete-and-steel buildings surrounding it. On my visits there I enjoyed examining the replica of the desk George Washington used. I imagined him sitting there and signing important documents with his quill pen.

A few African descendants lived in Harlem from the 1600s under Dutch colonial rule, and some slaves and free blacks continued to live in the area after Britain took over the colony. The estates of James De Lancey and Alexander Hamilton were also located there and Hamilton Grange, a National Memorial, is located at 414 West 141st Street, between Convent and St. Nicholas Avenues. Descendants of the original Dutch, English and French families lived quite comfortably in this country town.

By the end of the nineteenth century, abandoned farmlands in Harlem were used to build newer housing, populated mostly by old-line New Yorkers, German Jews and Irish and English immigrants. Harlem was considered to be an outpost of the core city. Pockets of blacks on East 122nd,

Deeper Roots

124th and 126th Streets and West 126th and 134th Streets provided enough children of color to populate an all-Negro school. The Garrison and Sumner apartment houses at 125th Street and Broadway had Negro residents dating from 1890, when Southern Negroes and West Indians came to New York and moved into Harlem in increasing numbers.

Land speculation began after 1890. The elevated train extended its route to Harlem, encouraging developers to build an abundance of good-quality housing for upper-and middle-class white residents from downtown New York to rent or buy. But the new housing stock exceeded the demand, so in order to protect financial investments, real estate agents very reluctantly opened apartments to those who could afford to pay the rent—but not just anyone. The Harlem Property Owners Improvement Organization, active between 1910 and 1915, was established to prevent rental or sale to African Americans. The organization failed in its goal as reflected in an April 7, 1911 editorial in the *Harlem Home News* that referred to "the black hordes eating through the very heart of Harlem."

The racial covenants designed to prevent Negroes from renting and owning these desirable properties did not hold; nor did these investors anticipate the arrival of Negroes north of the imaginary line at 145th Street that for years separated black and white residential properties. In 1917 one of the land speculators, the Atlanta-based Candler Holding Company, owners of Coca-Cola, had already committed to building 409. But by then Negroes were already moving north (as whites were moving to the suburbs) into the part of Washington Heights that is now considered "upper" Harlem. By 1927 Negroes had replaced the predominantly Jewish residents of 409.

Mr. Harold Thomas, occupant of apartment 13E, had lived in 409 for more than 60 years. During the 1931 and 1932 school summer vacations he was an elevator operator in the

Chapter Three: Home to Harlem and 409

"house" where his aunt, Dr. Buelah Gardiner and his cousin Billy lived at that time. Mr. Thomas's older sister, Thelma Wilson, told me, "I was hired in 1927 by Nail and Parker Associates, the successful colored realty firm, to manage the building and collect rents at a time when many apartments were still vacant because of the glut in the market. That was my first job after graduating from Wadleigh High that year, and I was offered an apartment in the house rent free. The Metropolitan Life Insurance Company owned the building, and John Thornton was the superintendent. It was a pleasure to work there because the tenants and staff were so friendly."

For the first twenty-one years of my life, until I married Hubey and moved to the Boston area, 409 was my home. Then 409 became a second home for our growing family. "I see Ba's house, I see Ba's house" my children would chorus from the rear of the station wagon as we motored down the Harlem River Drive to visit my widowed mother. Later on, the apartment was used by most of our eight children when they studied or worked in New York City and it is the place where I now do some of my research and writing. But 409 means even more to me because in its elegance, its glamour, and the pride reflected by the tenants who lived there, it represents a part of Harlem in its glorious days. A few of the people who were my neighbors when I was growing up still reside in the building today. These neighbors assisted my mother in her advanced years and they add a sense of continuity to my life.

My parents moved into 409 right before my birth. Thede, Meme and Maud literally and figuratively "moved up" to 409 from the fifth floor walk-up apartment next door when the flights of stairs were too much for Meme to climb when she was expecting me. Auntie Maud, Mom's domineering

65

Deeper Roots

older sister said, "Meme, get a room for me when you move. You will need someone of your own around."

Every day after Auntie Maud came home from work, she would dress me to go out for a stroll. She pushed my carriage down the ten-block promenade of Edgecombe Avenue while the bench-sitters across the street watched. "That mother gets her baby out religiously," Mrs. Simon said to Miss Long. "I always see her with the carriage." "That's not the mother, Miss Long. The real mother doesn't have snow-white hair, and she's not as thin as that lady. That's the baby's aunt. They live together. The mother is my hair-dresser, so I know."

It was not surprising that my nurturing aunt became my self-selected godmother, announcing to my parents after I came home from the hospital that "the baby will be christened at St. Philip's Protestant Episcopal Church on Whitsunday." It was typical of her to take command. My mother laughed as she recalled the directives. "You, Teddy," Auntie Maud said to my father, "get the godfather, and you, Meme, get *another* godmother." Auntie Maud purchased the white long flowing christening gown. On the appointed Sunday afternoon in May 1936, Auntie Maud and the other godparents, Edna Jackson and John Adams, all stood together at the altar for the ceremony while Father Shelton Bishop sprinkled holy water on my forehead. In photographs taken to document the day, you can barely see my face emerging from billows of lace. They said I cried.

My mother's brother, Oscar, also stayed with us occasionally. He was a waiter on the Cunard Steamship line and his layover was in New York. His bulging eyes looked right through you, although they were sometimes bloodshot when he had too much to drink. Even bloodshot, however, Uncle Oscar always looked dapper in the custom-made linen suits and Panama hats he purchased on his trips abroad. My Uncle Oscar called me Miss Betty when he didn't call me "moonface." In my room I had a bookcase with glass doors and a key, just like my dad's bookcase. On top of that bookcase I kept the curios my Uncle Oscar brought home for me from his trips to Asia. There was a seashell girl—her mischievous face painted on one seashell, her body formed by two shells glued together, her legs a pair of pipe cleaners attached to another shell. Next to her I placed a black-and-white speckled rooster with a red comb that looked so real. He had springs for legs and could bounce on his stand. Then there was a wooden jinrikisha, four inches high with a hand-carved man pulling the carriage and a couple riding in the rear. The wheels rolled when I moved the carriage. A Japanese paper umbrella with a toothpick-size frame rested next to the jinrikisha. One of the other souvenirs he brought me, a beautiful white silk kimono with quilted sleeves and a blue-and-silver dragon embroidered on the left side, hung in my closet.

Oscar's daughter, Edna, came to our house every day. Edna played the Hardman Peck piano in the living room every afternoon after school. She went to Wadleigh High, at 114th Street and Eighth Avenue, Harlem's premier all-girls school, and took the subway to our house. I would watch from the living-room window as she walked down the hill on 155th Street. Since well before I was born, Edna had come to my parents' apartment to prepare for her Saturday afternoon piano lesson—paid for by my mother—with Miss Shephard, the music teacher.

"My brother Oscar was away at sea most of the time and your Aunt Louise, who was also from Jamaica, worked in a factory doing piecework. So Edna had lots of time on her hands," mother told me. "She spent weekends with me when I was single. We went to the movies and window-shopped downtown. We had a ball. I was like her second mother."

Those excursions around the city were abruptly halted when I came on the scene and began monopolizing my mother's attention. Edna admitted to me decades later that, "at first it was hard having you around, Betty." Thirteen years my senior, Edna was like an older sister to me and I know I must have been a pest to her. "I was accustomed to having Aunt Meme all to myself but I got used to you being my shadow."

When Edna rang the doorbell, Mom was usually doing a customer's hair in the kitchen off the foyer, so I would open the door. I remember my cousin as a tall, lanky girl wearing a box-pleated skirt and a loose-fitting beige sweater and a blouse with a Peter Pan collar at the neck. Bobby socks and brown-and-white saddle oxfords completed her outfit. Her hair was combed into a neat pageboy style, parted on the left side. After she settled in, Edna would let me sit next to her on the piano bench while she practiced scales. Her long legs easily reached the pedals while my legs dangled in the air. I hoped that someday I could read those odd-shaped notations in the music book and know what keys to press with my fingers to make the living room fill with sound.

I liked to follow Edna and watch her brush her long hair over the bathroom sink as the medicine cabinet's rectangular mirror reflected the movements of Edna's graceful hands as she carefully applied deep red lipstick to her heart-shaped lips. Edna had the same space between her two front teeth that I had, but that was about all we had in common. My cousin was quiet and shy while I was talkative and inquisitive. But Edna loved to dance. Her face would come alive as she grasped the bed posts of the two-poster in my parents' room using it as an imaginary partner to pull herself back and forth, her feet flying in step with the rhythm of the lindy hop playing on the radio. Edna also loved fashion, spending hours intently paging through *Vogue* and *Glamour*. She ordered her high-heeled shoes from a Newport News, Virginia, sales catalogue and had them delivered to our apartment.

Chapter Three: Home to Harlem and 409

Then Edna and I would go into my bedroom, which I had inherited at age four when Auntie Maud moved to the Dunbar apartments on Eighth Avenue and 150th Street. In my room Edna kept the Remington Rand typewriter Mom gave her when she began a secretarial course at Wadleigh High, immediately after her 1941 graduation. "Won't you teach me to type, too?" I begged. "Okay, Betty. We'll set up the card table and put the typewriter on it. First get the telephone book to sit on so you can see what you're doing. Now you sit in this chair and rest your fingers on this middle row of letters. The next thing you have to do is to memorize the keyboard so that you don't have to look at the keys then you will know exactly where each letter is. But first, I'll put the paper in the roller and you can try pushing the letters down one at a time and see how the typewriter works."

My first of a series of lessons began. Eventually, after much patient help from my cousin, I learned to type. Edna let me time her speed in typing the exercises in the silver-covered instruction book. I can see her fingers moving effortlessly across the keyboard, hear the tinkle of the bell when she finished the line and moved the carriage back, always with her eyes on the sentences she had to type. That course preparation enabled Edna to be hired as a secretary when the scarcity of workers caused by World War II opened previously unattainable jobs to Negroes in white-collar positions and defense work. Edna continued to visit our home at least twice a week for many years while she pursued a lifetime career in government service.

But time passes and lives change. Family ties strengthen and weaken, ebb and flow. In 1951 Edna and I lost contact with each other when Meme favored her brother, Oscar (Edna's father), after the breakup of his marriage to Aunt Louise. Edna's allegiance was to her mother, and remained there past the death of her father, her mother, our Auntie Maud and Edna's favorite Aunt Meme. We met only at funerals of family members. A gnawing feeling of uneasiness and guilt prompted me to telephone Edna one evening at her St. Albans, New York home. A thin high-pitched voice answered the phone. "May I speak with Edna," I asked. "Who is calling?" the unfamiliar voice asked. "Betty Butler. I'm Edna's cousin."

"Betty who?" I felt as though I had traveled light years through space. Neither of us recognized the other's voice; it had been decades since we had seen each other. Once we had reintroduced ourselves, we tried to catch up.

"How many children do you have?" What did you say your husband's name is? When did you get married? I wish I had that Remington typewriter now, instead of this word processor—it keeps skipping on me," Edna laughed.

"You know I still keep the apartment at 409, I said. "I haven't thought about 409 for ages," Edna said.

♦ ♦ ♦ ♦ ♦

Unlike Edna, my attachment to 409 was (and continues to be) not only a physical attachment but an emotional one as well. The impact of my neighbors on my life was almost as strong as the influence exerted by my family.

The 409 tenants were an interesting and eclectic mix, representing the entire social and economic spectrum, the famous and infamous. It was a diverse vertical community of African Americans from all walks of life who treated one another with respect and courtesy. You didn't have to leave the building to encounter ministers, teachers, musicians, artists, red caps, lawyers, hot goods dealers, judges, gamblers, doctors and hairdressers in those 111 apartments. As a young man, after returning to New York from Jamaica, and before he became famous as a singer, actor, and social activist, Harry Belafonte hauled trash for the residents. His

Chapter Three: Home to Harlem and 409

recollection of these tenants was of a snobbish exclusive group. To me as a child, they were my friendly neighbors.

Long-time resident, Ms. Thelma Wilson recalls one neighbor in particular. "I remember Madame Stephanie St. Clair breezing through the lobby with her fur coat dramatically flowing behind her. She had a mystical aura about her, and she wore exotic dresses with a colorful turban wrapped around her head. She was always very pleasant to me. When I went to her apartment to collect the rent she invited me in to see her collection of gold coins embedded in a glass-topped table. I was impressed."

I was impressed too when I thought about the courage, intelligence, skill, and savvy needed for a woman of the 1920s to create and run one of the most lucrative policy banks in Harlem. Also referred to as "the numbers," policy banking was an illegal and lucrative gambling operation. When notorious gangster and bootlegger Dutch Schultz, who controlled the numbers in other areas of the city, attempted to encroach on Madame's territory, she resisted. This tall statuesque entrepreneur of French-Caribbean ancestry stated that she was not afraid of Dutch Schultz or any other man. She hired ten controllers and numerous clerks to operate the business, forty runners to collect bets and distribute winnings, and guards to protect her business. She also retained personal henchmen to protect her. Harold Thomas recalled, "One day during the summer of 1931 when I was operating the elevator, the hall man on duty signaled for me to come to where he stood, as a black limo stopped in front of the house. I saw the four doors open simultaneously and one man got out of each door. They closed the doors in unison, making a single sound. They were very businesslike in their appearance; they about-faced and walked into the building military style. I took them up on the south elevator to Madame St. Clair's floor. They rang for me about twenty minutes later and repeated the routine, leaving the building

Deeper Roots

the same as when they entered, without saying a word. These men were Madame St. Clair's protectors. My cousin, Billy, told me that Dutch Schultz sent one of his men up to see Madame. St. Clair. She pushed him in a closet, locked the door and called her men to take care of him," Mr. Thomas reported. When Dutch Schultz was gunned down by mobsters and taken to the Newark, New Jersey City Hospital, he received a telegram from his guileful antagonist. According to Dutch Schultz' biographer, Paul Sann, the telegram read, "As ye sow, so shall you reap" and it was signed, "Madame Queen of Policy." Shultz never recovered from his wounds; he died in the hospital on October 24, 1935.

The numbers racket was an integral part of Harlem life and it worked much like the modern lottery. Today's storekeeper sells tickets much like a numbers runner did back then. When I was living in 409, a Mr. Brown was the numbers runner for most of the tenants. A very respectable-looking man with mixed gray hair and a complexion like butterscotch pudding, "Brownie" came to the building every day except Sunday. His trousers were properly creased and his jacket well fitted and he unfailingly tipped his hat to the ladies as he came around the corner. His shoes were polished to a gleaming shine and he always had the New York *Daily News* tucked under his arm. For several hours he went from apartment to apartment to collect the numbers the tenants played for the day.

Our apartment was one of the stops Mr. Brown made. My mother had a piece of paper with a list of the numbers she wanted to play for the day, straight or in combination. It was always three numbers, playing 687 for five cents straight, for instance, or various combinations such as 876, 786, 678, and so on for two or three cents per combination.

Dreams and hunches determined my mom's selection, and she frequently referred to her "dream book" for listings of numbers associated with the content of dreams. Brownie sat down at the kitchen table, opened the New York *Daily News* to the centerfold of photographs, took a pencil sharpened to a needle point, and carefully copied the numbers in the minutest way possible so that you needed a magnifying glass to decipher them. Then he got up from the table, said his goodbyes, and tucked the paper under his arm on his way to the next apartment. He carried no evidence on his person of this illegal activity; no number slips could be found in his pocket if he was arrested.

If you "hit the number" (based on the results from the horse races), Brownie came the next morning to pay off the bet—twenty dollars, fifty dollars or hundreds of dollars, depending on the amount of money that you placed on the number(s). As far as I know he never got caught. I would get a special treat when Mom hit the number, maybe a new coat if I needed one, or a trip by subway to Radio City Music Hall. My dad never played the numbers and I never thought that there was anything wrong with this activity. It was a chance for working-class people to dream of striking it rich for a day. Nowadays, we call it Lotto and it is a legal activity.

In 1941 the United States entered into World War II, and during those wartime years 409 was the air raid shelter for the neighborhood. A yellow sign near the front door identified the building as the place to go in case of a bombing attack. When the singsong sirens blared to indicate an air raid practice drill was occurring, men and women called wardens wearing white helmets and armbands checked the streets to make sure that no lights showed from any apartment. Special black shades were pulled down, the streets were silent and everything was in total darkness. The sweep of searchlights across the sky created an eerie glow. I was not scared that enemy planes would drop bombs on us, even though I had seen newsreels of buildings in Europe reduced to rubble. In the films, patriotic music played as parachutes

Deeper Roots

billowed and American aviators dropped from the sky onto enemy soil, while deep-voiced male commentators reported scores of victories for the Allied troops.

The war propaganda made its indelible mark on my mind. Cartoon films depicting slant-eyed, yellow-skinned Japanese pilots shot down from the heavens brought roars of delight and applause from the audience. On the West Coast, where the largest number of Japanese Americans resided, real estate belonging to Japanese Americans was confiscated, and the owners were sent to internment camps. Japanese Americans also became easy targets for racism across the nation. "Japs" was the derogatory name frequently used in news reports, even in respectable media. Yet there was no similar use of derisive names for the German enemy and German Americans were not placed in detention camps.

While World War II continued overseas, African Americans still battled racism at home. On the floor above us, in apartment 13B, Walter White, Executive Secretary of the NAACP, entertained his guests. These included his neighbors on the thirteenth floor as well as poet Langston Hughes, author Claude McKay and pianist and composer George Gershwin. Mr. White and his wife Gladys had two adult children, Jane and Walter Jr. ("Pidgy"). The Whites' apartment was referred to as the "White House" because so many influential people partied there. Although Mr. White was light enough to "pass for white" when he traveled south to investigate lynchings firsthand, the Ku Klux Klan was capable of lynching him or anyone else suspected of gathering information to use in court against them. One day a volunteer came to our apartment collecting money for the NAACP and left a flyer with the picture of a Negro man hanging limply from a tree like a puppet on a string. When I saw that picture my stomach turned over.

Chapter Three: Home to Harlem and 409

Next door to Walter White and his family lived the poet and literary editor, William Stanley Braithwaite. The Braithwaites had three generations of family, including adult children, living in their large six-room apartment, 13A. Historian and social critic Dr. W. E. B. Du Bois, the most important Negro intellectual of our time, who predicted that the color line would be *the* problem of the twentieth century, also lived on the thirteenth floor, in apartment 13H. I remember Dr. Du Bois, carrying a cane on his arm, barely acknowledging my presence with a nod of his shiny domed head when we were riding on the elevator together. He was deeply engrossed in his own thoughts. Dr. Du Bois was so different from the friendly Mrs. White, who reminded me of a Native American with her copper colored skin and straight black hair; and the gregarious Mrs. Braithwaite, who could have passed for white. These ladies always asked me, "Betty, what did you learn in school today? What do you want to be when you grow up?" The elevator was the meeting place for tenants in this vertical community, and we had a long ride together from the twelfth floor to the lobby.

In 1953 lawyer and neighbor Thurgood Marshall was planning strategy and preparing to address the United States Supreme Court in the case of *Brown v. Board of Education* (Topeka, Kansas) which ultimately determined that segregation in the public schools was a violation of the Constitution of the United States. That summer I suffered a humiliating experience while swimming with other camp counselors, who were white, at a New York state park near Poughkeepsie on our day off. "You... get out of the water," a life guard yelled and pointed at me, as he frantically waved his hands in the air. Transfixed, I was motionless for several moments then I slowly waded to shore. Even though I knew that discrimination in public places was illegal, we all left the park. The experience was so painful for me at the age of seventeen that I buried the details in the recesses of my mind. I could hear the silence in the car ride back to camp. Thoughts ran through my mind. "This couldn't happen to me in the North. Segregation in the South was a way of life, but in New York State....?" My friends were determined to fight this violation of my rights through the New York State Commission Against Discrimination, chaired by Algernon D. Black, my high school teacher and a leader in the Ethical Culture Society. My mother wrote to me at camp, "You have a good case there. If you want me to, I will speak with Thurgood Marshall in 9E. I'm sure he can help." Although the lawyer was not a personal friend, my mother knew that she could count on Mr. Marshall because he was our neighbor in 409. I was elated when Mr. Marshall won *Brown* in 1954 and again in 1967 when he became the first Negro Justice to sit on the Supreme Court of the United States — where he served for twenty-five years. These national leaders in 409, people working for the cause of racial equality throughout the world, became my role models, although I did not know it at the time. Their accomplishments reinforced the idea that whatever I wanted to achieve was possible.

But it was not only the famous tenants of 409 that influenced me but also those tenants that did not appear on the national stage. In the first half of the twentieth century, Negro business and professional people usually served an exclusively African American population and found, despite their education and training, that most 'clean' jobs, (jobs performed in business attire) were closed to them. But the demand for labor during World War II, when men were drafted and factories converted to fulfill defense contracts, opened up jobs in sales, factory, secretarial and postal work, as well as the armed services that had been previously closed to both blacks and women (like my cousin Edna). Living in 409 during this period of transition, I sensed the upbeat spirit of the day, despite the war effort.

Chapter Three: Home to Harlem and 409

Frank Carter, in apartment 11A, livened up the house playing jazz piano duos with his musical partner, Arthur Bowie. They would be practicing for a gig, each at their own piano when I visited the apartment; I used to watch Mr. Carter's manicured fingers glide across the keys. Messrs. Carter and Bowie performed every night around the corner at Bowman's Lounge on St. Nicholas Place, where their glossy black and white photographs were displayed in the window. Mrs. Elsie Carter was a vocalist with her husband, and her melodious voice drifted through the halls when the apartment doors were left ajar during the summer. Elsie Carter stayed home with their toddler daughter, Frances. Occasionally Frances would climb up the steps to my apartment and we would play together. I was like her big sister, just as Edna was a big sister to me.

Another neighbor, Mr. James, whose first name I never knew, had two indentations in his chocolate-brown head. Had he been wounded in World War II, or injured in his work as an electrician? I was afraid to ask. Mr. James conducted himself in a very formal manner and always tipped his brown felt hat when I joined him in the hallway to wait for the elevator. He was a man of few words but when he did speak, it was in a high-pitched voice. Mr. James brought his war bride home from Germany when he moved into apartment 12H, directly under Dr. Du Bois's apartment and right next door to us. Mr. and Mrs. James were a couple with distinctive differences. Marie James looked much older than her husband, she was short and he was tall, she was light and he was dark, and she was German and he was American. Marie wore a hairnet over her dyed blond hair and a kerchief tied under her chin when she took their two dachshunds (one was named Fritz) on daily outings. Marie's housedress hung loose over her thin body, and she held her head down and wriggled into the corner of the elevator as though she were ashamed to take up space. Her only friends,

Deeper Roots

Mr. and Mrs. Seabeck, who also came from Germany, visited Marie frequently from their home in Connecticut but Marie was still lonely for company. Although her husband did not want her to be friendly with the neighbors, she would come to visit us in the daytime when Mr. James was at work. Her blue eyes danced as she conversed with my mother. "Mrs. Butler, may I bring Betty home with me for awhile?" she asked. Marie was an immaculate housekeeper who polished her parquet floors on her hands and knees each week. I took off my shoes at the doorway to slide across the gleaming surface. Marie taught me to count to ten in German and made delicious dumplings for me. After living in the building for many years, Marie finally overcame her reticence and sat on the bench across the street to talk with the neighbors. In this Negro community Marie was treated with respect as a human being, despite the prevailing negative attitude toward Germans in the aftermath of World War II.

When I was old enough to take piano lessons like my cousin Edna, I practiced on the studio grand piano for half an hour after dinner every day. Sometimes my mother played the piano with me. On Saturday morning I put my music books in a brown portfolio tied with a string and took the elevator to the fifth floor for my ten o'clock piano lesson with one of my mother's customers, Mrs. Blanche K. Thomas, who lived in apartment 5A. This was serious business because every young lady of proper upbringing learned to play the piano. When my teacher was not giving piano lessons, she was at church rehearsing the choir for their weekly Sunday performances.

Mrs. Thomas opened the door. "Good morning, Betty,'" she said. Her breath smelled of coffee. She led the way into her studio, the skirt of her navy blue dress swinging well below her well-endowed calf. Black laced shoes with low stacked heels supported her weight as she stepped to the piano bench and seated herself. I would sit next to her and

Chapter Three: Home to Harlem and 409

perform my lesson. The assignments included learning about the lives of the famous composers (Bach, Beethoven, Brahms and Mozart) and playing scales and pieces in major and minor keys. I used a manuscript book to place treble and bass clefs, tempo and notes correctly in each measure. My blue lesson-plan book was signed each week by my mother after my teacher placed on the page a colored star indicating the quality of the execution of the lesson. Red meant failure. Blue was fair, silver was good and gold was excellent.

Mrs. Thomas presented her students each year in a recital at the Little Town Hall on 43rd Street, and every family was expected to sell tickets to their friends at two dollars and fifty cents apiece. Butterflies fluttered in my stomach when I walked out onto stage one June Sunday when I was nine. Mrs. Thomas was at the piano to announce my name and what piece I would play. I sat down at the piano—by now my feet could reach the pedals—the black patent leather shoes I wore were lustrous from the Vaseline my Dad had rubbed on them. After I completed my solo, I curtsied to the audience's applause. I was so glad that I hadn't made any mistakes and my parents were proud of me. In the brown simulated-leather autograph book she gave me that day, Mrs. Thomas wrote, "May your life be like a piano, both Grand and Upright." The musical tradition continued into the next generation. My mother shipped her piano to our home in Massachusetts when our daughter Karen was old enough to take lessons. And although I do not play anymore, all six of our girls learned to play the piano.

Another musical neighbor was Laverne Williams in apartment 2E. Laverne was a few years older than me and took cello lessons as a teenager. I remember Laverne lugging her cello through the lobby; it was almost bigger than her diminutive five-foot-two-inch frame. Her rapid staccato speech pattern and effervescent personality have not changed, as I discovered when we talked by the mail boxes

Deeper Roots

during a recent visit to New York. Laverne has retired from her career as a music teacher in the New York public schools. Nowadays she checks with the senior citizens in the building to make sure they have the things they need, sometimes traveling late at night by subway to the twenty-four hour pharmacy to get prescriptions filled. She also makes frequent trips to New Jersey to assist her widowed mother.

My doctor, May Edward Chinn, who had her office on the first floor in her apartment, was a musician also. A short, stocky woman, Dr. Chinn wore her hair brushed back from her face in a pompadour. She was always punctual for my appointments with her. A consummate professional and aloof in her manner, Dr. Chinn devoted her life to the practice of medicine well into her eighties. She had spent her early childhood on the Tiffany Estate in Tarrytown, New York where her mother worked as a maid. But Dr. Chinn, according to her report, was treated as a member of the family. After graduating from Columbia University and Bellevue Hospital Medical School, she was the first Negro woman to hold an internship at Harlem Hospital and for many years the only female Negro doctor in Harlem. Before becoming appointed to the hospital staff, Dr. Chinn performed blood transfusions for her patients while they reclined on an ironing board. This outstanding physician never told me about the discrimination and obstacles she confronted as a Negro woman. It was only later, while conducting research that I learned how the system had prevented her from having access to hospital facilities.

Our neighbors in apartment 12A across the hall were named Butler too, but were no relation to us. In the summer, when our front door was kept wide open with a pinkish conch shell, their dog Chubbie, a brown-and-white chow would come to visit before his afternoon walk, with his leash dragging on the floor. He lavished me with licks or "kisses" as I called them. I loved dogs and adored Chubbie. Alfred

Chapter Three: Home to Harlem and 409

and Irene Butler and their teenage daughter, Arlene, lived in the big six-room apartment directly under the Whites' place, but they lacked the financial affluence of the Whites—the Butlers had two lodgers who helped pay the rent. Mr. Carrington was a bachelor who worked in the post office and invested his earnings on the New York Stock Exchange, which he followed assiduously. Seated in a club chair in the living room, his horn-rimmed glasses perched at the end of his nose, Mr. Carrington pored over daily market fluctuations in the business pages of the New York *Times*. His deep baritone voice rumbled when he spoke. Perhaps thanks to his successful investments, Mr. Carrington retired from the post office in comfortable style and lived for more than a century. Mr. Lee, the Butlers' other lodger, was a tall, stocky man with a ruddy complexion and worked with Mr. Butler as a red cap in Grand Central Terminal where they carried luggage for tips. At 2:00 p.m. I sometimes peeked from my kitchen window across into their kitchen window to see the household gathered around the table, eating the meal Mrs. Butler prepared before the men went to work. Mrs. Butler often brought a plate of hot rolls to share with us.

When I was old enough, the Butlers' daughter, Arlene, took me for hour-long rides on the number 2 bus down Seventh Avenue (now Adam Clayton Powell, Jr. Boulevard), through Harlem and all the way to the end of the bus route in Washington Square in Greenwich Village. We climbed the spiral stairs to sit on the open top of the double-decker bus. I loved to feel the wind blowing in my face on a hot day. When the man came to take the fare, Arlene let me push the nickel into the slot of the metal coin collector the conductor held in his hand, which jingled every time a coin was deposited.

Seventh Avenue is a broad street with a grassy strip down its middle. We passed Smalls' Paradise on 135th Street, a popular cabaret with a shimmering facade of multicolored glass and as we approached 125th Street, the main concourse in Harlem, I could see the famous Apollo Theater between Seventh and Eighth Avenues. Arlene pointed to a building on the corner. "Betty, there's the Hotel Teresa," she said. A white brick and stucco building thirteen stories high, the hotel was a gathering place for Negroes visiting New York when hotels downtown refused to accommodate them. However, Negroes had been excluded even from the Teresa until 1937 when the hotel was purchased by Mr. Love Woods, a Negro businessman.

On the corner across from the Teresa, men standing on a raised platform spoke into microphones about political and religious topics. In the 1960s, Malcolm X would talk to the people of Harlem about the Black Muslims from this same platform. Many of the buildings we passed along the way were well-kept, but some buildings had boarded-up windows, and jobless people sat on the stoops idling away the time.

After the bus turned right at 110th Street (the north end of Central Park) to continue its route along Fifth Avenue, I noticed the Negro women exiting from the rear of the bus to enter service entrances of the large apartment buildings overlooking the Park, where they worked as maids. Meanwhile, white women boarded the bus to visit the Metropolitan Museum of Art and to shop at Saks and Bergdorf Goodman department stores. By the time we reached 59th Street, nearly all of the passengers were white. The worlds of Negro and white women were so different, yet their lives were inextricably connected. And while the servants knew intimate details of their employers' lives, the employers often knew little or nothing about their help.

However, commerce in Harlem was another matter—all of the merchants in my neighborhood were Jewish, as were most of the business owners in Harlem. Their success depended on being familiar with the day-to-day needs of their customers. I liked to run errands for my parents and the Butlers to the stores around the corner.

Benny the butcher had sawdust sprinkled on the floor of his shop and blood on the front of his apron. Neatly trimmed cuts of meat placed on white enameled trays were arranged in the display case. At the rear of the store was Benny, slicing a loin of lamb into chops on the butcher block. "Three pounds of bottom round ground, please," I said. "Just a minute," he replied. He disappeared into the cold storage box, the door slamming firmly behind him. After a few moments, Benny emerged and placed the chunk of meat in the grinder, turning the handle and pounding the meat with a pestle through the strainer until it all fell onto a piece of white glazed paper, which he wrapped, sealed with tape, and handed to me in a paper bag. "Thank you," I said, paying him with a dollar bill from my pocket. During World War II, the Federal Department of Price Administration judiciously allocated such items as meat, sugar, butter, gasoline and nylon hosiery, giving each household a certain number of ration stamps to prevent hoarding and to minimize black marketeering. Auntie Maud gave us her extra stamps, which boosted our supply.

Next door was the grocery store, presided over by Jack. He had a gap between his front teeth and stubble of beard on his face. Jack wore a plaid flannel shirt underneath his apron, to keep warm, and behind his left ear he kept a short yellow pencil stub which he used to total up the prices on the brown paper bag. He was a whiz at adding up the columns of numbers for the things I bought.

When I retraced my steps around the corner to Edgecombe Avenue, I stopped to get toffee for a penny from the elderly couple that owned the candy store. The vegetable man and his horse-drawn wagon were in front of the house

Deeper Roots

when I returned. I asked permission to pat the horse after the gray oat bag was removed from his mouth.

When I returned to 409 after my errands, Wilbur, the hall man, would teach me to run the elevator—I was thrilled. First, he pulled the red outer door closed and slid the brass accordion-like safety gate shut. Then I took my position at the back of the cubicle to manipulate the controls. I held the lever down until we approached the twelfth floor, then gradually released the handle to slow acceleration for a smooth and even stop at the landing. It took me many tries before I got it down pat, but in time I became an expert.

Every other week peddlers made their rounds in the building. Mr. Meir had a slight German accent and a mole on the right side of his forehead. He brought a bundle or two tied with twine which he placed on my mother's side of the bed, near the nightstand. "Mrs. Butler, I have some special things today," Mr. Meir said. He untied the package and spread out his wares. Nylon slips, boxes of stockings and blouses came cascading out of the brown wrapping paper onto the pink chenille bedspread. I sat in the lounge chair by the window to watch the salesman trying to convince my mother to make a purchase. Mom had a running credit account, which Mr. Meir recorded in the light brown sales book he pulled from his vest pocket. Each visit Mom paid him two or three dollars to reduce her balance and often bought one or two new items to keep her account in the red. "Do you need any tablecloths or mats today, Mrs. Butler? I have some very special ones right here in this package." "Don't bother opening that one, Mr. Meir, I get all of the plastic placemats I need from my sister; she works in a stitching factory where they are made, you know," my mother would inform him.

The other tradesman who came every other week was an immigrant man from Armenia. I watched him from the window, slowly walking down the hill toward 409, leaning from left to right with each step he took, burdened by the weight of his heavy parcels. His thick hair was graying, and his eyes drooped sadly like the eyes of a beagle dog. I always felt sorry for this peddler with his worn rumpled suit, and his shoes with run-down heels. His name was too difficult for my mother to pronounce or remember so she simply called him Mr. Macy, in tribute to her favorite department store.

◆ ◆ ◆ ◆ ◆

There are no flowers in the lobby at "409" today. No Oriental rugs cover the tiled floor. No draperies hang at the windows. There are no doormen or elevator men who stand in the lobby, only a uniformed security guard who oversees people coming and going from the house. The older residents lament that "409 is not what it used to be." The house became the property of the City of New York when the a group of entrepreneurs of West Indian heritage, the Antillean Holding Company headed by A. A. Austin, declared bankruptcy. Then 409 was rehabilitated under HBD, and each apartment was sold to its occupant for $250 if they wished to purchase. The building is now a cooperative managed by a fractious, ever-changing owners' board of directors.

In 1995 the house received a new adornment: a plaque designating 409 as a City Landmark Building, bestowed by the New York Landmark Preservation Foundation. "The home of numerous prominent and influential African American intellectual and cultural personalities," the plaque reads in part. The plaque is in the exact place where Dr. Chinn's office sign used to be.

Now when I walk down Edgecombe Avenue I hear children speaking Spanish as they play stick ball outside the buildings where they live. 409 is one of the only houses on

Deeper Roots

Edgecombe Avenue between 150th and 155th Streets that still has a majority of African American residents.

Beginning with a trickle of Negroes around 1900, by the 1920s Harlem had became the Negro capital of the world. Today the Latino population and immigrants from Africa are making Harlem a more heterogeneous community than it was when I grew up there. Change keeps happening, just as the residents of 409 changed from Jewish to Negro in the early 1920s. Each generation will have its memories. For me, the 409 Edgecombe Avenue of the 1930s through the 1950s was simply a wonderful place to grow up.

Chapter Four:

Lift Every Voice and Sing

The Modern School (1940–1944)

Every three weeks Meme's customer Rhoda Smith, put jet-black dye in her hair, dried it thoroughly and wrapped her head tightly with a bright kerchief. Then she would come to our apartment for a press and curl. I opened the door when Rhoda rang the bell.

"How are you doing, gal?" she greeted me. Rhoda dropped a fifty-cent piece in the red metal tea box on the kitchen counter where some of my favorite customers left

Deeper Roots

money for me. In a good week I collected about three dollars. "Play some Chopin on the piano Betty while your mother does my hair," Rhoda said.

Rhoda settled her willowy body into the customers' chair by the kitchen window, extending her long trouser-clad legs. Meme ran the hot comb through her short thick hair. "You know, Meme," Rhoda said in her thick Bajan accent, "I don't take no foolishness from those lodgers of mine. I lay down the rules. No noise. No guests in the room. No late rent either or you're out. They know I mean business."

I remember walking up the twelve steep concrete steps to the front door of the white brick attached house where Rhoda lived. It was on tree-lined 154th Street, two long blocks from my house. All of the homes on the street looked very much alike to me, but there was only one Rhoda's Villa. That is what the gold letters written in script across the glass pane on the front door said. ...*Rhoda's Villa.*

Behind that glass-paned door, Rhoda plastered ceilings, painted walls, fixed faucets and collected rent *on time* each week from her lodgers. One lodger was Ann Lewis, also a customer of Meme's. Ann was a live-in maid at a duplex apartment on Riverside Drive. She came to use her room at Rhoda's on Thursdays—to shop, to run errands and, most importantly, to pay her rent.

The lodgers weren't the only ones who knew Rhoda meant business. Her husband, Moulton, knew it too. In the basement of Rhoda's Villa, he had set up a room with swinging doors where he could entertain his gambling friends. A fully-stocked bar stood in one corner; it had a shimmering front panel made of glass squares. Two padded green card tables, each with four folding chairs, awaited his guests who would sit and shoot craps until the early hours of the morning. But from this subterranean haunt no cigar or cigarette smoke was ever permitted to wend its way upstairs to foul the air in Rhoda's place. I never knew how Moulton

Chapter Four: Lift Every Voice and Sing

earned a living because he was usually home when I visited during the day. The money from the night gambling may have kept him solvent.

When I came to visit, I often saw Rhoda raking leaves in front of her house in the fall or shoveling snow from the steps in the winter. When the weather got very cold, Rhoda went on a cruise to the Caribbean, using the money she earned from her rooming house. In the summer this enterprising businesswoman played tennis at the Metropolitan Club on Convent Avenue, a few blocks from her house. One day, Rhoda told me she observed a neighborhood girl playing stickball on the street. "You're a good athlete," Rhoda told the girl. "Would you like to learn to play tennis?" The rest is history—and a story that Rhoda loved to tell. Rhoda Smith outfitted Althea Gibson with a tennis racquet, tennis shoes and tennis whites, and took Gibson to the Metropolitan Club for lessons. Althea was tall and lanky, with rounded shoulders like Rhoda's, but she was very shy and awkward. (I met her at Rhoda's house one day, although she didn't say much to me.) But in 1957, after years of intense coaching and practice, Althea Gibson became the first black woman to win the U.S. National Singles Championship and Wimbledon competitions, breaking racial barriers in a previously all-white amateur sport. The trophies that Gibson won were left on display in Rhoda's recreation room, apparently given by the athlete to her mentor. When the house changed hands, the new owners discovered the trophies and conveyed them to the Schomburg Center for Research in Black Culture.

"Betty will be ready for school in the fall and I don't know what to do," Meme said to Rhoda. She twirled the last curl in her customer's hair and gently removed the curling iron. "Sometimes I watch the children at dismissal time at the public school on St. Nicholas Avenue, and I don't like the way the students behave when they come out of school.

Deeper Roots

They're noisy and undisciplined. There's a new school that opened up two doors from my house, at 411, called the Modern School," Rhoda said. "Why don't you send Betty there?"

Miss Mildred Johnson, the school founder, interviewed me and showed me around the building. I don't know how my parents made the decision, but in September 1940, at the age of four, I started kindergarten at the Modern School. There were a total of sixty-six Negro children enrolled in kindergarten through sixth grade at the school and the principal and teachers were black as well. Mildred Johnson, who was also the headmistress, directed the first private school in New York City staffed by African Americans.

On my first day of school, my mother and I walked up the steep hill at 155th Street to St. Nicholas Avenue, passing the Cities Service gas station and the mustard-colored brick garage that took up the whole square between St. Nicholas Place and St. Nicholas Avenue. We crossed the street to the opposite corner, where the red neon lights of the well-known Fat Man Bar and Grill flashed on and off all day. Men and women walked past us on their way to work, descending the steps to the bowels of the IND subway station next to the restaurant. Only one block from here on 154th Street was the Modern School. As I entered the building, the daily routine began. "Good Morning, Betty," said the lady standing with her cane at the door. "Good Morning, Mrs. Johnson," I replied. Nora Johnson, the headmistress' mother, was a tall, stately-looking woman with a tawny complexion who wore her gray hair pulled back from her face and pinned firmly with gray hairpins in a bun at the nape of her neck. The greeting was cool and a little stern as her milky blue-gray eyes swept over each arriving student from head to toe.

Each morning I hung my coat on one of the hooks in the hallway cubby-hole compartment with BETTY BUTLER neatly printed on a red-bordered label. I took my smock from

Chapter Four: Lift Every Voice and Sing

the other hook and put it on, holding the cuffs of my dress sleeves so that they did not get clumped up in the smock sleeves. We wore smocks to protect our clothing, not just during art lessons but all day long. Headmistress Mildred Johnson always wore a colorful smock, usually one with large orange flowers on it. Mine was a solid maroon color with white buttons down the front. (My mother made it for me, buttonholes and all. She was a very good seamstress.) I bent over to put on my beige doeskin slippers (called rhythm shoes) we wore to keep the noise down. Now I was ready to start my day.

I climbed the stairs to the second floor, where the younger classes met. Mildred—we called the teachers by their first names—not only ran the school but taught the sixth grade. Her classroom was the large first-floor room with a bay window facing the street. Although the sliding doors muffled some sounds when closed, I could often hear Mildred's commanding voice echoing through the hall. "Sit *down*, Stanley," she ordered. Mildred was tall like her mother and had her mother's impervious air. She too wore her hair in a bun pinned at the nape of her neck but her hair was dark brown.

I remember when the mothers of my first-grade class-mates came to hear us read. They sat in chairs arranged in a row at the back of the room. We were so proud of our books and their smell of newness. We were the first students to open the stiff binding and move our fingers along the pages and under the rows of words. Although we had practiced for weeks to show off our newly-acquired skill, I was afraid that I would make a mistake when it was my turn to decipher, "run, spot, run" from *Dick and Jane*. Ann Davidson sat next to me. Everyone said that we looked alike. We both wore our hair with an ever-so-straight part down the middle and two thin braids tied with ribbon at the ends. Curled bangs covered our high foreheads. We had the same chocolate-

Deeper Roots

brown complexion and the same toothpick legs, and we measured the same height when standing up straight. Posture was important at the Modern School. Ann was my best friend then. I visited her home in the Bronx, and she stayed overnight at my house sometimes.

At noon the pungent aroma of homemade soup filled our nostrils. We sat silently at the long oil-cloth covered table. In the basement lunchroom we waited for our portion of soup to be ladled into the metal cups. Heads upturned, we drained the cups then banged on the bottoms with the palm of our hand to dislodge the clinging vegetables. There were no spoons.

Our lunch and lessons were sometimes punctuated by air raid drills in those wartime days, as we ducked under the desks when the warning blasted its shrill blaring sound. I never sensed danger, although we all wore identification bracelets engraved with our name and address in case we were injured in a bombing attack. I have my silver bracelet in the jewelry box on my dresser.

At the Modern School there was an emphasis on music and the arts. Thelma Teasdale, short and squat and with bulldog determination etched on her face, played the piano loudly and forcefully to accompany—or to drown out—our young untrained voices. She led our chorus, her head bobbing, in the rendition of *Lift Every Voice and Sing*. The song known as the Negro national anthem, had been written by Mildred's father, J. Rosamond Johnson and her uncle, James Weldon Johnson. We learned all three verses and I can still recite them now. We sang the song with the parents and friends who came to see our annual presentation of scenes from *The Nutcracker*, which we performed in the auditorium of I.S. 136 on Edgecombe Avenue. This was a fundraising event for the Modern School. Our mothers made the costumes—I was a sugarplum fairy and danced around the

Chapter Four: Lift Every Voice and Sing

stage with my spindly legs protruding from a frosty blue net tutu.

I later learned that Mildred was a well-rounded educator whose experiences gave her the necessary training to direct our performances. Each summer during her high school years, Mildred travelled on the road managing the details for the musical productions created by her father and his collaborators. The professional cast of dancers and singers performed for audiences along the East coast comparable to what we now call summer stock. Although her dream was to follow in her father's footsteps in the theatre, her parents did not consider show business to be an appropriate career for their daughter. However, Mildred apparently never lost her love of show business. She poured that love of the arts and music into her school and would eventually create and produce over fifty musicals and write two books of poems. We, her students, benefited from her love of the arts in more ways than words can ever express.

I loved school—I loved the Modern School. But one day when I was in the second grade, my daily trip to school hung in the balance. Mom was sick. For three days in a row she had been sipping a strong brew she concocted from roots boiled in the white enamel sauce pan. But despite her home remedy, the severe cold and the cough that settled in her chest would not go away. "I can't take you to school today Betty. I feel as sick as a dog. Do you want to go there by yourself?" It was almost time for class to begin and I didn't want to miss a day of school. I was seven years old. Mom had taught me how to cross the street by myself while she watched me from the other side of the street. But this time she would be watching me from her bedroom window twelve stories up. I made my first crossing with traffic coming from five directions—Edgecombe Avenue, the Speedway, St. Nicholas Place and 155th Street from both east and west. I was not afraid. I waved to my mom before and

Deeper Roots

after I crossed the street. Then I ran up the hill to the next street, crossed over to the Fat Man Bar and Grill on St. Nicholas Avenue, turned one more block at 154th Street and waved once again to Mom before going up the steps to the school. "Where is your mother?" Mrs. Johnson asked from her station at the door. I'm sure she expected me to say, "She's coming," but instead I replied, "She's home sick."

"Who brought you to school then?" "I brought myself," I replied. It was only later when I overheard conversations and exchanges among other adults that I learned the impact of what I had done. "Why didn't you call me?" Rhoda asked my mother. "I would have come and gotten Betty."

"Mrs. Butler, why didn't you ask me to take Betty to school? One of the other boys would cover for me," Wilbur, our doorman, said. "I thought she was just going around the corner for you."

"Woman are you crazy?" Dad asked when he came home from work and heard the story. He seldom got perturbed but he was beside himself. "Betty could have been hit by a car."

"Oh," my mother replied, "I knew she could manage. I wasn't worried at all. I could see her from the window all of the time." This abiding faith and confidence at the core of my mother's character was unique. That same type of faith and confidence enabled Mildred Johnson to create and run the Modern School for over sixty years.

I was a student at the Modern School when I reached the age to go to Sunday school. There was no question about where I would be enrolled. Auntie Maud had made that determination. At the time, I am sure that she was not aware of the unique connections that existed between her church, her pastor, Mildred Johnson and my school. I learned of these links during conversations I had years later with Mildred Johnson as part of my independent research.

My dad rode with me to St. Philips Protestant Episcopal Church on the subway. We got off the train at 135th Street

Chapter Four: Lift Every Voice and Sing

and from there we walked three blocks to the church, past the rectory where Mildred Johnson had first started her school. Dad read the newspapers in the nearby park while I went to Sunday school where my name was neatly printed on my St. Philips attendance card. We sat at long tables to color our bible story books and listen to the teacher tell us about "Noah and the Ark," "Jonah and the Whale," "Joseph and his Coat of Many Colors," and "Daniel and the Lion." I was bored.

Some Sundays Auntie Maud would emerge from her room and say to my parents, "I'll take Betty to church with me. She'll go to Sunday school after the service." I remember the loud organ music. "Turn around Betty and pay attention," my aunt directed me as the celebrants of the service began their procession. Father Bishop, short and balding with skin as white as ivory, and Father Harrison, the assistant minister, tall, thin with skin as dark as ebony, were an odd pair I thought. Father Harrison wore a long black robe over his long black body. He would stride down the aisle to the altar to light the candles and genuflect at the cross. The organ played its melodious chords and the congregation rose to sing the first hymn. When the last amen reverberated through the cathedral, the assembled worshipers would kneel on the green pads to pray. The mood was serious and somber and the silence was deafening to my ears. There was no celebration of joy in this church; the atmosphere was staid and reserved, just like Father Bishop.

Auntie Maud was enthralled by Father Bishop, I thought. I could tell by the way she looked at him adoringly when they shook hands at the door after service. "Your sermon was so inspirational," she would sigh. "Oh, thank you Maud," said the unctuous pastor. "Do you remember my niece, Betty?" Auntie Maud inquired. "Indeed I do, and my, how you have grown," Father Bishop would say, bending over slowly from the waist to study me from head to foot.

Deeper Roots

Auntie Maud was in church every Sunday all day, for both services, including afternoon tea.

Every Sunday the women vied to outdress each other, so it seemed to me, donning their fur coats, lavish full-brimmed hats plumed with feathers and, of course, white gloves. I later learned that St. Philips, the largest black Episcopal congregation in the country, reserved pews for families who made large donations to the church. Most of these people were of light complexion, representing the "elite" of Harlem. Most West Indians from British colonies attended St. Mark's Church on Lenox Avenue, where the Episcopal service had more reminders of "home." But not Auntie Maud; she preferred the formality of St. Philips, which was reminiscent of the Church of England, like the parish church in Falmouth to which her Jamaican family belonged.

Decades later I met with Mildred at her summer home on Martha's Vineyard. This is when I was made aware of the connections that existed between Mildred, Philip's Episcopal Church and its pastor, Reverend Bishop. I originally wanted to learn how and why she took on this huge endeavor.

She told me, "When I graduated from Ethical Culture Schools in 1932, I was the only Negro in my class and a member of the first class to graduate from the newly-built Fieldston High School campus in the Bronx at Riverdale. I enrolled in a preprofessional course sponsored by the schools. I was assigned to Midtown Ethical on Central Park West for teacher training. It was the same school that I attended from kindergarten but the program director discouraged my participation. When I arrived on the first day, she said, 'a Negro will never get a job in a private school in New York. Why waste your time?'" Nevertheless, Mildred Johnson persevered. But after two years of outstanding practice teaching in the first and third grade, often assuming full responsibility for the classroom, the director's prophesy

Chapter Four: Lift Every Voice and Sing

became a reality. No private school would accept Miss Johnson for the third year of internship.

"You see, a placement in another school was mandatory to obtain a license, so I was caught in a difficult situation," Miss Johnson continued. "So I approached my minister, the Reverend Shelton Hale Bishop of St. Philips Church, where I taught the nursery and kindergarten Sunday school classes. He allowed me to use the parish house to set up my own classroom." Algernon D. Black (Miss Johnson's and later my ethics teacher at Fieldston), who became a leader in the Ethical Culture Society, contributed a hundred and fifty dollars to Miss Johnson's school and helped her fledging idea to become a reality. "I was ready to begin," Mildred told me. "I called up friends of my family and enrolled eight students. We added a grade level each year and expanded to fourteen students. The church received ten percent of the net receipts for rent. After three years I moved to the basement of a friend's house, and then I borrowed money from my parents to buy the townhouse on 154th Street."

The Modern School opened in 1938 and was modeled after the Ethical Culture schools. It became a lab site for Columbia University and students from New York University and student teachers at other private schools came to observe the program. The student body at the Modern School represented a cross section of the socio-economic levels of the community the school served. Children of physicians, teachers, actresses, clerks and maids attended. Neither Mildred nor Nora Johnson, who was a full time helper, ever received a salary for their work. In 1941, the teachers earned one dollar a day while students paid up to two dollars a week, lunch included, depending on what their parents could afford. According to the annual report of 1941, some parents couldn't afford to pay anything at all and their children were unable to continue. Food, clothing, medical care and temporary housing for those in need were offered.

97

Deeper Roots

During the Depression, many parents had lost their jobs, causing families to be dispossessed.

The connection between the Johnson family, the Bishop family, and St. Philip's Protestant Episcopal Church was strong indeed. Mildred Johnson's request for use of the parish house was given high priority because Miss Johnson was a niece through marriage, of the prominent entrepreneur, John E. Nail. A loyal member of St. Philip's Church, he had helped negotiate land purchases made by the church in Harlem in the early 1900s, and as a member of the New York Ethical Culture Society, he had suggested that his niece be enrolled in kindergarten at the Society's Midtown school. Mr. Nail, president of Nail and Parker, was the key figure in the real estate transactions that permanently changed the color of the face of Harlem.

It was the Reverend Shelton Hale Bishop's father, the Reverend Hutchens Bishop, who actually bought the land on which St. Philip's now stood. The pastor also purchased other property in Harlem, which he later sold to the church. The Reverend Hutchens Bishop acquired this real estate because he could pass for white at a time when there were racial covenants signed by owners and realtors to prevent infiltration of the area by colored people. Reverend Hutchens Bishop was the father of Auntie Maud's crush, the short and pale Reverend Shelton Hale Bishop.

Today Miss Johnson's voice, "like the brook's low song" as described in her senior class high school yearbook, is the same voice that I remember from childhood. And she remembered me, even though I left her school at the end of the third grade. Miss Johnson was delighted to meet with me, especially after I told her that I had followed in her footsteps, choosing a career in education and setting up innovative educational programs for black youth. I had followed in her footsteps, too, in attending the Ethical Culture Schools— Midtown Ethical and Fieldston—the same schools that Miss

Chapter Four: Lift Every Voice and Sing

Johnson graduated from before I was born. At the time of our conversation, Mildred was planning a celebration of the sixtieth anniversary of the Modern School, then located at 870A Riverside Drive in Upper Manhattan, serving sixty children from kindergarten through sixth grade. As she and I talked, I realized that Mildred Johnson, now Mrs. Mildred Edwards, retired educator, had been a role model for me, subtly influencing the development of my lifelong career.

In 1989, at the age of 75, Miss Johnson handed over the day-to-day affairs of the school to professional administrators. For the next ten years, the school continued on as an oasis in a neighborhood that was besieged by the crack epidemic. The building itself became a landmark of another variety with drug dealers standing in front of the school, directing buyers and sellers. The students watched arrests from their classroom windows and heard gunfire on occasion. During the same period, the school suffered internal difficulties as well; the school's enrollment declined as its financial troubles grew. In a 1999 interview with the New York *Times*, the school's director, Sandra A. Carter, claimed that the school's financial difficulties stemmed from expensive repairs on the building and the bad economy. In that year, Mildred and her daughter, K. Melanie Edwards (co-owners of the school building) sold the four-story edifice. The Modern School continued until 2007 and Mildred died the same year at the age of ninety-three.

On reflection, it would be unwise to focus on the circumstances surrounding the demise of the Modern School. The important thing to keep in mind is the impact on the students who attended the school during its sixty-year existence. The majority of those students received an education that was unique—an education that would not have been offered to them, as students of color, anywhere else in any part of the country. The Modern School and Mildred Johnson are testaments to the power of faith and the

Deeper Roots

acts that flow from that faith. That is a powerful lesson in itself.

Chapter Five: What's in a Name?

Midtown Ethical Culture School

(1944 – 1947)

My birth certificate reads Catherine Elizabeth Butler, in honor of my two grandmothers, Catherine Elizabeth Simpson Clark and Elizabeth Anna Weeks Butler. But everyone who knew me in childhood called me Betty. That's what the nurses at the hospital nick-named me because I had big brown eyes and long eyelashes that beaded when I cried, like Betty Boop, the popular car-toon character of the 1930s. My mother and father called me Betty and that was my name for the first nine years of my life. Then, at my interview for admission to the Midtown Ethical Culture School, Mrs. Victoria Wagner, the principal, leaned over her desk peering at me with mischievous blue eyes, and asked, "If you came here to school, what would you like to be called?" A funny thing happened. I heard myself saying, without a moment of hesitation, "I wish to be called Katherine."

From then on Kathy, Katie, Kay, and Kate became my new names in my new life. The new spelling of my name — with a K — would make the transformation complete. This interview came about because Mom did not feel that I was being challenged enough at the Modern School; my friend, Barbara Patrick and I were always the first two names at the top of the list in every subject area. We also had skipped grade 2B, but Mom still was not satisfied. She consulted with her customer, Maudester Newton, who was an employment counselor at the Harlem YWCA. Maudester suggested that application for admission be made at several of the other selective schools in the city: Lincoln, Horace Mann, Hunter Model School, The Little Red Schoolhouse and Ethical Culture Schools. I had interviews and took entrance examinations for them all.

Apparently my studies at the Modern School had been challenging enough that I passed my exam and earned a scholarship. My acceptance at the Midtown Ethical Culture School (where most of the students were upper middle-class and predominantly Jewish) was a time of celebration. "Betty, you are so fortunate to have this opportunity. I know that you will set an example for the race," my crinkled-faced art teacher whispered in my ear. Miss Wilcher had been fired from the New York public school system for "subversive activity" — she was a Negro teacher suspected of communist leanings. In lieu of permanent employment, Miss Wilcher maintained a livelihood by teaching arts and crafts classes in her home on Saturday mornings to neighborhood children, some of whom were my school friends and playmates. Edgar Thomason, red-haired and freckled, was in my group, so was

Chapter Five: What's In A Name?

his younger sister, Laura, a light-skinned girl who spoke with a lisp and Regina Mason, with skin the color of dark chocolate. They all lived in the apartment building next to mine, and we all attended the Modern School together. In art class we made clay animals and dabbled with finger paint while we developed our latent artistic talent.

On Thursday morning, the 26th of September 1944, my mother had me scrubbed, oiled and powdered; my hair was pressed and sectioned into two braids tied with ribbons, all in preparation for the first day in my new school. The lisle socks we had bought at Macy's department store to match the color of my dress were turned in a neat cuff over the new brown oxford Buster Brown shoes with the arches built in to support my flat feet. The "A" express train whisked my mother and me beneath the world of Harlem to Central Park West and 61st Street in just ten minutes. We walked two short blocks, past a few of the skyscrapers that lined the avenue, to the red brick school building on the corner of 63rd Street, without speaking a word to each other. Somehow I knew that I was a pioneer embarking on a new adventure, not only for myself but for family, friends and neighbors who counted on me to succeed. As we mounted the steps to the entrance I am sure my mother said a silent prayer.

Seated on a stool to the right side of the doorway was a man, a nameless middle-aged colored man in a dark blue suit who watched the procession of students and parents coming to and leaving the school each day just as Nora Johnson had done at the Modern School. But this man did not greet the students with "good morning." Instead he watched us in silence and we did not speak to him directly either. He was there exuding an assumed permanence, part watchman, part doorman, observing my entrance to this new world. He was the only adult person of color on staff that I would encounter during my three years as a student at the

Deeper Roots

Midtown Ethical Culture School. He was a daily reminder that I was part of another, different world.

The clank of the closing elevator door jarred me to attention as I rode to the fourth floor. My assigned room, the corner room diagonally across from the elevator, was 4C: 4 for the grade level and C for the last initial of my teacher, Miss Laura Clements. She was a slight woman, prim and proper, standing in the doorway wearing a navy blue dress, a white frilly collar complementing her steel-gray coiffure. After brief introductions and an exchange of pleasantries I gave my mother a good-bye kiss and wrapped my arms around her neck, smelling the soothing aroma of her gardenia perfume. "Everything will be just fine, Betty. I'll see you this afternoon at dismissal time," she said as she turned to retrace her steps back to the elevator.

I crossed the threshold into my new life, absorbing everything around me like a sponge. Desks were arranged two by two in rows three deep, leaving open space in the center of the floor. Burnished orange leaves framed themselves in the windowpanes overlooking Central Park, while the windows facing 63rd Street seemed to be smack against the Century apartment building. You could actually see the people in their apartments when they stood near the window. One female tenant chose to dress each morning without the shade drawn, creating a stir in class that must have prompted a call from the office of the principal, Mrs. Wagner, since this diversion lasted only a few days.

Sharp-nosed Miss Clements probably greeted me warmly and escorted me to my assigned place but I don't remember that encounter. I do remember smoothing down the skirt of my red-and-green plaid dress so it wouldn't get crushed as I slipped into my desk chair. When I heard the girl behind me say to her seatmate, in a whisper just loud enough for me to hear, "There's a colored girl," I felt the blood rush to my face

104

Chapter Five: What's In A Name?

and felt my skin became warm and moist. Oh, how I wished that Barbara Patrick, my classmate from my former school, was in this class with me now. We were neighbors on Edgecombe Avenue, so our mothers had taken turns walking us to and from the Modern School each day. Although Barbara had also been accepted at Ethical, she had been placed in the third grade as she was seven months younger than me. Donald Johnson, Mildred's adopted brother, had left the Modern school the previous year to attend Ethical, but he was in the fifth grade. Both Barbara and Donald were light-skinned and could have passed for white, but at least I knew them and they knew me. How would I, a decidedly brown-skinned girl, fare in this place?

The experience of entering a new and different educational environment with the dimension of racial attitudes and expectations influenced me greatly. In 1966, as a founder and director of an educational program bringing children of color from Boston to suburban schools in response to de facto segregation, I made certain that each elementary school child in the program was placed in a homeroom with at least one other student of color.

The envelope with a purple three-cent stamp in the corner addressed to Miss Katherine Butler, 409 Edgecombe Avenue, New York, New York, let me know immediately that it came from a new schoolmate, since everyone else in my life called me Betty. My mother watched as I pulled out the card with pink and blue balloons on the front. Joyce Jacobs, the same girl who had whispered behind my back on my first day in class, was inviting me to her birthday party at her home in the Essex House on Central Park South. We were to see Walt Disney's newest film, *Dumbo*, at the party. (Joyce's family owned the Globe Theater chain in New York City.) I jumped up and down with joy. Even though I had made friends at

Deeper Roots

school, I breathed a sigh of relief to know that I was also a part of the group outside of the classroom.

One Saturday afternoon Joyce, her mother, and I were seated at the oblong dining-room table at their apartment waiting for lunch to be served. A pair of eyes in a coffee-brown face peered at me through the square pane of glass in the door between the kitchen and the dining room. When Mrs. Jacobs pressed the button under the rug with her toe, a buzzer in the kitchen rang and a Negro maid emerged through the swinging door dressed in a black uniform with a white ruffled apron. "What can I get for you, Ma'am?" she said to her employer. While the question was directed at Mrs. Jacobs, the maid's eyes were riveted on me, her eyebrows raised quizzically. Her eyes, full of astonishment and curiosity, locked with mine. It may have been the first time she had seen a person of color seated at the table. No words were spoken. No other acknowledgments of each other's presence passed between us. Although it never happened, I dreaded the day when one of the maids emerging from a kitchen would turn out to be one of my mother's customers sitting in our kitchen.

I did, however, have other disquieting encounters with those who questioned my "place." New York City was safe enough in 1947 for children to travel alone by subway, but there were other hazards. When I arrived for the birthday party of another classmate at the Majestic Hotel on 72nd Street, the doorman directed me to the service elevator. "You are to use *that* elevator," he said, glaring at me and pointing to the back of the lobby. My vision blurred with tears. My heart beat so hard I thought it must be echoing through the hallway. The muscle in my right leg cramped and ached. I stood there as if my black patent leather shoes were glued to the floor. I thought to myself, "I don't ride the service elevator in my apartment building, so why should I ride it

106

Chapter Five: What's In A Name?

here?" "You must be mistaken," said I, faking calm. "I am here to visit Maxine Leff. Please announce me."

"I have this colored girl here who says she's visiting you," the doorman said over the intercom. "She refuses to use the service car. You know the building policy." I could not hear the voice on the other end of the receiver, but when the conversation was completed, my interrogator turned to me with a purple face, nodding in the direction of the passenger car. "14F," he brusquely instructed the elevator operator.

These educational encounters with uniformed "gatekeepers" occurred regularly when I visited friends on Central Park West. After this first experience, I braced myself for a similar confrontation each time, and each time I rode on the passenger elevator with a sense of pride for asserting myself. I never told my dad or mother about these incidents. I was eleven years old and I didn't want my parents to worry about me. I could handle these situations on my own, or so I thought.

When I shared these experiences with a fellow alumna at a Mount Holyoke College trustee meeting in 1976, she vehemently protested. "Katie, this could *not* have happened to you. This type of discrimination could *not* have occurred in New York City." I felt my whole body stiffen and I wished that I had kept my mouth shut.

At eleven and twelve years old, my friends and I did indeed keep our mouths shut about the racial incidents we experienced in the world outside of Harlem. On Sunday afternoons, I would visit my Auntie Maud and play with some of my former classmates from the Modern School in the courtyard of the Dunbar apartment complex where they lived. They were my friends but we shared something more—we were Negroes who attended predominately white, elite schools. I would play hide-and-seek, red rover and ring-a-levio with Jean Carey and Marion Booth, former

107

Deeper Roots

school mates at Mildred's who now both attended the Little Red School House, a private school in Greenwich Village. Anne Raven Wilkinson would come to join us, too. She was in the other fourth grade class, 4S, at Ethical; she had started school there in the first grade. Her family lived at the opposite end of the Dunbar. Anne's father's dental office sign, placed on the street side of the brown brick building, read *Frost B. Wilkinson, D.D.S.*

We played as children and *never* talked about racial slights occurring in school, or about what it felt like to be the only person of color in the class after attending the all-Negro Modern School. We were silent on those subjects; we were children dealing with matters of adult racism and we spoke to no one or to each other about it.

But when my friend Anne Wilkinson and I were placed in Miss Gardner's fifth grade class, that silence was broken. It was Miss Gardner's first year at Ethical; she had come north to teach. One morning my mother rushed to school to speak to Mrs. Wagner. "I did *not* send my daughter here to listen to incorrect English," my mother stated in her clipped, precise way. She was objecting to Miss Gardner's reading of the Uncle Remus tales with a Southern Negro dialect. That was the last time we heard those Joel Chandler Harris stories. Although I did not comprehend the significance of my mother's action, I was proud of her for standing her ground. As a representative for my class, she came to school each month to pour tea for afternoon mothers' meetings, always dressed to suit the occasion, always carrying herself with elegant regal bearing. She always made me feel proud.

Anne Raven Wilkinson would later learn to rely on the silence we had cultivated as children. Anne and I met many years later at Lincoln Center in New York City where a panel of successful African American dancers related their experiences setting up African American dance troops,

Chapter Five: What's In A Name?

teaching dance in black urban communities and dancing on stage in white troupes in the 1950s. During our conversation I learned that through her mother's determination, Anne was enrolled in The Children's Professional School in ninth grade so that she could receive the intense training necessary to pursue a career in ballet. Anne became the first African American dancer to join the world-class ballet company Ballet Russe de Monte Carlo.

Anne has a light olive complexion and many people did not know she was black and so she performed as a leading dancer around the world without revealing her racial identity. However, while performing in the American South during segregation a hotel maid identified Anne as a Negro and raised the delicate question with the manager of the ballet company. Anne refused to say that she was white, and her contract with the troupe was terminated. She spent the rest of her dancing career with the New York City Ballet.

The Ethical Culture schools had a long history of racial diversity. According to the former registrar, Sally Rust, "from the very beginning there was an occasional Negro in the school and after ten years an occasional Oriental pupil. If a dark-skinned child appeared and passed the test and there was room for him, he was admitted." Known at its inception as the Workingmen's School, Midtown Ethical began as a free kindergarten in 1878, enrolling immigrant children of English, Scottish and Irish descent, as well as a few African Americans. Two students of color, Martha and Walter Mason, were in the classes of 1889 and 1890, respectively.

In its report of the dedication of the Ethical's new school building site on 63rd Street on October 24, 1904, the *Nation* noted that gender or color presented no barrier to admission to the Ethical Culture School, which may have been the only private school in New York City at the time that accepted

Deeper Roots

Negro students. Varsity team pictures in Ethical's high school yearbooks indicate that everyone was eligible to compete. School archives reveal that this rigorous school policy prompted cancellation of a 1910 basketball contest with a school that objected to the presence of Negro athletes on the opposing team.

During my years of matriculation at the Ethical Culture schools, teachers attempted to ignore race as an issue and no distinction by race was made. There was a conscious denial of racial differences. Prejudice and intolerance were unacceptable and their existence at school was denied; such behavior was perceived to exist only in the world beyond the protected environment of the school. The view conveyed to students was that discrimination based on race or religion was practiced by a minority of less educated people and with education these people could be taught to behave differently. What our educators did not (or could not) teach us, however, was how to navigate among the 'less educated' in order to get from one world to another—from one protected environment (school) to another (home and community).

During the early years of the schools, Jewish parents enrolled their children in response to quotas and institutionalized anti-Semitism at New York's private schools. However, those of us with darker complexions could not "blend in" or "pass" when needed and as such, assumptions were made about our place in society no matter how well-educated we were. That was a gauntlet we had to traverse on a daily basis.

Regardless, we were still innocent and sweet children who acted, and were treated as such, by our loving adults and by each other. All of my friends from school were welcome in my home, and they came. "Don't forget to invite Mendy here," my mother reminded me one day. "You've been to her house two times already." No customers were

Chapter Five: What's In A Name?

scheduled on afternoons when my company was expected; my mother would make hamburgers for lunch, medium rare, which we ravenously consumed. "Mendy," short for Mendelson, was in my fifth grade class and wore her hair in braids like me, with short bangs across her forehead. Her hair, though, was light brown and straight. Mendy loved to pinch my pug nose, so different from her bony nose. After school we often stopped at the luncheonette of the Century apartments across the street. We climbed up on high stools to place the order at the soda fountain. "One chocolate malted with two straws, please," I said to the soda jerk. Mendy and I exchanged friendship bracelets in fifth grade. Mine sits in the jewelry box in my bureau today. We are still friends, although I call her Marguerite now.

At Ethical, Central Park was our front yard. We had gym class there each day when the weather allowed. We lined up in front of the building, holding hands, two by two. When the light turned green, our gym teacher, Mr. Craven, his red hair slightly disheveled from the breeze, led us across the street. He stood in the middle of the avenue until we were all safely on the opposite sidewalk. Then we were off... Some days we played kick ball with a large red rubber ball. I was always picked first when we made up teams, because even though I was short and skinny, I ran like lightning and kicked the ball so far. We climbed the huge rocks that seemed to emerge out of nowhere, racing up over the boulders and sliding down on the other side. It was fun. The Central Park Zoo was right there too. You could smell the fishy odor near the seals' pool at feeding time. I loved to watch these aquatic acrobats catch the fish in midair and to hear the low yelping, barking sounds they made. I loved to see them stretch their sleek, shiny, iridescent bodies erect, their whiskers aflutter, their noses held high in the air—just sniffing.

Deeper Roots

Given Central Park's rich racial history, it was preternatural that it would be located so close to diversity-driven Ethical. In 1825 on the acreage in Central Park at 80th Street, Seneca Village was created by an African American, Andrew Williams, who purchased three plots of land. The community that evolved brought black skilled workers to the area who bought land, built homes, a church and a schoolhouse. Seneca Village (which extended downtown for about twenty blocks) was destroyed in 1858 when the city acquired the land through eminent domain in order to build Central Park. Central Park now extends from 59th Street to 110th Street between Fifth and Eighth Avenues.

Midtown Ethical Culture School, by its very location as well as its philosophy, defied delineations that separated races and cultures in New York City. The residential geographic lines separating blacks and whites were clearly defined in New York City in the years when I was growing up. On 155th Street, just three blocks west of my house, a white population resided between Broadway and Riverside Drive. That's where my classmate Stuart Auerbach lived. Those three blocks that separated our living spaces made different subway lines convenient for going back and forth to school. Both lines stopped at 59th Street but the Eighth Avenue subway line I rode went uptown through Harlem, while the Broadway subway line went up the avenue known in the theatre district as the Great White Way. Sometimes I would make believe I was operating the subway train— standing with my nose pressed against the plate-glass window in the door of the first car next to the conductor's compartment. I shifted weight between my feet, standing astride to keep my balance while I checked out the signal lights in the pitch-black tunnel. When the conductor left his door ajar, as he would sometimes do on stifling hot days, I watched in rapt attention. He moved a lever to govern the speed of the train, speeding us up or slowing us down to approach the station. I had about the same amount of control over that subway train as it hurtled through the tunnel as I did over the subtle and unexpected aspects of racial discrimination that affected me periodically.

After World War II, a concerted migration of the Jewish middle class from the Bronx to more luxurious accommodations on Manhattan's East and West Sides occurred, as discriminatory barriers for Jews in housing were diminishing. A comparison of the student address lists for my class in fifth and sixth grades reflects this pattern. But before my friend Diane Drachman's family moved to Riverside Drive, she would often pick me up in their chauffeured limousine, crossing the 161st Street Bridge and stopping at 409 on her way to school from her apartment on the Grand Concourse near Yankee Stadium in the Bronx. Diane and I would chatter together in the passenger seat as we traveled down Eighth Avenue, and she would occasionally speak with the chauffeur in the most friendly manner, always addressing Jim by his first name. I wonder if the Negro doorman at Ethical gave a nod of acknowledgment to the Negro chauffeur who escorted us up the steps when we arrived at school. Both men were trapped in an aura of anonymity because of their positions and because of their race.

The Ethical Culture Schools were strongly influenced by John Dewey's philosophy of experiential education. We were paired in teams to plot maps; we would trace them from the atlas onto tissue paper, and then transfer them onto huge pieces of oak tag, using a graphing grid to make the proportions accurate. We worked on the floor to paint the continent of Africa. I used pink tempera paint for the interior

113

Deeper Roots

of the continent, and with a flat broad-tipped pen dipped in black India ink I outlined the borders. The map was my first personal encounter with the continent as a geographic entity. When I Scotch-taped the completed map to the wall in my room at home, I had no idea that my ancestors had a direct connection with Africa or that various cultures lived there under European colonial domination.

On Tuesday afternoons we brought our chairs to form a circle in the middle of the classroom. I sat on the edge of my chair waiting for the door to open and our storyteller to come to tell us the next episode in the adventures of Odysseus. Although he looked tall to my young eyes, Dr. Henry Neuman's shoulders were stooped with the weight of many years. He was a senior leader in the Ethical Culture Society. His thinned gray hair barely covered a balding scalp. As he lowered himself into the large chair in the circle we could smell the sweet odor of pipe tobacco that permeated the air around him. I noticed that his suit vest buttons strained to cover a slight paunch. This was our ethics class, a class taught to every grade by the religious leaders of the Ethical Culture Society. In his deep melodic voice Dr. Neuman introduced us to Greek literary heroes at an early age.

One of the very special days at school was Fathers' Day. I was so happy to have my dad there with me. He was a lot older than the other fathers in my class, and his balding head gave evidence of that fact. He must have taken a sick day or vacation day from his job as a clerk at the post office to come.

We showed our work to our dads on Fathers' Day and we took them with us to the science lab. We worked in pairs and my friend, Phoebe Gaynin, was my partner as we shaped glass tubing to use in experiments. Our dads sat in the back of the room to watch us; Phoebe's dad wore a khaki uniform because he was in the military and my dad was dressed in his suit. We placed our Bunsen burner on its asbestos pad, lit

Chapter Five: What's In A Name?

it, took our narrow tube of glass and measured and filed the tube to the proper length, rounding the edge with the blue-yellow flame. After heating the tube of glass until it glowed, we bent it on the corner of the pad to form a right angle. Mr. Denslow, the science instructor, always wore a gray lab coat when he taught our class. It made everything seem very important and very serious. "I can't believe they let you do these things by yourselves. They're going to make real scientists out of you," Dad said as we left the room and walked down the hall to the next class, cooking class, where the smell of baking cookies filled the air. We served these snacks, prepared from ingredients measured from scratch, to our fathers that day. We rolled the dough and shaped the cookies on the metal sheet. Both boys and girls took cooking class. I was happy things went well that day. I remember the afternoon I lit the gas oven with a match and the oven exploded in my face, searing my eyebrows and lashes. I was very careful after that to make sure no gas had escaped in the oven before lighting it.

By fifth grade most of my activities were outgrowths of the Ethical Culture Society programs. I transferred from St. Philip's Church Sunday School to attend Sunday school at Midtown Ethical, run by the Ethical Culture Society, and I spent the summers in Cooperstown, New York, where the Ethical Culture Society ran a camp attended by some of their school students and staffed by some faculty from the high school. The Ethical Culture Society was the organizational expression of the Ethical Culture movement, founded in 1876 to promote moral and ethical behavior toward people irrespective of race, class, or creed. The society served as the governing board for the three Ethical Culture schools: Midtown, Fieldston Lower and Fieldston (the high school).

In Sunday School we discussed current events and interesting issues like euthanasia, capital punishment and discrimination in the South. Ethical Sunday School was a striking contrast to the formal atmosphere, the African American population and the Christian orientation of Sunday School at St. Philip's Episcopal Church. I liked it better. We met in the same classrooms as in regular school and I felt right at home. Although all of the teachers were different, a few of the students were the same. One such classmate and Ethical campmate looked at me in class one day and said, "Katie, let's not speak to each other when we're in Sunday school, all right?" I understood that although we would remain friendly in regular school and at camp, where I was accepted as part of the larger group, Michael didn't want his white Sunday School peers—most of whom attended public schools—to know that he had any association with a Negro girl. I complied with this request without a challenge. We ignored each other in Sunday School.

But I could not ignore the fifth-grade visitors from a public school in Harlem who met with Mrs. Brown's fifth grade class one year at Ethical and then reciprocated the hospitality at their school in Harlem. These visitors drew my attention as they lined up two-by-two with their host partners to walk through the hall. The buxom Mrs. Brown led the way, her pocketbook swinging at her side. I felt a tingle of self-consciousness on the days these students came to visit even though I never heard *any* discussion regarding the class visits. They were a group of students who looked like me, lived near me, yet had a different school experience in their daily lives—an experience that I knew nothing about. What factors separated me from them? I wondered what they thought about my school. Perhaps Anne Raven Wilkinson and I had been placed together in Miss Gardner's class because we both lived in Harlem and both were Negroes. Supposedly we did not need to experience this student exchange. Yet I knew that I was a bridge between

Chapter Five: What's In A Name?

two contrasting worlds with my feet firmly planted on both sides of the abyss.

Another educational and social conundrum involved the matter of sex education. Sex education was not yet part of the curriculum, even in this progressive school but when challenged by events in the classroom, the school evidenced remarkable flexibility. One day my classmate began excusing herself from class every twenty minutes. "Katie, guess what? I have my period," she whispered to me in a hushed voice. None of the other girls in the fifth grade had experienced this life change, so she became the center of our attention, disrupting the planned lessons for the entire week. I think Miss Gardner sent her to the nurse's office.

Our parents must have been notified and called to a meeting to discuss the issue of sex education, because all of the girls in our class were summoned to the nurse's office for group sessions to learn the facts of life. Where did babies come from? How were they made? The boys met with Scully, too—separately. Nurse Sculthorp was a kind and gentle person whom we knew and trusted. So our sex education began in fifth grade, prompted, I believe, by my classmate's precocity. Somehow we learned that in her case imagination had replaced reality—but the furor created in the classroom demanded an adult response, so the teachers and staff adjusted the curriculum to meet the learning opportunity. Soon after these sex education sessions I remember sitting on the living-room couch with my mother and reading the book, *Growing Up,* together.

Ethical again rose to the occasion to respond to social issues of the day in sixth grade when we rehearsed Earl Robinson's *Ballad for Americans* for our graduation ceremony. Our music teacher, Miss Hanson, taught us how to tuck our chins into our chests to make the proper tones for the ballad, which begins with the Revolutionary War and gives a

Deeper Roots

synopsis of American history, emphasizing the different ethnic and nationality groups that make up America. We sang with gusto:

> *Our country's strong, our country's young.*
> *Her greatest songs are still unsung.*
> *From the plains and mountains we have sprung*
> *to keep the faith with those who went before.*

This ballad was controversial at the time (1948). The Negro singer Paul Robeson had recorded it and both he and the composer were blacklisted as alleged communists. Despite Ethical's liberal orientation, I believe that the school still took a substantial risk to perform the *Ballad for Americans*.

On graduation day the boys looked so different in their white shirts, ties and suits, each with a carnation sprouting from the lapel of his jacket. The girls wore pink corsages pinned on the left side of their white dresses. We paired off, boy and girl, to walk down the green-carpeted aisle to our seats in the auditorium of the Ethical Culture Society building, which was connected by a corridor to our school. Donald Scherl was my partner. We had been classmates, campers together, and good friends for three years. It was a solemn occasion. The organ played the school anthem to accompany our procession. As I entered the wood-paneled hall I could see that the pews were full. Our relatives and the entire school population came to this event. I spotted Mom and Dad and Auntie Maud sitting in the audience and gave them a reassuring smile. The gold lettering above the stage read, *THE PLACE WHERE MEN MEET TO SEEK THE HIGHEST IS HOLY GROUND*. I wondered what that meant. Miss Hanson rapped her baton on the music stand then, turning her palms upward, signaled us to rise. The

Chapter Five: What's In A Name?

enthusiastic sound of our young voices filled the auditorium with our well-rehearsed rendition of *Ballad for Americans*. I felt very important.

It was the last time that we would be together as a class. A cutoff point at sixth grade determined our fates. Some of my friends had not been selected to go on to Fieldston, the Ethical Society secondary school located on a spacious campus in the suburban-like Riverdale section of the Bronx. But all of my progress reports at Midtown had been good, so I never had any doubt I would go to school at Fieldston.

When Leonard Brook's name was called, I knew that I would be next to go up to the platform to receive my diploma. All eyes would be on me then. "Take the diploma with your left hand, and shake hands with your right," I repeated to myself as I navigated the six steps up to the dais. "Katherine Elizabeth Butler," I heard the principal announce, and I reached out to receive my prize. Only a dim memory of my first interview in Mrs. Wagner's office crossed my mind, the interview when I, as Betty Butler, began the process of renaming and redefining myself.

The conflict between the aspiring Negro middle class, desirous of integration, and the problematic lower classes that were believed to interfere with the attainment of that objective, was a struggle my family was engaged in. Therefore, I was raised with the belief that it was my responsibility and all of the other young people that I had contact with "to set an example for the race" in order to gain acceptance for Negroes in the white world. Langston Hughes has written this poem that sums up our dilemma. I have reproduced this poem as it was written.

Deeper Roots

High to Low

God knows
We have our troubles, too--
One trouble is you:
you talk too loud
cuss too loud
look too black
don't get anywhere,
and sometimes it seems
you don't even care.
The way you send your kids to school
stockings down, (not Ethical Culture)
the way you shout out loud in church,
(not St. Philip's)
and the way you lounge on doorsteps
just as if you were down South,
(not at 409)
the way you clown --
the way, in other words,
you let me down --
me, trying to uphold the race
and you --
well you can see,
we have our problems,
too, with you.

Chapter Six:

Ethical Culture School Camp

(1946-1951 & 1955-1957)

The Main Concourse of Grand Central Terminal is the length of one and a half football fields with a domed ceiling seemingly rising to the heavens. The vast vaulted area is jammed with campers, counselors and parents saying last goodbyes with hugs and kisses and first greetings to fellow campers as we gather under the historic brass and opal four-face clock. It seems like all the camps are traveling this day in the last week of June 1946; the Concourse is so crowded you can barely move. It is as noisy as a barnyard, with shrieks of recognition from last year's bunk mates. I feel like I could be gobbled up in the enormity

Deeper Roots

of the place, and the enormity of the change I am about to make.

Previous summers Dad and I spent two weeks in Windsor, Connecticut with my Dad's sister, Aunt Jessie and her family. The postal address was RFD 257, and although we were just half an hour away from the capital city of Hartford, we were light years away in a country setting with no sidewalks. We got off the commuter train at Hayden Station and the white shingled farmhouse sat beside a dirt road, near endless rows of tobacco. Sue and Mary, Aunt Jessie's adult children, lived with her while their husbands fought in World War II and Mr. Garrett, Aunt Jessie's second husband, with his copper skin and white hair looked to my young eyes to be pushing 100.

There were acres of land on this property with space to grow rows of corn and peas, cucumbers and lettuce, and all the other vegetables you could imagine. I learned to tell what was growing in the soil by the shape of the leaves that peeked out of the ground. There were two pigs in their sty and a barnyard from which the roosters crowed to wake me up every morning. I begged Aunt Jessie to let me go with her to collect the eggs and she let me pick them ever so carefully and place them in a basket that she carried. The eggs were so warm having just been laid, and the baby chicks were so cute. Aunt Jessie let me hold them in my hands. There was so much for me to see; things were so different from the city.

Summers in Harlem could be hot in more ways than one. A race riot had broken out there and I remember the newspaper photographs marking the story—yet it seemed so far away to me. I felt so safe in these sylvan surroundings. My grandmother Elizabeth, I was told, once had a country stand on the road. Other cousins lived nearby: Edward Weeks, named for his grandfather, had his family there, and long and lanky Earl, who always looked so sad to me, perhaps because his eyes drooped down at the corners. There was little work for black men here except in the tobacco fields so the other brothers, Alfred and Elmer, and sister Redie had left the farmhouse to put down stakes in Harlem. But there were always family members going back and forth between Windsor and New York. My grandmother also traveled back and forth between Connecticut and New York where she lived with my Dad and his first wife. My father also owned property in Windsor which I inherited but never used. I subsequently gave it to the black church, Archer Memorial, just up the road from the family farmhouse. I played with other kids my age during those summers, but now I was going off to the unknown.

In Grand Central Terminal, the camp counselors hold sticks high in the air with the number indicating the group we will travel with. I bid my parents goodbye as we move in a pack on our way down to the track. Dottie Meltzer is my group leader for the ten-year-old girls and she leads us down the ramp to the train where the conductor calls out, "all aboard."

The train wheels screech against the steel rails of the New York Central coach (the predecessor of Metro-North Commuter Railroad) pulling out of Grand Central Terminal. The car reverberates with the laughter of campers coming together again—sharing stories of fun they had at Ethical Culture camp the previous summer. I sit staring out of the window feeling the smooth rhythmic motion as the train brings us from the darkness of the tunnel into the pink/orchid glare of the early morning sunlight reflecting off the windows of the East Harlem tenements we whizz by. The seat next to mine is vacant. I am ten years old and scared. I hope the adventure of eight weeks at overnight camp will be fun, but the thought of being away from my parents for the

Deeper Roots

first time makes me blink back tears when I see 409 across the Harlem River.

I was so excited the day the doorbell rang and the man in the brown khaki uniform announced, "Railway Express." He came to pick up the black brass-studded trunk and burlap duffle bag stuffed with army blankets and a pillow shipped to camp two weeks in advance of my arrival there. My mother sewed red-lettered name tapes into all the clothes we packed in neat piles—a pair of navy blue shorts that buttoned up the front with two rows of white pearl buttons, a dark blue polo shirt with thin red and white stripes, and the polka dot halter top that reminded me of a bandana scarf. I wish I was sitting in my room now instead of riding on this train.

I take my Walt Disney Donald Duck comic book from the brown paper bag that also holds my lunch and thumb through the pages of familiar characters that make me feel more comfortable. Judy Hershson, my classmate from school and a veteran camper must sense my growing uneasiness. "You'll have a good time this summer," she assures me, "there's so much to do." Classmates Stephen Peck and Michael Bokat are on the train too along with upper grade students that I also recognize from school. We sing camp songs on the bus that meets us at the special stop at Fort Plain, New York to begin the seemingly endless trip over unpaved and bumpy country roads along acres of neatly-plowed farmland. We ride past the "tin top" yellow barn near the narrow road leading to the camp grounds in the Hyde Bay section of Lake Otsego in Cooperstown, New York—the town noted for the National Baseball Hall of Fame. I feel like a caged bird finally freed as I get off the bus. I run so fast across the sweet-smelling newly-mowed grass that the wind whistles in my ears.

Chapter Six: Ethical Culture School Camp

Dottie introduces the people in my bunkhouse to each other. There are six of us and we all wore braids: Barbara Flaster, Roberta Elmer, Frances Hardy, Victoria Beller and the daughter of my principal, Victoria Wagner. We have lots to talk about because Frances and Barbara are veteran campers and they would show us the ropes. The row of nine bunkhouses comprises the girls' line, numbered in order by logs of birch bark forming Roman numerals fitted across each porch — I am assigned to Bunk Six. Since I have already made friends on the train with my bunkmates I am feeling more comfortable when the screechy screen door slams shut.

I read the two letters resting on my pillow (one from my mother and one from my father) and they immediately help me feel a connection between camp and home. The letters that my parents sent to me those summers bore three-cent postage stamps on the envelope and no zip code. Mom and Dad took turns writing, so that I would be sure to get mail every day. I kept them posted on all of the activities and friends that I had made during the summer. When my children left for camp I always wrote a letter to them that would arrive before they set foot at camp because I remembered how important those letters waiting on my pillow were to me.

Our trunks had arrived and were arranged next to our respective cots. We begin unpacking our things, arranging our individual shelves on the wall next to the cots with magazines, books, hair comb and brush. We hang our raincoats and warm jackets on the hooks in the cubby in the rear of the cabin. We each write our name on adhesive tape and place it under our individual metal rack where we hang our towel and washcloth. Finally, we place our toiletries in the bathroom on the shelf.

Deeper Roots

That first summer was my first away from both of my parents and despite my initial misgivings, it was a wonderful experience. It didn't take me long to feel at home on the beautiful camp grounds nestled in the Otsego mountain range. The Main House, a Tudor-style mansion dominated the grounds. We ate our meals in the Main House's three dining rooms, with the oldest campers supping on a screened-in porch off of one of the dining rooms. The counselors' room and the kitchen were the only other rooms on the ground floor. Camp offices, the infirmary, the doctor's office, the library and science room comprised the second floor.

Soon after our arrival at camp we chose the activities that we wanted to participate in, and it was expected that we would attend these classes. There were so many activities to keep us busy all day long including, but not limited to, square dancing, group singing, campfires and picnics. There was no television or radio but there was the rehearsal for the annual Gilbert and Sullivan operetta performed for Parents' Weekend. Many campers chose this activity but it demanded so much preparation and I preferred to do more athletic things. There were no color wars between teams. Collaboration, not extreme competition was the ethos. Woodworking shop, social hall and jewelry bunks were situated near the tennis courts. Down the road a quarter of a mile were the banks of Lake Otsego where the camp waterfront was located. We had rowboat, canoe and sailboat instruction based on our swimming level. This is where I learned an important skill.

During the normal school year at Midtown Ethical Culture School, we sometimes went to the Y to swim. The first time I jumped in the pool the water was over my head. I could not touch the bottom when I tried to stand up—I could

Chapter Six: Ethical Culture School Camp

not swim a stroke and I could not breathe. My nostrils filled with water and it felt like I was swallowing water by the gallon. I was coughing and thrashing around underwater so unlike the Central Park Zoo seals which glided through the water with ease. Each time I came to the surface for air I would go down again. I was in a panic, fighting for my life. I thought I was drowning. I do not remember who pulled me out, but I emerged determined to master swimming. I had signed up for swimming lessons, but found floating on my back insurmountable. Each time I tried that feat under the watchful eye of the waterfront instructor, I found my feet sinking to the sandy bottom. Floating was not for me. "You can do anything that you set out to do," my mother said.

It took me several summers to get out of first area designed for non-swimmers. But eventually I did learn to overcome this liability and later I became a Red Cross water safety instructor and director of the waterfront. I also made certain that my children learned to swim—I taught them myself and it is a moment of great pride for me today when adult men and women remind them that I taught them to swim when they were campers at ECSC.

I also learned to play tennis on the clay courts and hit softballs on the baseball field. The baseball field separated the row of nine bunks that comprised the girls' line from the eleven tents on the boys' line and the rule preventing boys and girls from crossing over from their respective lines was strictly enforced.

I did, however, manage to pick up one bad habit— smoking. Dad was a smoker, and I would sneak cigarettes from his pack and smoke them out of the window. At camp we would sneak cigarettes out of the counselors' boxes in the counselors' room and go into the field in back of the tents where we lived to smoke. I asked for my mother's permission (I was fifteen) so that I would not be smoking without

Deeper Roots

her knowledge—she grudgingly gave it to me in 1951 when she came to visit me at camp. A few years later when I was at Mount Holyoke, she included this post script in one of her letters:

> *Oscar* [my uncle] *has gotten your special cigarettes. Hope you are cutting down. Saw Dr. Chin* [my physician] *yesterday and went over the same story--how injurious it is etc., etc., especially for youngsters. So there. Can't say we didn't warn you. If you want to fall in with the crowd, it is entirely up to you.*

Neither Mom's nor Dr. Chin's warnings stopped me from smoking. During my senior year in high school a chemistry experiment conducted by one of my classmates, John Reiner, proved that filter cigarettes did not accomplish the advertised benefit of trapping tobacco tars. The white fiber filter purportedly reduced the danger of lung cancer as evidenced by the fact that the filter turned grayish. That was important information for us to have, although it did not do anything to curb smoking at Fieldston. It took my own children to put out my lighted cigarettes and get me to give up the habit. As more information appeared about the dangers of smoking, I limited my smoking to four cigarettes a day—four too many. I quit during the SmokEnders® campaign in 1978. Three of our children smoke, but they do not smoke around me.

I was a camper at Ethical Culture School Camp for six summers and a counselor at the camp for three summers, eventually earning a position as director of the waterfront in 1957, my last summer at camp. I was a work camper at University Settlement, run by Charles Cook, my first form (7th grade) ethics teacher. The following summer I worked as a junior counselor at Camp Felicia, run by Fieldston faculty

Chapter Six: Ethical Culture School Camp

member Phillips Houghton and his wife, Vera, who were my social dancing, shop, and jewelry instructor at Ethical camp. My first and only interruption in this revolving door of Ethical Culture Society programs was the summer I spent after sophomore year in college as co-waterfront director at Forest Lake Camp, in Meredith, New Hampshire. The camp was under the auspices of the Harlem Presbyterian Church of the Master, whose minister was the Reverend James Robinson, my neighbor in apartment 12F at 409.

But the ECSC was a different experience altogether. People made this place so special. The adult community, directors and staff treated us with respect and caring which was reflected in the way that we interacted with each other. We formed a diverse community from different socio-economic, racial and national backgrounds and we lived together in this protective environment for a part of each summer. The majority of campers came from the New York City public school system. Those who could not afford the camp were awarded scholarships and the camp strove to dispel the economic and social differences among us. For example, you could not bring any food or money with you so everyone, at least for those eight weeks, was equally hungry and poor. There was also a policy of rotating seating assignments during meals. The assignments served two purposes: first, it required campers to eat and interact with other campers of different ages and backgrounds and, secondly, the camper sitting in the first seat was required to bring the food to the table from the kitchen—we served each other. We were also encouraged to eat one meal consisting of soup and bread each summer. After voting, the campers would choose which charity received the savings derived from that simplified meal.

During one particular year at camp I also lost and gained the two most important men in my life. Hubey was seventeen-years-old and had been hired as a helper in the kitchen the summer my father died. Hubey came back to ECSC as a counselor for the interceding four years when I returned as a counselor. It was a small camp and we got to know each other, beginning our relationship that has lasted to this day. One of my former bunkmates was matron of honor at our wedding in 1957 and Hubey's best man, his closest friend through high school and college was a counselor that I dated the summer before I returned to ECSC as a counselor. All of our connections were interconnected — and never more so than during that August of 1951 when I was fifteen years old.

While I was away at camp each summer, my parents took their one-week vacation together in the Catskills. It was on one of those vacations that my father was hospitalized for a kidney operation. He insisted that Mom come to see me for Parents Visiting Weekend at camp so she complied with his wish. Dad wrote me a letter that weekend from Presbyterian Hospital with regrets for not being able to visit. He was looking forward to getting home and seeing me at the end of the month when camp ended. Three days later I was called to the office of the co-camp director, Marg, who explained to me as gently as she possibly could that my father had died. I went to my tent, packed some belongings and travelled to Grand Central Station with my camp counselor. How could this happen to me, I wondered. I knew that my life would never be the same again. That four-hour train trip seemed interminably long—much longer than it ever seemed in previous years. As I looked out of the window at the farmlands that we rode through I thought about Stephanie, my good friend from school and camp. I had visited in her home and we went on car rides on country roads with her parents on many occasions. We sang songs on those trips and the fun we all had together was now seared in my mind.

Chapter Six: Ethical Culture School Camp

Stephanie just lost her dad after a long illness during the last school year and I had expected her face to change when she returned to school because of the severity of her loss. How could you look the same when your life is so abruptly and tragically altered? I felt so different inside that I thought I would see a different person when I next peered into a mirror.

Our family friend met me at the train gate when we finally pulled into Grand Central Terminal. My counselor returned to camp, and I went to my apartment where Mom greeted me with a big hug as I crossed the threshold. We went directly back to my room leaving Dad's family, Aunt Jessie, my cousins Redie, Mary, Elmer and Alfred in the living room. Mom and I tried to reassure each other that we would manage somehow. We would "bind the belly" as the Jamaicans would say. It would not be the last time we would use that term.

The funeral was to take place a few days later, and this would be the first time that I ever attended such a ceremony. I spent the next days reading *The Great Gatsby*, focusing my mind on whatever I could to distract me from the reality that I had to face. When the black limousine carrying my family arrived at the Walter B. Cooke Funeral Home I did not know what to expect. I intentionally managed to sit far enough away from the front of the room so that I could barely see the profile of my father's face in the coffin.

I don't remember what happened next. Luckily for me, I was headed back to camp the next day to be reunited with my bunkmates who warmly greeted me on my arrival. Hubey recollects looking out from the kitchen and seeing "everyone running out" to welcome me back. He was struck by the racial neutrality and caring spirit of the ECSC and its campers and this show of support resonated within him.

131

Deeper Roots

Hubey now reflects back that it was his experience at the ECSC that convinced him that integration (and not fringe activism) was the key to solving America's race problems during the tumultuous 1960s. The spirit of the ECSC changed him forever and embraced me at a time when I needed it most. This was my haven. This was my bridge over troubled water—my place to invest in friendships and activities. I was lucky in love too, wearing the Fieldston jacket of my boyfriend that summer.

The letters I received from Mom only a week after Dad's death did not reflect her loss and sadness. "Wish you were here...Went to General Post Office to get info for pension benefit application. People helped me to find the way to government offices." I imagine she was trying to cheer me up by reporting on baseball scores and telephone calls from family and friends. "Edna called to ask me what I wanted from the store just as I was getting ready to go food shopping for myself. Wasn't I lucky?"

In the summers after my father's passing, my friends at the Ethical Culture Schools and ECSC always kept in touch with my widowed mother. The relationship between my friends and our parents was very close, and in her letters my mother was always interested in the wellbeing of my friends. In a typical letter, she writes:

> Judy E just called to say she and Victor are coming to visit you at camp, and they invited me to join them. ... Annette called the other day and we talked for half an hour... Mr. Silver offered you a job for July and August (summer of 1954, you better take it)... Phoebe called, her mother is sick again...Dottie Milman's mother called to tell me all about the place." (the University Settlement where Dottie and I were both work campers).

Chapter Six: Ethical Culture School Camp

Throughout my lengthy ECSC and Ethical Culture School history, there was one person who remained a constant. "Netsy Bumps" is what we called her. Annette Winter went to ECSC, Midtown Ethical, Fieldston, and Ethical Sunday School with me. We became good friends over the years partly because we were the only two Negro girls who shared so many of the same experiences at the same time. We also shared a Caribbean background. Both of Annette's parents were from the Caribbean just like my Jamaican mother (her mother was from Antigua and her dad from British Guyana). Although we were born in the same year, Annette was a grade below me.

We would often visit each other on the weekends as we lived only a mile away from each other, a short bus ride down Seventh Avenue from her house to mine. The golf-playing Winter family lived in a cream-colored three-story brick row house not far from St. Philips Church on tree-lined Strivers Row on 139th Street off Adam Clayton Powell Boulevard. When I called on the telephone, Annette's mother would answer, "Dr. Winter's Office" in her soft West Indian accent, but we could not talk on the phone at all during the doctor's visiting hours.

Although Annette and I were alike in so many ways, our camp experience highlighted our differences. At camp Annette enjoyed reading while I played sports. An awkward lefty, Annette could hardly swing a bat in the softball games or stroke a racket on the tennis court—things that I could do. But she could write, and she wrote in her journal every day for hours and hours. Although I also read books at camp, I was more social than solitary Annette. We were close though and we told others that we were cousins and I called her mother "Aunt Victoria" when she came on Parents Visiting Day. Annette's older brother, Walter, was at camp too and

133

teased her all the time when he was not ignoring her. Annette followed in his footsteps through Midtown Ethical, Fieldston, ECSC, and Brown University (back then it was the women's college, Pembroke, which later merged with Brown). Annette and I remain friends and in contact with each other to this day.

My memories of ECSC are rich but it was still, after all, camp. There were moments when the benevolent philosophy of the camp was subsumed by the bad behavior of the campers. However, the behavior never escalated to anything beyond rhyming taunts and teasing among the kids and although it was not pervasive, it still did occur.

Sixty-six years have passed since my first bus ride to ECSC. Our daughters Karen and Lauren and children of my other former bunkmate Barbara Flaster spent their summers there too. I received a call from a former ECSC camper, now a professor at the University of Massachusetts at Dartmouth who told me of his visit to the camp last summer with his daughter. Another fellow camper bought a home in Cooperstown, across from our Lake Otsego camp dock. There is a loyalty to the place that meant so much to us. Since we keep in touch with many former campers and counselors, we know personally of the individual and family trips revisiting ECSC. One of these former campers rents a place on Lake Otsego each summer and invites former ECSC campers and counselors to come for a weekend where we eat together, sing camp songs, set lighted candle boats on the lake at night, revisit the camp grounds with spouses and significant others, reunite, share stories and photographs, and get to know each other in our present lives. The beat goes on.

It is at these reunions that I hear what I was like as a counselor from the campers that I had in my bunk, and it is

134

Chapter Six: Ethical Culture School Camp

where I connect with the person who taught me how to play tennis when I was a camper. I am so glad that our two oldest daughters had the opportunity to attend ECSC before it closed. They tell me that of all the camps they experienced, it was the best one of all.

Hubey and I stand on the same spot where the bus dropped us off on the camp grounds. We have come to claim our piece of this land where our hopes and dreams were formed. This place was so important to our development as human beings, reinforcing our values and concern for others. Now the field is overgrown with weeds so high they bend their heads like chaffs of wheat. The field where we once played softball for hours is marked only by the rusty metal backstop lilting to one side. A tarred surface amidst the un-bridled growth marks the place where we played tennis while the rays of the sun beat down on us. I recall the rhythmic solid sounds of the volleys back and forth and the sound as the ball hit squarely on the racquet strings.

Of all the buildings, the Social Hall is the only one left standing on the acreage sold to private individuals. The Hall is now a summer home, retaining the colored markers which preserve the names of former campers on the walls. The owners of the home tell us that former campers come by each year to reminisce about their summers spent at ESCS. The Main House where the dining rooms once reverberated with camp songs and the voices of chattering children is boarded up, displaying remnants of a fire that burned the building many years ago. Yet the House stands tall, like an old dowager who refuses to yield to the passage of time. The foundation remains intact, so the mansion will not fall. If I stand quietly I can hear the clanging of the camp bell that Hubey used to ring, calling us to meals.

Deeper Roots

Day and night great trains rush toward the
Hudson River,
Sweep down its eastern bank for 140 miles,
Flash briefly by the long red row of tenement
houses south of 125th street, dive with a roar
into the two and one half mile tunnel which
burrows beneath the glitter and swank of Park
Avenue and then Grand Central Station—
crossroads of a million private lives! Gigantic
stage on which are played a thousand dramas
daily!

Chapter Seven:

Higher Hopes and Greater Goals

Fieldston School (1947 – 1953)

On a crisp September morning in 1999, I walked up the hill from 409 to retrace my daily route to the Fieldston School. The local uptown subway train at 155th Street brought me to the 168th Street station; I got on the noisy elevator connecting to the Seventh Avenue/ Broadway Interboro Rapid Transit (IRT) on the upper level where I boarded another train. Part of the line's northern route runs on elevated tracks and I stayed on the "el" to the terminus at 242nd Street. I descended the metal stairway from the platform overlooking part of the 1,122 acres of public space of Van Cortlandt Park. The park forms a huge green carpet in the midst of the asphalt and concrete of the West Bronx. Some people stretched out on blankets were watching a pickup baseball game on the field. I trudged up a street away from the small shops and bustling traffic on Broadway. The white-steepled red brick building of Manhattan College dominated the hill to my right. The Christian Brothers founded this school in upper Manhattan in 1853 as a Catholic liberal arts college for commuting male students and moved it to its present location in 1923. I crossed Manhattan College Parkway to climb twenty steep steps bringing me a tier above the bustling city in the residential section of Riverdale. This particular subdivision of Riverdale, called Fieldston like the school, is a privately owned 250-acre enclave of expensive, mostly Tudor-style homes and mansions. The idyllic setting makes a striking contrast to groups of cooperatively owned high-rise apartment buildings that have sprouted up along the nearby Hudson River.

Four independent schools serving different populations coexist in Riverdale within a one-mile radius, yet when I was a student there, there was very little contact between the respective student bodies. The students at Fieldston and at Horace Mann School for Boys were predominantly Jewish. Riverdale Country Day School students were predominantly Protestant, and Manhattan College catered to Catholic men. Each school group observed a rigid but unspoken taboo regarding interreligious social intercourse. The older Fieldston girls dated Horace Mann boys, but the boys at Manhattan College ignored the girls when we congregated after school at 242nd Street to ride the "el" back to Manhattan or to other parts of the Bronx. We all rode the train together but usually in separate cars.

During my high school years I made this trip to Fieldston by public transportation. However, most of the students who lived in Manhattan rode to school by chartered bus and a few mothers made round trips by automobile to transport their children to and from school. Sometimes I rode the A train to 207th Street, took the Riverdale Avenue bus to the

Chapter Seven: Higher Hopes and Greater Goals

brick monument at 243rd Street at Fieldston Road, and walked the few blocks to the Fieldston School. I usually met other classmates en route and we studied and talked during the hour-long trip. This time I made the journey by myself. I wanted to recapture those six important years of my life. It was a happy and transformative time for me.

I decided to walk through the neighborhood to absorb the tranquility of my surroundings before visiting the school campus. The purple asters, the yellowing sycamore leaves and the crispness of the air reminded me that autumn was near, but the song birds had not begun their seasonal migration. I could hear their chirping because no car horns or noisy jackhammers disturbed the quiet natural beauty around me.

The circuitous Fieldston Road led me past the sign to the entrance of Riverdale Country School, but the buildings were set back on expansive grounds beyond my view. I continued until the white flecked grey fieldstone buildings of my former school took shape. The eight-building complex, built here in 1929 on eighteen acres of land, frames a grassy quadrangle. Beyond the main complex is a wooded area where the tennis courts and the arts and library buildings are located. I sauntered past the classroom buildings—unlike Riverdale Country School these buildings are clearly visible from the road—and up the sloped gravel surface leading to the athletic fields where I spent many afternoons playing varsity soccer, field hockey and co-captaining the cheerleading squad for the boys' varsity sports teams.

Pre-season practice was underway, and the maintenance staff was installing goal posts at either end of the field. Some members of the Fieldston football team performed calisthenics while another group of varsity players in their orange-and-white uniforms rifled long and short passes to

Deeper Roots

each other under the watchful eye of head coach Clarry Miller.

Memories flood back. I see myself leading the field hockey forward line across this same chalk marked field. I shift my body to receive a pass from fullback Anne Silver. My hands sting when the hard ball slams against my stick, but I don't pause. I dash down the field, dribbling the ball past the defense, and position myself. I glance up momentarily at the goalie poised in a crouched position, and then I angle the ball to the left side of the cage and score the tiebreaking goal against our arch rival, Riverdale Country Day School. The piercing sound of the referee's whistle ends the game. Our shrill screams reverberate across the field and we run to the fifty-yard line to jump up and down in a circle, the pleated skirts of our navy blue uniforms billowing. Then we drop our sticks and huddle with our arms around our teammate's waists, throw back our heads and give a rousing cheer. "Two, four, six, eight, who do we appreciate? Riverdale! Riverdale! Riverdale!" The teams form two lines. We 'high five' our opponents to salute each other before heading into the athletic building to shower and dress. Pat Katzenstein, our short, husky-voiced coach, who has taught most of us how to play hockey, wears a tailored green suit, brown oxford shoes and white athletic socks over her stockings, to referee our games. After we eat chocolate chip cookies and drink hot chocolate in the cafeteria, the Riverdale girls return to their campus on buses parked in the driveway.

That driveway separates Fieldston from the adjacent Fieldston Lower School both literally and figuratively. The buildings are also separated by another athletic field used mostly by the lower school students in preschool through sixth grade. First form (7th grade) students at Fieldston consisted of children from the Lower School plus new entrants

Chapter Seven: Higher Hopes and Greater Goals

from Midtown Ethical and from public schools in Manhattan and the Bronx—about a third from each group—to make up a class of seventy. I was a member of the first form class in 1947.

Some of the Fieldston students in the classes above me spent their summers at Ethical Culture School Camp in Cooperstown, New York and my classmates were part of the revolving door of Ethical Culture programs, Ethical Culture School Camp and Ethical Culture Sunday School. Faculty members at Fieldston worked as counselors at ECSC and all of the leaders of the Ethical Society sent their children to the Camp. Some of the faces of faculty members were familiar to me because they sent their children to the camp and came to visit on Parents Visiting Weekend. Exchanging greetings with these people in the Fieldston hallway made this new environment a more welcoming place for me.

The move to Fieldston was an important demarcation for me. After sixth grade I was left out of mixed-gender social events outside of those sponsored by Fieldston or the Ethical Culture Society. Although I had lots of male and female friends at school, my social life on weekends was spent with girlfriends from school and camp. Barbara Tessohn, my camp friend and I chatted on the phone for hours at a time and ate hamburgers together at her family-owned, counter-style restaurant, the Robin Dell, a hangout for nearby Columbia University and Barnard College students. Other Saturdays I ate lunch at Stark's Restaurant on 90th Street and Broadway with classmates Phoebe Gaynin or Anne Silver. After lunch we often went to a movie at the 86th Street Loews Theater or hung out at their apartments.

My mother's customer, Hilda French, was like a special aunt who helped me fill my Saturdays as well. She took me to lunch at Toffinetti's restaurant in Times Square and to Saturday matinees of Broadway shows. Hilda was a frustrated tap dancer who made her living as a postal clerk since the opportunities for breaking into show business were miniscule for Negroes. Hilda introduced me to the theater and, along with my artistic experiences at the Modern School, I developed a lifelong appreciation of drama and dance.

But as I went through high school I was sorely aware that I was missing out on a lot of boy-girl dating and parties that engaged my peers. Fifty years after graduation at our Fieldston reunion, my classmate Steven Peck reminded me that I had asked him if I was welcome to attend a party he was having at his East Side apartment at the time of our graduation. I do remember going to the party and having a good time although I did not remember making the request. However, Steven's memory of this event was vivid; he was perplexed and dismayed that I was doubtful about my being welcome although we had known each other since fourth grade. I explained that a cut-off in invitations to coed parties from school friends began at Fieldston for me when race apparently began to matter. That was the time that we lived in and remnants of that social structure exist to this day in our society. However, my Fieldston experience was unique and quite extraordinary because of the people there.

Like the educators at the Modern School and Midtown Ethical, there were certain teachers (and the issues that they raised) at Fieldston who come instantly to mind. In some instances the teachers continue to influence and impact me — that is the power of an educator.

Kendall Bassett, our balding science teacher, introduced us to Mr. Bones, the human skeleton, when we began studying anatomy in the lab located above the corridor. Mr. Bassett was the head of the first (7th grade) and second (8th grade) forms, and he wore jeans and plaid flannel shirts when he led us in square dancing at the Friday evening parties in the cafeteria. He was the first of the many male major subject teachers I encountered at Fieldston. We had very few men teaching academic subjects at Midtown Ethical, but the Fieldston faculty was evenly divided with respect to gender. Mr. Bassett's son, Kendall, Jr., who was tall with the chiseled features of a Greek god, joined our class from Fieldston Lower. It must have been difficult to have a parent who was a teacher, with octopus-like tentacles gathering information about every move you made at school. Kendall Jr. was viewed as a "catch" by my friends Anne Silver and Gwen Barrera who had crushes on him at various times. We spent many conversations discussing how cute Kendall was.

We had faculty (and classmates) with disabilities at Fieldston. One faculty member and Fieldston alum suffered from cerebral palsy, and because of his awkward walk frequently became the subject of ridicule by students. A classmate of mine also had cerebral palsy which affected her speech and physical mobility (there was never any explanation made to us about her handicap). Another student carried sugar cubes in his jacket pocket but we were never told that he was diabetic. Personal privacy was protected, but in retrospect, perhaps we could have understood something more about these illnesses and how they affected our community if presented as part of our curriculum.

My homeroom teacher, Eleanor Whalen, was new to Fieldston when I entered first form (7th grade) in 1947. Miss Whalen was in her mid-20s, and was one of the youngest teachers I had. She was a tall, slender brunette who parted her hair on the left side in a page-boy style. She had a relaxed, easygoing manner and a ready smile that revealed two slightly overlapping front teeth. Miss Whalen was also our instructor for basic courses in math, English and social studies, and she prepared the narrative reports to parents in those basic subjects under the categories of performance described as superior, very good, fair, barely passing and failing. (The school, in a successful attempt to deemphasize competition, did not give letter grades.)

On Valentine's Day a bouquet of a dozen red roses was delivered to our classroom. "Miss Whalen has a boyfriend, Miss Whalen has a boyfriend," the boys chanted unmercifully. Miss Whalen's face turned the same deep red as her flowers. I think the boys who teased the loudest had a secret crush on our teacher and were really jealous of her suitor, who won out and married Miss Whalen the following year. I felt lucky to be assigned to her class. However, that feeling would change during the school year.

Miss Whalen assigned the class Charles Dickens' *A Tale of Two Cities* and Dad allowed me to take the leather-bound copy from his bookcase to read at home. I loved reading books and I felt very grown-up when I was entrusted with this special volume. Madame DeFarge captivated me and I focused my book report on her. "Click, click went the knitting needles," I began my paper. I worked diligently to make my essay both lively and dramatic, and knew that I had done a good job.

I eagerly awaited the day the papers were returned. But on that fateful day Miss Whalen asked me if I had written my paper by myself; I was totally devastated. Why would she doubt my honesty? Why did she question my ability? Was it because my skin was brown? From that moment my feelings toward Miss Whalen soured precipitously and irreparably. Once again, I didn't share my disappointment with my parents or ask for their advice. I felt that I should be able to deal with these experiences independently.

Mr. William Bell, my fourth form (10th grade) ethics teacher, was the first Negro teacher I had since leaving the Modern School after third grade. As a general rule, leaders of

Chapter Seven: Higher Hopes and Greater Goals

the Ethical Culture Society teach an ethics class at every grade level and Mr. Bell, as a leader-in-training, was assigned to my form.

I feel an instant connection with this man. He sits back in his armchair, slowly puffing on his pipe. He studies the circle of faces in front of him. His gray pants are immaculately creased over his long outstretched legs. His blue shirt is adorned with a gold collar pin, and a narrow red tie complements the tweed sports jacket that hangs smoothly from his shoulders without a pucker. Mr. Bell's caramel-colored face is set off by a neatly trimmed mustache. He is simply knockout handsome. He smiles benevolently at us as we explore the moral questions of our individual lives and the ethics of society at large.

"What about dating?" Mr. Bell asks in his melodious baritone voice. "Would you kiss a guy on the first date?" he asks. Carol responds, "No, I wouldn't let any boy kiss me on the first date. They would think I was fast." "Oh come on now, get real." Don says. "You sound like a prude." The boys have very different ideas from the girls about the appropriate time for necking and petting, or so they say.

I try to gather up the courage to ask the question that bothers me. "What do you do when boys don't ask you out because your skin color is different or you have different religious beliefs?" Will I embarrass Mr. Bell or will I embarrass myself if I raise the lid of Pandora's Box?

But I never did ask that question. The reality of social norms conflicted with the humanistic philosophy on which the school was founded. Of course, I could talk with Mr. Bell after class but I believed he wanted to continue the game of racial denial that we were all playing. Eye contact, body language and non-verbal communication often give cues to how a person will respond to you. As a person of color you become sensitized to those messages and assess who can be

145

approached about delicate questions in a reasonable comfort zone. I got no cues of this kind from Mr. Bell, while Ms. Wilkerson, our African American modern dance teacher, was warm, self-assured and open.

I can vividly re-create in my mind images of English classes with Georgine Peasley. The tiled floor of the hallway would echo with the click of Miss Peasley's high heels as she approached our fourth form (10th grade) English classroom. She entered like a sparrow, pausing momentarily, tilting her head to one side as she took short quick steps to the front of the room. A few strands of brown hair fell away from the upsweep of loose curls on top of her head—which I believe she thought added inches of height to her diminutive five-foot frame. Miss Peasley was both my English teacher and my advisor. We met in monthly conferences to redraft creative writing assignments and to review the books I read other than required reading for school assignments. I was a voracious reader, filling out many three-holed cards listing author, title, date read, and a brief synopsis of the book. John Dos Passos, Fyodor Dostoyevsky, Pearl Buck, Leo Tolstoy, Langston Hughes, and Howard Fast were my favorite authors.

The soft murmur of conversation quieted when Miss Peasley stood at the side of the desk in the front of the room. "Class, will you please turn to page 32 in your poetry anthology," she requested. I opened my book and scanned the page of the poem entitled:

THE CONGO: "A Study of the Negro Race"
1. Their Basic Savagery

The words sizzled through my brain like a red-hot branding iron. I have no idea what Miss Peasley said next. Perhaps she explained that Vachel Lindsay's work was intended to be read aloud in choral style, effectively dramatizing poetry by making it dynamic and alive. My eyes glanced down the page.

> Fat black bucks in a wine barrelled room...
> Barrel-house kings with feet unstable,
> Sagged and reeled and pounded on the table
> Pounded on the table,
> Beat an empty barrel with the handle of a broom
> Hard as they were able,
> Boom, Boom, Boom,
> Then I heard the boom of the blood-lust song
> And a thigh-bone beating on a tin pan gong
> And "BLOOD" / screamed the whistles and the
>   fifes of the warriors,
> BLOOD screamed the Skull-faced lean
> witch doctors.......Mumbo Jumbo will hoo doo you.

The Negro race? The Congo? But this isn't about me. No, I am another Negro. Like the people who live in 409. Like my family and friends. Like the other Negro students at Fieldston. Don't you know this isn't about me? Can't you tell? I play the piano. I am the example of the Negro race.

The images presented in the poem of savages, cannibals, pagans, criminals, evoking fear and fascination in white civilized societies were the images that I was responsible for contradicting and eradicating. But no matter how hard I tried, these negative stereotypes of Negroes and Africans prevailed. This poem added to my difficulty defining my identity as an African American.

"Aren't the rhythm of the words just marvelous? You can almost hear the beat of the drum," Miss Peasley commented.

Deeper Roots

It was not the beating of the drum that I heard, but a cacophony of voices in my head. "That's not you they're talking about. You have nothing to do with those people," I said to myself.

I didn't know enough about Africa to verbally contradict the images, but I did know enough to realize that something that I saw in print was very wrong. Yet because of my adolescent need to conform, I was no longer prepared to confront authority as I did with the elevator operator at Joyce's house who directed me to the service car. My world in some ways had become too fragile for me to take that risk so I pretended not to be offended and dutifully memorized the poem. I practiced the cadence of the words, absorbing the mystery, the danger, and the poison so enticingly offered. To recreate the feelings stirred up by this poem is to peel off a scab from an unhealed wound.

The Congo: And Other Poems, published in 1914, eloquently epitomized the notion of "the white man's burden," dehumanized Africans and reaffirmed the innate inferiority of people of African descent. Audiences and readers of this work were convinced of the necessity to contain and Christianize Africans, because they were born dangerous and evil. Vachel Lindsay, a Midwesterner by birth, crisscrossed the country and received artistic commendation for reciting his work.

On March 11, 1915, Lindsay made an appearance at the Mount Holyoke College Chapel. The following day, according to the Mount Holyoke campus newspaper, Lindsay recited his poems for the 19th century American poetry class. Sophomore Ellen Riggs included this comment in a letter written to her mother dated March 15: "It was perfectly fearful and very unconventional. I liked them (the poems) very much, because they were so different, but some did not. "

148

Chapter Seven: Higher Hopes and Greater Goals

When I researched *The Congo* in the Mount Holyoke College archives I found an autographed volume in the rare book collection inscribed:

> To all the fair ladies on the Mount: Greeting and God-speed
> and so—I remain your slave and servitor,
> Vachel Lindsay   March 11, 1915

Lindsay presented this book to the college on the occasion of his campus visit. What unusual words he chose to describe himself in the inscription. Slave, servitor—the same terminology used to describe the Africans and Negroes he seems to despise and fear.

Mount Holyoke College was founded in 1837 as a women's seminary and many of its graduates pursued missionary work on the African continent, motivated and reinforced, in part, by the same attitudes and perceptions Lindsay expresses. The film *Birth of a Nation*, which degraded Negroes and justified Ku Klux Klan lynchings, made its screen debut a year before *The Congo* appeared in print. It took many years for me to unlearn and replace these perceptions regarding people from the African continent and their descendants—perceptions that are so deeply embedded in the ethos of this country.

When I was a student, media advertisements, films and radio programs like *Amos and Andy*, were public statements about the role of Negroes in American society that constantly bombarded me and my classmates. The image depicted on the box of Aunt Jemima Pancake Mix was a plump, smiling, round-faced black maid or cook, with a plaid kerchief on her head. Uncle Ben—the butler on the box of rice with the same name—was a white-haired black man with a kind face whom you could depend on to make and serve delicious unsticky rice. *Beullah* was another radio program featuring a Negro maid in the title role played by Amanda Randolph, who spoke in a "negro" dialect. And Rochester, the valet of comedian Jack Benny, played a raspy voiced straight man for his "boss," "Mr. Benny" on the weekly nationally-broadcast radio program. Obese Hattie McDaniel also wore a kerchief on her head, as Scarlett O'Hara's maid in *Gone With the Wind*; a performance for which McDaniel won an Academy Award as best supporting actress for her sympathetic role catering to the whims of her mistress. Butterfly McQueen, the thin, giggly maid in the same film, couldn't remember anything, and got her words all mixed up. What else could you expect from a Negro? There was also the contrasting image of the Negro woman as sultry and sexy temptresses played by slim, sharp-featured, light brown skinned actresses like Lena Horne and Dorothy Dandridge. Miss Peasley and that poem made me think about perceptions about me, and the people who held them, outside of my insular world.

Thankfully, not all of the classes were that thought-provoking or intense; some classes were fun with entertaining teachers. For instance, group singing was an important part of Fieldston's program. The entire school met in the gymnasium once a month to harmonize rounds and learn international songs under the direction of tall, bald, Bernie Werthman. We knew Bernie had a bad temper, although his bark was worse than his bite, but we were on our best behavior when Bernie raised his baton. It was rumored that Bernie became enraged at a disruptive student, and threw a 78 rpm record one day in music class. Luckily his aim was askew, and the record hit the floor and shattered. Every Wednesday morning Bernie Werthman scheduled Special Chorus—a block of one and a half hours in which upper classmen and two tenor-voiced teachers prepared to present a major oratorio. Students in fourth form (10th grade) through sixth form (12th grade) could go to study

Chapter Seven: Higher Hopes and Greater Goals

hall or to the library if they chose not to participate in this activity, so nearly 100 per cent participation was guaranteed. No other courses were offered in this period. Special Chorus was our opportunity to construct a beautiful musical work that depended on collaboration and rigorous practice. Each individual was part of a whole, and I was a very enthusiastic participant.

Bernie Werthman took on the challenge of working with our mostly untrained voices, and each year he proudly presented the chorus to the parents and underclassmen in an annual performance of a work such as Mendelssohn's *Elijah*, Haydn's *Creation* or Handel's *Messiah*. We were good. One of the soloists, my classmate and lifelong friend, Stephanie Diamond, began private tutoring with Werthman and launched a career as a professional opera singer, voice instructor and concert critic.

Ironically, as pleasurable as Fieldston's music program was for many of us, the program was also a pathway that allowed Fieldston to venture into the social discourse as well. Pete Seeger led us in folk songs at these monthly all school assemblies before and during the time that his singing group, The Weavers, were blacklisted. Recording companies and concert halls were advised not to engage the group, which included Ronnie Gilbert, Lee Hayes, and Fred Hellerman. The Weavers were outspoken supporters of civil rights, labor unions, and peace at a time when the resurgence of fears of a Soviet takeover or attack reemerged after World War II. Despite the blacklisting, The Weavers' songs made the hit parade; *Goodnight Irene, This Land Is Your Land,* and *When the Saints Go Marching In,* had record sales of four million in 1953. The group disbanded for two years during the McCarthy communist scare period, and regrouped at a 1955 sell out concert at Carnegie Hall that Hubey and I attended. The Weavers symbolized my political and social philosophy.

Deeper Roots

They shaped and influenced popular culture before being succeeded by Peter, Paul and Mary, who were the folk singing gurus for the next generation. Pete Seeger continued his career as a soloist and social activist and led a successful campaign to clean up the Hudson River which flowed by Beacon, New York where he lived. When I was a work camper in 1951 at University Settlement Camp (also in Beacon, New York), Seeger and his Weavers partner Lee Hayes often came to sing.

This "reign of terror" regarding left-wing associations decimated many lives and careers without substantial evidence or fair judicial process to determine seditious intent, or involvement with the Communist Party or "communist front" organizations—often spuriously listed as "un-American" by the government. Many people were pressured to testify against friends and colleagues in Congressional hearings in order to retain their own jobs.

Fieldston graduate, J. Robert Oppenheimer, the renowned physicist who developed the atomic bomb, was labeled a communist conspirator and denied security clearance to continue his work. Julius and Ethel Rosenberg were found guilty of conspiring to pass classified information to the Soviet Union and were put to death in the electric chair. In 2000, we learned that their conviction was based on false testimony.

The "red scare" would hit a lot closer to home and directly affect my friend. I met her in 1952 when we were both work campers at University Settlement Camp. She became good friends with my classmate from Fieldston when we were all work campers together; they became a couple that summer. His father had some rumored leftist political involvement and my friend was advised by her parents not to continue their relationship. Apparently, her father was on the New York State Supreme Court and his tenure in that position might be jeopardized by his daughter's association. I was crushed by the unfairness of their dilemma and the ethical implications involved, but they decided to continue to see each other.

Needless to say, it was a social and financial risk and incredibly courageous for the Fieldston School to associate with individuals that had been blacklisted. However, the philosophical foundation upon which the Ethical Culture Society is based demanded that they enter into the socio-political debate.

Felix Adler, founder of the ethical culture movement, formed The Workingmen's School in 1878. The school was named for the original population of immigrant children it served but that name would later be changed to the Ethical Culture School to identify the school with the movement and its philosophy. John Lovejoy Eliot, one of the original leaders of the Ethical Culture Society, founded the Hudson Guild as part of the settlement movement on the lower east side of Manhattan. University Settlement, the first settlement house in the United States and a model for more than 400 settlement houses in the city and beyond, was also closely affiliated through its leadership with the Ethical Culture Schools.

The Workingmen's School was a confluence of these nineteenth century movements. The School offered literacy programs and trade skill instruction through the Hudson Guild and social support and health services for arriving immigrants through University Settlement. These programs all functioned together seamlessly within the Workingmen's School under the philosophy of the Ethical Culture Movement. In keeping with these origins, manual labor and hand craft skills infused the curriculum of the Ethical Culture schools as a highly valued component echoing these educational programs offered in the settlement houses. Girls and boys met in separate skills classes in first form (7th grade) and second form (8th grade) to make lamp bases on lathes in shop, saw wood to build sturdy bookcases, hand set type and print personalized stationery, cut out and sew skirts and aprons, and prepare meals in the lab kitchens. We threw clay and molded it on potters' wheels, and we wove mats on desk-sized looms. We didn't know that we were learning about measurements and reinforcing math skills through these enjoyable activities.

The leaders of the Ethical Culture Society also promoted a social movement for political change and part of that ethos involved participation in the relevant social issues of the day. Our mandatory class trips gave us exposure to the many different ways people lived in America. In third form (9th grade) we visited the coal mines of Wilkes-Barre, Pennsylvania, at a time when coal was the major source of energy used throughout the world. We descended the mine shaft in a narrow elevator to see the dangerous work performed in cramped tunnels, where the light from miners' helmets cast eerie shadows on the walls. We ate with families of the miners and learned about labor and management issues confronted by the controversial and powerful United Mine Workers Union under the direction of gruff voiced, bushy-browed John L. Lewis. The union was so powerful that it ordered strikes that crippled industries throughout the country including railroads, and automotive and steel manufacturing. An injunction was issued by President Truman calling the miners back to work. The experience of seeing the hazardous and impoverished conditions of the miners made a lasting impression on me. I still have a chunk of anthracite I brought up from the Pennsylvania coal mine.

◆ ◆ ◆ ◆ ◆

Chapter Seven: Higher Hopes and Greater Goals

My life had been enmeshed with the Ethical Culture Society for many years. Not only was I a student at the Ethical Culture Schools for nine years, but I attended Ethical Culture School Camp for nine years as a camper, counselor and director of the waterfront. In addition, the Friday Evening Clubs for high school students, under the direction of the Ethical Culture Society leader Henry B. Herman, drew me to the Society building each week where students, mostly from New York public schools, met in discussion groups followed by square dancing and refreshments.

After graduating from the Ethical Culture Sunday School, I attended the Sunday morning meetings. Ethical Culture talks were also broadcast live at 11:00A.M. on WQXR from the Meeting House. There I heard speeches by A. Phillip Randolph, founder and leader of the Negro Brotherhood of Sleeping Car Porters and AFL/CIO Vice President, and by Eleanor Roosevelt among other distinguished national leaders.

I remember Mrs. Roosevelt stating that independence would come to the colonized sub-Saharan African countries when they were ready for self-government. The representative of one of these countries on the panel asked, "When someone steals your coat, does the thief determine when it should be returned?" The colonist nations of France, England, Italy, Germany, Portugal, the Netherlands and Belgium, made all of the political and economic decisions for these African countries. This analogy helped me to understand the parallel situation between colonized African countries and the African American population whose right to fully participate in the life of their country had been denied. This continued exposure to sets of ethical principles about the worth, equality and dignity of human beings became an integral part of my belief system. That belief system would soon be tested in a practical way and I would learn a valuable lesson in political activism.

In 1948 President Harry S. Truman initiated legislation to outlaw lynching, provide reparations to Japanese-Americans interred during World War II, and reinforce and expand the scope of the Fair Employment Practices Commission to include discrimination by unions and employers. Southern democrats rebelled at these liberal proposals put forth by Missouri-born Truman. The proposed legislation was seen as a betrayal of the accepted way of life of a majority of white southerners, leading to the formation of the "Dixiecrats"—the conservative southerners in Congress who banded together. However, Truman moved forward and desegregated the military and all means of public transport.

During my senior year at Fieldston, Algernon D. Black, the chairman of the Board of Leaders of the Ethical Culture Society, was my ethics teacher at the time he served as Chairperson of the New York State Commission Against Discrimination.

In 1952 air travel was used mostly by businessmen as an elite and high status means of travel. Full course meals of excellent quality were graciously served by attractive young women. These hostesses would, hopefully, lure more people to aviation travel, which was just beginning to replace the rails as a more popular form of transportation. Unlike our flight attendants of today (post 9/11), the air hostesses of the twentieth century catered to passengers, making them as comfortable as possible during the flight. There were more hostesses on each flight than there are today, and the service in coach class was comparable to what we now expect in first class. Air hostesses had to be high school graduates and meet stringent criteria regarding height, weight, and physical proportions to acquire the glamorous job. These positions were vigorously pursued because they offered the novelty of ex-

156

tensive travel for single women (who were the only people eligible for these jobs at the time).

Mr. Black wanted me to apply for a job as an airline hostess in order to breach the barrier that existed in the industry that prevented the employment of black women. I rejected Mr. Black's request to be a test case although I met the qualifications for the position. I was going to college and would be misrepresenting myself to seek a job I was not prepared to accept—it seemed unethical. In my naiveté I thought that I would be hired and be morally obligated to take the position, thereby denying the slot to an earnest applicant.

In hindsight, I may have been reluctant to face the inevitable rejection since the first Negro airline hostess was not hired until 1958, six years after I was approached by Mr. Black. She was Ruth Carol Taylor, also a New Yorker, hired by Mohawk Airlines, an upstate New York-based company. NAACP's *Crisis* magazine, June/July 1958, describes the hiring of Miss Taylor 'The First Colored Air Hostess' as "one of the most important events of the year in the field of American race relations." It was of particular importance because of the impact on the world stage. *Pravda*, the Soviet Union's government-controlled publication, cited the absence of Negro stewardesses as proof of discrimination in the United States. This issue, therefore, became a concern to the State Department in the propaganda war between the United States and the Soviet Union. Shortly thereafter, Miss Grant was hired by Trans World Airlines (TWA) as the first Negro hostess to work on international flights. The New York State Commission Against Discrimination, still chaired by Algernon Black, was instrumental in these negotiations. Ironically, when I graduated from college and was hired by the Boston Public schools during an acute teacher shortage, the school system was so desperate for teachers that they hired airline stewardesses to work as substitute teachers when they flew to the city.

I was very young but anxious to contribute in some way as I had been taught. I found that way doing something that I enjoy doing to this day—writing. My peppy, enthusiastic friend, Peggy Gray, was the only Negro girl in the form above me at Fieldston. Peggy wore bangs over her forehead and preceded me as captain of the cheerleading squad before being accepted at Simmons College in Boston. When she graduated from Fieldston, she asked me to take over her weekly column in the New York *Age*, a Harlem newspaper that is now defunct. I was thrilled to have this job and the five dollar weekly stipend for my expenses. "The Younger Set" reported on social events and achievements of teenagers and college-age young adults in the city. I listed as many names as possible in each column, hoping to increase the readership of the paper as more teenagers bought the paper to see their own and their friends' names in print.

I used Betty Butler as my byline. That was what I was still called by family members and neighbors in Harlem. As my name from childhood, it symbolized my anchor to the African American community and in an analogous way my column bridged the gap between the Negro world of Harlem and the white environment in which many of the people I wrote about were being educated. I was raising my voice to let my readers know some of the positive things about Negro teens in New York City. This was who we were and what we were about. Vachel Lindsey take notice—I had a profound need to prove our worth, both individually and collectively. It was my responsibility to validate us to one another, as well as to the white world that was so skeptical of our worth. I kept my ear to the ground to gather information from friends, as well as from youth organizations like the YWCA and YMCA.

Chapter Seven: Higher Hopes and Greater Goals

I felt very grown up when I typed my first column as a newspaper journalist/society page writer to present to my editor, sports columnist Lester Matthews. When I arrived at the blue-tiled fronted office building on 135th Street and Martin Luther King Boulevard, I expected to hear the noisy clatter of typewriters and to see people frantically moving around the pressroom. I envisioned reporters grabbing coats from the rack and bowling me over as they rushed out of the door to cover fast-breaking stories. I may have read too many Superman comic strips featuring mild-mannered Clark Kent, as a *Daily Planet* newspaper reporter. I found instead a morgue-like atmosphere of deadly quiet. Lester Matthews didn't even raise his head from the copy he was reviewing when I approached his desk. I stood there for a while before Matthews finally peered at me from under his eyeshade and gruffly thanked me for my piece—so much for the glamorous excitement of the newsroom. Matthews never said more than two words at a time to me during the year I worked for the newspaper—those two words were, "thank you."

On September 13, 1952, when my first column appeared with my photo and byline, I became a journalist cheerleader, telling my readers about the great team of Negro youth in the community who were preparing themselves for competition in the larger adult world. I praised accomplishments that otherwise might go unnoticed: scholarships won, awards given, volunteer work recognized. In a casual way I affirmed that black people rode horseback. I affirmed that Negro people pooled resources and bought country homes in the suburbs, where some black families were beginning to relocate. I affirmed that Negro students were going to Ivy League schools in a limited but steady stream—long before affirmative action was national policy. I affirmed that

Deeper Roots

Negroes from New York also went to black colleges in the South.

My upbeat tone of encouragement and confidence represented my own naive belief that young people of color had achieved, and would continue to achieve, all they desired. I was confident that opportunities awaited us when we moved into the adult world. We would make it. We would fulfill the American dream—and we would give back to the community. Sometimes invisible barriers of race stood in our way, but these barriers would not deter us. We would run through them, run around them or jump over them. Our communities expected us to be successful. We were the "talented tenth" that Dr. Du Bois wrote about. (My naiveté also lead me to believe that Negro women were considered a part of the talented tenth.) Our role models were our families who surrounded and encouraged us although we did not think of them as role models; we knew them as our neighbors and our relatives. "Take advantage of everything," my father urged me in the letters he sent me at camp. We were the young people who would lead our generation and we would be prepared.

I was right. The Negro Fieldston upperclassmen whom I frequently mentioned in my column included Audrey Penn, Madison Jones, James Boone, Clifford Alexander, Jeanne Allen, James Teasdale, Walter Winter, and Peggy Gray. Many of these graduates became well-known physicians, educators and governmental appointees. Clifford Alexander, a Yale Law School graduate, became Secretary of the Army in President Carter's administration. Both Audrey Penn and Jeanne Allen became physicians (their dads were also physicians). Our emergence into adulthood at the cusp of the civil rights movement certainly helped make my prognosis a reality. We were often the ones to break racial barriers and to become the first Negroes to win elected office or head programs. The schools we attended prepared us to succeed in college and beyond.

A column from 1953:

Hi There:

Well the summer is over and we're all settling down to our old routines, specifically school. Cliff Alexander is returning to Harvard to continue his studies. Clay Bates goes into his junior year at Manhattan College majoring in engineering...Don Johnson is off to Bard... Joe Bostic, Jr. is entering Morgan to become a big name track star...Phyliss Murphy made the grade at Fisk...Madison Jones will resume taking athletic honors at Columbia..Our own Jeanne Allen goes into her senior year at Sarah Lawrence....Good luck kids!!!

Glamorous Mimi Coates spent part of her vacation gallivanting in Lexington. (Ky?) Mimi has just returned to town to try her hand at modeling luscious clothes for the ultra modern Etienne Fashion Salon located in the Hotel Teresa. Demure Annette Winter has just breezed in from her extensive vacation traveling by land, sea and air to South America and the West Indies. Her older brother Walter is training in St. Albans, Long Island after attending Brown University (editor's note) as a guest of the U. S. Navy.

Marion Booth entertained Saturday afternoon in her lovely home in Croton-on-the Hudson. The day was spent roasting franks and hiking around the beautiful Hudson Valley. Among the guests

161

were Audrey Penn, Sandra Mann, and Brenda Birdy. It's in the air that the Equestrian Club sparked by Sandy Jones is launching a new season and planning a lot of bang-up parties. Word has gotten around that Barbara and Joan Perry are doing volunteer work in Harlem's drive to combat tuberculosis...Keep up the good work gals! Representatives of the YWCA teenage groups are meeting to plan a gala reunion on Sept. 26th...Eloise Williams, president of the Y Debs, Yvonne Mulings, also of the Y Debs, Muriel Williams from Velveteens, Ruth Gray of Secluded Debs, Jean Dubose, Vipra Harps, Ruth Dalton from Dubs and Debs, Delores Saunders of Silver Slippers and Alma Walter also of the Y Debs will help to make the reunion a tremendous success..

Well, that's all the news for now from this corner. Don't let that homework get you down. We'll see you next week.

Clubs may contact me, Betty Butler, at 409 Edgecombe Avenue, New York, 32, N.Y.

I was very surprised when Les Matthews mentioned me in his column in June 1953.

Bye Bye Betty

It seems that we no sooner get used to an exuberant "young set" columnist electrifying the office, when it's time for her to graduate and leave. First it was Peggy Gray and now that enthusiastic

162

Chapter Seven: Higher Hopes and Greater Goals
editorial writer, Betty Butler is leaving the scene
for plateaus of higher learning. Good luck.

When I went off to college I bequeathed my column to my friend, Mimi Coates. Mimi lived around the corner from me on St. Nicholas Place and attended Elizabeth Irwin (the high school of the Little Red Schoolhouse located in Greenwich Village). Mimi's dad was the first Negro policeman that I knew because, for some reason, black officers did not patrol Negro neighborhoods. Only white cops and white mounted policemen patrolled our neighborhood, especially on the days when the New York professional baseball or football games were played at the Polo Grounds. Officer Coates wore his patrolman's hat low down on his forehead as he rode the bus to work.

◆ ◆ ◆ ◆ ◆

In October 1998 (forty-five years after I graduated) the Fieldston student government held an all-day meeting for the entire school community to reexamine the mission of the school and to ask if the Ethical Culture Schools movement had changed its values or practice over its 110-year history. I was invited to be part of a panel of six alumni (each representing a decade from the 1940's onward) who would share the things we remembered from our experiences at Fieldston. I represented the decade of the 1950s, sometimes called "the silent generation" because we tended to conform to authority and initiated few protests—an accurate assessment indeed.

This event was part of a self-assessment project that would guide the direction of the school for the new millennium. Had Fieldston become just another good preparatory school without any special commitment to racial and economic diversity? Had pressure for college acceptance made the students more competitive for grades and SAT scores? What about the human values that were such an integral part of the learning experience? In preparation for this conference, students had organized a display of school archives and planned small group follow-up discussions in classes in which the panelists were encouraged to participate.

This was the first time I had returned to Fieldston to discuss how the school had influenced my life and my role as an educator. Although I had kept in touch with the school in many other ways, I was excited and a bit apprehensive about addressing the meeting. After all, Walter White, Executive Secretary of the NAACP spoke from this same platform. I recalled the event and was very proud then to have my neighbor at 409 speak to the assembly. He was the only person of color I remember who addressed the student body when I was at Fieldston. Now it was my turn to talk to the students. It was awesome. The panelists offered their perspectives on the whole sweep of the mid-to-late twentieth-century.

World War II affected the students of the 1940s directly because many of their fathers went off to battle. Patriotism and sacrifice were the watchwords of that era. These students had grown up as children of the Depression, and scarcity and rationing became prevalent again during the war, making this generation more appreciative of what they were later able to acquire.

My decade was idealistic. We studied the organization of the United Nations after World War II and made many visits to sessions of the General Assembly. We learned about atomic energy and its possibilities and its dangers and the threat posed by the military-industrial complex that developed during the economic recovery after World War II. The 1950s radio broadcasts, and later television programs, such as *Father Knows Best*, epitomized what was expected of postwar middle-class white America. Women were once again relegated to the private sphere as men returned from military service.

I was reassured by the serious attentiveness of the audience and the stimulating questions. When a student asked how my experience at Fieldston had affected my life's work, I shared how my experience had provided a model that I used in forming, designing and implementing an educational program, the Metropolitan Council for Educational Opportunity (METCO), which still enables over 3,000 inner city Boston black, Hispanic and Asian students to attend suburban public schools. All of my work in education was based on a belief in the unique strengths of individuals and a belief that the school was the place for these qualities to be identified and developed in an atmosphere of excitement about learning—beliefs developed and fostered in my experience in the Ethical Culture Schools of my day.

The 1960s generation was viscerally impacted by the Civil Rights movement. Donald Harris ('58), a black member of the Student Nonviolent Coordinating Committee (SNCC), was arrested and jailed in Americas, Georgia for leading a civil rights march in that city. Fieldston and the Ethical Culture Society again chose to become a part of the social and political discourse. The alumnae and Fieldston parents put pressure on federal governmental officials to intervene on his behalf.

The 1970s was marked by the Vietnam War, the anti-war movement and student unrest. On March 23, 1970 Fieldston experienced its own internal conflict in those tumultuous years when young people felt free to challenge adult authority in unprecedented fashion. After two years of unsuccessful discussions and petitions, a student protest was staged in the administration building demanding more faculty and students of color, curriculum reflecting African

Deeper Roots

American and Hispanic history, and volumes of literature in the library written by authors of color. A three day sit-in of mostly black and Hispanic students resulted in a major confrontation when the administration called in the police to arrest the (fourteen) student demonstrators. However, the Board of Governors agreed that the goals of the students fit the philosophy and mission of the school. This demonstration confirmed that change could be made in an institution through radical action—albeit slowly.

Over thirty years later, the deep wounds from that confrontational experience (manifested in divisions within the Fieldston community and the resignation of Principal Spenser Brown) would partially heal and Fieldston would move forward and embrace the inevitable change. In 2002 a course offering, "United States History Since 1940," taught by the head of the history department, included an oral history project involving interviews with members of the Class of 1970, other students, faculty, parents and Board members associated with Fieldston during the "takeover." Three of the members of that demonstration returned to Fieldston to attend the Martin Luther King Day celebration in 2002 and John Hewitt ('70), a leader of the group, spoke to the assembly.

On Thursday, January 17, 2002, the evening of the Fieldston Martin Luther King Day assembly celebration, Hubey and I attended the reunion of Fieldston Alumni of Color held in the dining room on the roof of the Midtown Ethical building where I ate my lunch every school day in fourth through sixth grade. The room was gigantic then—the size of a dance hall—but the intervening years had considerably reduced its dimensions.

As the oldest graduate present, I had a cumulative fifty-eight years as a student and alumna. The gathering of sixty alums and staff of the Fieldston School began with informal conversations in small groups while we served ourselves from heaping plates of delicious Caribbean food. David Schwartz who was a student at Amherst when I attended Mount Holyoke, and spent most of his career as an administrator at Fieldston Lower and Fieldston demonstrating his involvement in diversity issues was there too. Parents and present students attended the session and participated in lively discussion with alums and staff about the strains of being a member of a minority group. Do you all sit together at lunch? Why? Why not? Can the majority Jewish group of students understand the significance of a Catholic religious experience? Is it worth taking the risk to explore these emotional moments?

One Fieldston graduate had a particularly interesting story. Edna Bell, a 1960s student, told us that when she arrived at the school dressed in African garb for an admission interview for her daughter, she was ignored by the other parents present until they learned that she was a Fieldston graduate. Then she became the center of attention. Her education in the Ethical Culture Schools had given her the ability to handle situations like this with aplomb and she wanted her daughters to learn those skills as well as benefiting from a good education.

We also discussed the financial challenges of the day. Although Fieldston maintains one of the largest financial aid funds among independent schools, the annual tuition can be prohibitive for lower- and middle-class parents. In 2002 (the year of our reunion), the annual tuition was $23,000. (During the 2011-2012 academic year, tuition was over $35,000.) Can enough scholarship aid be made available to avoid a marked division between wealthy and poor or even middle class? An alumna established a fund to provide monies to support students of color whose alumni parents are unable to meet the tuition costs.

Deeper Roots

The conversation was stimulating, the participants articulate and courteous. What we all agreed on was that the experience at Fieldston had a positive impact on the lives of those who attended the session. Lasting friendships were formed across racial and religious lines. This session was a fine tribute to the education that we received, and a tribute to the sense of caring about others. What made this school so special? It was not a boarding school. It was not a traditional religious school, and it was not a neighborhood community school. Students came from far flung places. Why was there so little fighting, intimidation, and scapegoating? Why were there no drugs or violence during my sojourn? I don't know. Perhaps it had something to do with the diversity that existed within the classes.

Matching cashmere sweater sets, family winter vacations in sunny Florida, and nose "jobs" for girls were part of the lifestyle of some of the upper income Fieldston students. Anne Silver and Sue Levy quietly rebelled against this conspicuous affluence by wearing their hair pulled back in pony tails, refusing to use cosmetics, and wearing lab coats over their clothing. Two fathers of my classmates owned local businesses in Manhattan: Brook's Haberdashery in Times Square, and Wucker's Furniture Store on 125th Street. Some fathers worked in finance and stock brokerage houses on Wall Street while others were physicians, dentists, professors, and writers. For me, the most fascinating occupation introduced to us in school was diamond cutting—and Sue Getter's dad came to science class to tell us about his work. Mothers usually stayed at home and did volunteer work, although a few were teachers.

I learned that economic status had little to do with the quality of family life and that we all had our own cross to bear. Problems of depression, alcoholism, separation, and divorce affected many of my friends' families, but we accepted each without blame or reproach. We were economically and socially diverse but we knew, as sentient beings, we were more alike than different.

The Fieldston School continues to do well.

Chapter Eight:

A Lesson in Higher Education

Mount Holyoke College

(1953 — 1957)

In 1952, during my senior year at Fieldston, Ann Nueberger (Nuey) who had graduated the previous June visited the school. She encouraged me and Anne Silver to come see her at Mount Holyoke. The three of us were close because we had all played varsity tennis together. Anne and I had already filed applications to the college but Anne had made interview appointments at Mount Holyoke and at

Deeper Roots

Smith College, members of the group of elite women's colleges called the "Seven Sisters." When Anne invited me to take the college tour with her and her mother, I accepted gladly.

Nuey was bubbling with enthusiasm as she greeted and showed us her dormitory. It exuded a luxurious ambiance with its wide circular stairwell, carpeted floors and a formal living room complete with baby grand piano. Then we wandered through a wooded area of the campus near two lakes linked by a small waterfall. The splashing foam of the waterfall was just a stone's throw away from the newly-constructed gymnasium where we gazed at the Olympic-sized swimming pool. Nearly every student we saw said a friendly, "hi" to us as we toured the grounds. The admissions officer, Clara Ludwig, was friendly as well and made us feel at ease. Miss Ludwig encouraged Anne and me to be interviewed at the same time. We agreed, even though I did not have a scheduled appointment.

At the much larger Smith College campus, where twice as many students were enrolled, the atmosphere and the people seemed less welcoming. They reminded me of a neighbor in 409, attorney Eunice Carter. She was a 1921 Smith graduate, summa cum laude with both an undergraduate and graduate degree. In 1937 she became the first Negro woman to serve in the New York State Attorney General's office. Carter was a very serious woman who never engaged in banter or discussion. When she came to our apartment to have her hair done, she always brought a book and read in silence and the few Smith students I met on that brief campus visit in 1952 seemed just as remote and serious as Carter. On the spot Anne and I decided that if we were accepted we would go to Mount Holyoke together.

The following February of 1953, two members of the Mount Holyoke Club of New York and alumnae of the college, paid my mother and me a visit ostensibly to answer any questions I had about the college. In retrospect, I believe they must have come, in large part, to determine whether I was in need of financial aid.

When the hall man announced that the expected guests had arrived in the lobby, I went to the apartment door to greet them. Standing next to my father's bookcase in the foyer, I realized how much I missed my dad. It had been only a year and a half since his death and I missed his love and support during the college interview process. I so wished that he were here to advise me about entering this new phase of life. The doorbell rang.

There stood two white women. The tall one, with a shock of bobbed gray hair said, "I'm Mrs. Sloan," removing her white gloves and placing them in her pocketbook.

"I'm Mrs. Gleason," the lady in the tailored green suit said in a high-pitched voice. She extended her hand. And then the two ladies sat down next to each other, side by side, on the edge of the cushion of our living room sofa.

My mother breezed into the room with a tea tray — gold-trimmed Limoges teacups placed next to the saucers, tea steeping in the matching pot and thin slices of pound cake on a doily on a green glass plate. "What a lovely view you have here," Mrs. Gleason observed, glancing out the window at the George Washington Bridge and the New Jersey Palisades framed by our red velvet drapes.

Ms. Sloan asked, "Who plays the piano?"

"I've been taking lessons for about eight years now," I replied. "But preparation for the college admission tests has left me less time to practice."

I knew our visitors didn't expect the resplendent lobby of 409 when they ventured into Harlem. Our standard of living must have astonished them — I'm sure that Mrs. Sloan and Mrs. Gleason were surprised to see the inlaid brass Chinese lamp placed on the antique table and the red cloisonné lamp on another. The Nile green-bordered Oriental rug also may

173

have captured their attention. I didn't realize how valuable these types of objects were until I saw similar ones in Beijing, China at the Winter Palace. More likely our visitors expected to climb up flights of stairs to a dingy apartment in a tenement house, which more precisely fit the image of Harlem most often depicted in the media.

The fact was that my mother had some of these pieces on consignment from her friend and neighbor, Robert Harris. He lived in a cramped basement apartment with his sister Edith who was one of my mother's customers. Robert was constitutionally unable to pass up a good auction-buy and Edith had threatened to throw her brother out if he brought one more piece of furniture into their tiny space. As a favor to them both, Mom agreed to display a few pieces she selected and to inform her customers that the articles were for sale. When one item was bought, another took its place. I believe Mom received a small commission for helping Mr. Harris with his "antiques problem."

Mrs. Sloan asked what I wanted to do after finishing college. I told her I hoped to attend graduate school at the New York School of Social Work, which was then part of Columbia University. "I wrote a paper last year about the field, after interviewing the director of guidance and counseling at the Harlem YWCA." I shared with our visitors how much I enjoyed being with people, listening to them and helping them solve problems, both as a camp counselor and with my friends at school. I also mentioned how much I had enjoyed my visit to Mount Holyoke and the interview with Miss Ludwig who had answered my questions about the college.

"It sounds as though you have everything worked out, Katherine. I hope you will be accepted." Mrs. Gleason said. She adjusted her gray felt hat and rose from the couch to end the visit. Although I had not been apprehensive about the visit, I was relieved that the encounter had gone smoothly.

Chapter Eight: A Lesson in Higher Education

Mom and I both hoped that the alumnae would put in a good word for me.

On May 15, 1953, college decisions were due to arrive by mail at our homes. Anne and I joined the long line at the Fieldston telephone booth to call our mothers to learn the results (we knew nothing of cell phones back then). We felt that our lives depended on the outcome of college acceptances. My finger trembled as I dialed WA 6-6296; the rotary phone dial seemed to turn in slow motion. After two rings, which seemed like an eternity, I heard my mother's melodious, "hello."

"What did I get, Mom?" I blurted out as my heart pounded in my chest.

She replied, "Two pieces of mail from Mount Holyoke, a package from Simmons College and a thin envelope from Sarah Lawrence."

"Open them Mom please and tell me what they say."

"Simmons and Mount Holyoke have both accepted you," she sighed with joyous relief. "Sarah Lawrence said no. Sorry about that."

I was elated! For the rest of the day the senior corridor at Fieldston was abuzz with college acceptance news. Not everyone got into their first-choice school so there was dis-appointment mingled with joy, but we were all going to college *somewhere*. That was certain. Anne was accepted at both Smith and Mount Holyoke, and we reaffirmed our decision to go to Mount Holyoke together.

But when I got home that afternoon and opened the second envelope from the Mount Holyoke financial aid office I learned that I had not been granted scholarship aid. Mount Holyoke had an "aid blind" admission policy, meaning that the college accepted students solely on merit. The financial aid office then considered those accepted students for scholarships based solely on need. Those Chinese lamps?

Deeper Roots

Neither my mother nor I believed we could challenge the decision of the financial aid office. Yet, it was impossible for us to pay the $1,800 annual expenses for tuition, room and board. I learned later that a white candidate two years ahead of me (living in a handsome apartment and whose father was a furrier), also had two visitors from Mount Holyoke pay her a call. She was given financial aid to begin her freshman year although, by comparison, my financial circumstances were probably just as dire, if not more so. If we had known of her success in obtaining aid, my mother and I would have had a basis on which to challenge Mount Holyoke's decision regarding scholarship aid. I believe that Mount Holyoke's decision not to offer me financial aid was influenced by expectations regarding standards of living based on race.

A few days later I went to the office of Henry Herman, my favorite Ethical Culture Society leader, to discuss my dilemma. Mr. Herman suggested that I stay in New York, where I would be company for my mother and attend one of the free colleges: Hunter College for girls or the coed City College. I had already applied to Hunter as an "insurance" college, but my mother would not even consider the idea of Hunter as an alternative to Mount Holyoke. She wanted me to have the experience of a residential college campus, and Mount Holyoke was it. "What will we do?" I wondered. "I'll sleep on it," she said. "A way will be opened. I'll pray for an answer." I had full confidence that Mom would come through with a solution to what seemed an insurmountable problem.

By morning Mom announced she had decided to cash in the life insurance policy she carried, since I was the beneficiary and I needed the money now. "Sophomore Year will take care of itself," she predicted in her indomitable fashion. I would use my $125 camp salary and fifty dollars from my week of work at Young and Rubicam for books and supplies and I would live on a very tight budget. When I told Mr.

176

Chapter Eight: A Lesson in Higher Education

Herman of my decision to attend college away from home, he rallied to the cause by recommending me for a $250 grant from the Sarah S. Ollisheimer Foundation, funded by a member of the Ethical Culture Society. The financial pieces were falling into place.

However—at least in some minds—I had not taken into consideration all of the realities that awaited me, and I was surprised by who expressed those doubts to me. On a spring evening in May I was talking on the phone with my friend and classmate, freckle-faced Gwenith Barrera. Gwen said, "Katie, my mother wants to speak with you." Gwen's mother was a practicing physician who kept her maiden name (Jones) and lived near Columbia University with her son and two daughters.

"Katie," Dr. Jones said, "you know that you're going to have a hard time when you go off to college. Fieldston has been a very protective place for you as a Negro, and you're in for a rude awakening. I just want you to be prepared so your feelings don't get too hurt." I swallowed hard.

"Don't worry about me, Dr. Jones. I'll be just fine. I've experienced discrimination already, and I do have friends from school and camp who will be there with me. So I won't be alone." The warning from Dr. Jones took me aback. I was not ready to hear her words, nor did I want to confront the possibility that I had made the wrong decision in choosing to attend a predominantly WASP (White Anglo-Saxon Protestant) school with a strong Christian missionary tradition. I had never considered applying to a black Southern college. I had heard too many stories from my mother's customers about Jim Crow in the South. I did not want to have the curtain drawn on me to make a "colored" railroad car—always the one closest to the engines—when the train crossed the Mason-Dixon Line into the South. I did not want to be refused service at soda fountains or to confront public accommodations that displayed signs for "white" and

Deeper Roots

"colored." "White" and "colored" schools, separate and unequal, were then the law of the land in the South. I had even decided not to go to Washington, D.C. with my classmates on the annual senior class trip because I didn't want to be relegated to a separate hotel (although I knew there were special funds available). I had too much pride.

But Dr. Jones was referring to the racism found in the Northern, less urban areas of the country and she was not the only parent who was cognizant of these discriminatory behaviors. In 2001, during a conversation with Nuey's 100-year-old father, Roy Neuberger, he told me about a motor trip he and his wife, Marie, (Fieldston '26), made with my mother to visit Nuey and me at Mount Holyoke.

"We picked your mother up at 10:00A.M. at 409, and as the lunch hour arrived we were still en route," Mr. Neuberger remembered. "I didn't say anything to your mother, but all the while I wondered if we would be discriminated against if we stopped to eat at a roadside restaurant." Luckily, his fears were dispelled and the trio had a nice meal before continuing on to Mount Holyoke College. My mother never suspected the apprehension Mr. Nueberger experienced, at least she never shared any concern with me about this expedition. This was racial prejudice northern style — the tactic you never knew when to expect: no service, bad service, or a table next to the kitchen or bathroom even when the establishment was virtually empty. As an adult, I learned to be constantly on alert against it, reviewing possible scenarios in my mind and creating responses to these obviously intentional insults and indignities that we as Negroes were often exposed to. "I would prefer not to sit next to the table-clearing stage, it's a bit too noisy. What about seating us at the empty table by the window?" I would say, and still say to this day.

So many years ago, I thought I had protected myself from some of the harsher forms of discrimination by choosing a small liberal arts women's college. Also, I had wanted to avoid being swallowed up in a larger institution and continue the closeness I was accustomed to from my personal contact with teachers at Fieldston. I stood by my decision.

In September, the trunk Mom had purchased from Macy's when I was going off to summer camp was brought out to pack for college. I had acquired the wardrobe of a well-dressed college girl of the 1950s — a pair of green watch plaid Bermuda shorts, a gray cable-stitched turtleneck sweater, a pair of brown-and-white saddle oxfords, and a pair each of grey and red cable-stitched knee socks. My summer earnings paid for these items. To keep me warm in the chilly New England winter, Mom gave me her raccoon coat, saying it was too heavy for her to wear. I think that she just wanted me to have it.

On my last Sunday before leaving my childhood home, I visited a family friend from Jamaica who had lived near my mother's family before immigrating to New York. Aunt Ida, as I called her, lived alone in one room on the first floor of a brownstone on East 129th Street. She worked in service and prepared her food on a hot plate and shared a bathroom off the narrow, dark hallway with the woman who rented a room next door to hers. Her housedresses drooped on her slight frame as she shuffled about in worn slippers. Because Aunt Ida spent so little on herself she was able to send money each month to help her nieces and nephews in Jamaica go to school, and she always remembered my birthday with a very wonderful gift. Each year Aunt Ida purchased a dress for me at Arnold Constable, an elegant Fifth Avenue department store. The package always arrived at 409 wrapped in beautiful glossy gift paper and tied with a bow. Since my birthday was close to Easter, I wore my new dress when Annette and I joined the Easter Parade on Fifth Avenue after Sunday school. And each time I came to visit

Deeper Roots

Aunt Ida, she would faithfully rummage through her bureau drawer and find a crisp five-dollar bill to place in my hands. When I graduated from Fieldston, she gave me a portable radio.

As it turned out, Aunt Ida's ties to my family was far more complicated than I would ever have imagined. Long after Aunt Ida's passing and during one of those informative dinners with my cousins, Methlin told me that Aunt Ida was indeed a blood relation and not just a family friend. She was the biological daughter of my grandfather, Sargent Major Clark, born outside of his marriage to my grandmother. I never learned the details of this family secret. All I know is that Aunt Ida consistently and generously gave of herself... and that fairy godmothers come in all forms.

That Sunday afternoon at the end of my visit, my fairy god-mother placed a neatly folded $100 bill in my hand. I had never held a bill of such a high denomination in my life. I was elated. "You can't imagine how much this gift means to me," I said with tears welling up in my eyes. Aunt Ida's generosity helped me to go off to college with fewer financial worries. Now I had enough money to take the train home to New York for vacations.

Two days after my visit to Aunt Ida, my $100 bill safely tucked deep in my wallet, I began my journey to Mount Holyoke with Anne and her mother, squeezed into the back of their blue sedan surrounded by boxes, lamps, and hangers. My trunk was shipped ahead by Railway Express. I was so excited about beginning this new adventure and happily waved goodbye to my mother as she stood in the doorway of 409.

In her first letter to me from home, Mom gave no indication of the loneliness she had already begun to feel:

Chapter Eight: A Lesson in Higher Education
Wednesday 4:30

Hello Darling,

You can imagine how happy I was to learn from Mrs. Silver you arrived safely and got all your wishes. She said the room is lovely.

Gee, wouldn't I just love to see what you and Vera have made of it. Then Anne is in the same house? Guess you feel quite at home. That's very very nice and I am so happy for you.

Mrs. S. got home at 12 midnight and I was here waiting. In fact I phoned her home around 10:30 thinking she had forgotten, but no one answered. She says she hopes to visit Anne in October and will take me. Isn't that ducky.

Take good care of yourselves and be good.

Much love, Mother

Twenty-four years later when our oldest daughter, Karen, went to college I understood how painful this great separation was for my mother and many years after that Mom finally told me that she had cried herself to sleep the day I left home. Although Uncle Oscar continued to stay with my mother whenever he was on leave from his cruise ship, she was now without her husband *and* her daughter. "Bind the belly."

As for me, I remember clearly that for the drive Mrs. Silver was dressed in a gray tweed suit and black high-heeled shoes. Her nails were a brilliant shade of red, her hair gray with a bluish highlighted tint. Mrs. Silver's face was long and oval, like her daughter's, and they both had large, dark almond-shaped eyes. Mrs. Silver was accustomed to driving many hours at a time, taking people to Red Cross centers to donate blood as part of her volunteer work. Our five-hour trip took us through New Haven and Hartford, Connecticut, through the Connecticut Valley and into Massachusetts. We passed Springfield, then Chicopee, where Westover Air Force Base was located. Fifteen miles north we reached South Hadley and Mount Holyoke College. Every sight and sound seemed to stand out. The gold charm bracelets on Mrs. Silver's thin wrists made a soft clicking sound when she turned the steering wheel right, and drove us through the arched wrought iron gate of the main entrance to the campus.

We came to a stop at Mary Lyon Hall, the administration building named after the founder of the college. The four sides of its tower enclose faces of a clock reminiscent of Big Ben, with a bell that tolls every fifteen minutes, adding a measure each time until it strikes the hour with deep sonorous tones. It reminded me of home — we had a German-made clock in the foyer of our apartment that chimed in similar fashion — the clock that sat on top of Dad's bookcase. Mary Lyon Hall was also familiar to Anne and me from our interview there the previous winter. This time we climbed the long flight of stairs to get our dorm and room assignments and the keys to our post office boxes and rooms. This time there was no return trip to New York City.

Anne and I were elated to find that we were assigned to the same dorm, Mead Hall, where Nuey and another classmate from Fieldston, Sheila Israel, were also assigned. Anne Silver had requested a single room and Vera Barad and I had decided before we arrived on campus that we would be roommates. Vera, a vivacious brunette from Hempstead, Long Island, and I met while working as counselors at Camp Felicia in 1952. Vera and Nuey had met at the same camp the previous summer when Nuey convinced Vera to apply to Mount Holyoke. (Vera, Nuey, and I all worked together when the life guard ordered me out of the water at the New York State Park.) Vera and I became close friends and when we found ourselves both bound for Mount Holyoke we decided to room together. So I had a group of friends on campus that I knew quite well when I began my freshman year.

Anne's room was on the first floor, across the hall from Judith Kramer from Long Island. Judith, Anne, Sheila, Nuey, and Vera were among a scant handful of Jewish students at Mount Holyoke in 1953. And despite their religion, they were required to attend Christian chapel services on campus three times in each two-week period, as well as five church services each semester on campus, although Catholic students could go to the nearby Catholic Church for religious observance. For all of us, attendance at church and chapel was based on the honor system.

As we commenced life at Mount Holyoke, every freshman was teamed-up with a junior class member. My "big sister" was Nancy Leech, who paid a courtesy visit to meet me the day we moved in to make sure that everything was fine. At the time I did not think that any special arrangement had been made to link us together, but in a conversation with Nancy years later I asked her how she became my big sister. She recalled that she had been asked by the administration if she would take on such an arrangement. Nancy gladly accepted. She had never known a black person as an equal before her contact with me, even though she lived in Bronxville, New York, not too far from Riverdale, where I had attended Fieldston. After graduation, with the encouragement of her roommate, Nancy became a consultant for the Penn Center on St. Helena's Island, off South Carolina's coast. Dr. Martin Luther King often brought his staff there on retreats and former slave children from the

Deeper Roots

other islands were educated on St. Helena's Island after the Civil War until the 1954 Supreme Court decision desegregated the schools. When I visited Penn Center for research in African American history I learned from director Emory Campbell of Nancy's involvement with the Center.

The housemother of Mead Hall was Mrs. Knowlton. Students took turns sitting at Mrs. Knowlton's table in the dining room with the other adults who resided in the hall— austere Miss Voorhees, the career advisor who wore her snow-white hair in a bun at the nape of her neck and shy Miss Alvarez, a Spanish professor who hardly spoke a word.

The only word for the rules and regulations that governed life at Mount Holyoke circa 1953 was *formidable*. The honor system, which all we students agreed to uphold in both academic and social areas, recognized us as mature young women. All the rules—and the punishments for infringement of the rules—were enforced by an elected student judicial board and were printed in a thick, twenty-nine page blue booklet given to each student.

The abundance of rules and regulations was in direct contrast to the diversity of the campus. There was a distinct paucity of Negro students when I arrived. There was only one African American student in each class of approximately 300 students. However, Carolyn Anderson from Pennsylvania was in my class as a freshman, but she did not return for sophomore year. The only Negro in the sophomore class was Frances Thornhill, from Montclair, New Jersey, and she too lived in Mead Hall. My first year was Fran's last year at Mount Holyoke; she returned to New Jersey to complete her education close to home. The Negro student in the junior class, Kathryn Coram of Wisconsin, had a dynamic personality, conviviality and flair that suited her choice of drama as a major. In the senior class was diminutive Mary Ellen Williams from Washington, D.C. who we called "Mew." After completing her master's degree in

Chapter Eight: A Lesson in Higher Education

English, Mew returned to the college with her husband and children as a member of the English department—one of the first Negro faculty members of Mount Holyoke.

Mew and I became reacquainted when I was elected to the Board of Trustees in 1973. The loquacious person that I had known was now almost mute on issues of race. Mew was in a difficult position during the 1970s when the numbers of African American students on campus increased and administration and students alike turned to her for guidance and support.

In conversation with a doctor (and fellow Newton resident) who attended Mount Holyoke during the 1970s, we discussed just how difficult things had become for blacks on the campus. She indicated that during her years there, she had been ostracized by the black student community and feared by the white student community. She felt compelled to 'pick a side' although it was her wish to attend a college where she could mix comfortably with all the students, and she was disappointed because that was not the case. But, in all fairness, what was occurring on the Mount Holyoke College campus was occurring on many other campuses across the nation. Things were so different from what we, as Negro students of the 1950s, encountered and how we dealt with racial matters.

We few Negro students seldom discussed the issues we were facing in this racially isolated community. Also, during my college years, there was no Negro faculty or staff. We were five (then four) Negro students in a population of 1,200 who often endured insensitive comments about race. "Susie" told a "hilarious" joke at our lunch table about a coed who was fixed up with a Negro for a blind date. I was shocked, angry, and I felt isolated. A lump came into my throat and I found it hard to swallow the morsel of food in my mouth. "Susie" didn't see me. I was invisible and I did not say a word. I made a conscious decision not to challenge this

185

insult. One must pick and choose one's battles. I was aware that these types of comments are made when people of color are absent, but I was stunned that they would be made in my presence. I lacked the emotional strength to take this on at the time. Once again, I realized that I seemed better able to respond to racial insults while I was in elementary school. Only later, in adult life, did I regain the self-confidence to stand up for my rights.

On May 17, 1954 the headline of the New York *Times* announced the unanimous United States Supreme Court ruling to end segregated public education. I was elated by the decision, but my excitement was not reciprocated by my dorm mates who merely continued to play bridge in the basement smoker of Mead Hall. Luckily, Mom phoned that evening and we celebrated the victory won by our 409 neighbor and NAACP lawyer, Thurgood Marshall, who had pleaded the *Brown vs. Board of Education* case before the Court. I felt such a surge of pride that this long-standing battle for more equal educational opportunities had been won, and personal satisfaction that the victory was in a major way attributable to my Harlem neighbor. However, the passive response to this historical decision by my dorm mates was prophetic. Demonstrated resistance on the part of whites, including violence directed against black children in both the North and South (Boston is an excellent example) made a mockery of the Court decision. More than half a century later, public schools in the United States are more segregated by race and class than they were in 1954. We continue to offer separate and unequal education for students of color. But Mount Holyoke College made some effort to provide quality education for a few selected Negro girls.

Years later in a conversation with Charles Merrill, the founder and former director of the Commonwealth School, a small independent located in Boston, Charles informed me

Chapter Eight: A Lesson in Higher Education

that Clara Ludwig, of Mount Holyoke's admissions office, encouraged him to refer candidates of color to her attention for slots at the college. I presume that is why our guidance counselor at Fieldston recommended Mount Holyoke to me and to Peggy Gray, knowing that we were well qualified and would be accepted.

However, despite the outward friendliness on the part of most faculty and students, there was this sense of uncertainty about how to classify Negro students. Without any Negro faculty or staff to consult with, we were on our own to explain ourselves. *No, we are not foreign students. Well, how did you get here?* The implication being that we didn't really belong in this place. Ruth Elvedt, of the physical education department, and my water safety instructor, always treated me warmly and fairly and we remained in contact until her passing. My major, Economics and Sociology, was a combined department and I remember so well the ease and comfort I felt in economics Professor Everett Hawkins' class. But that level of ease and comfort did not exist in all my classes.

A sociology professor taught a course in comparative cultures that focused on South Africa, the Bantus and the Boers, in which he justified the treatment of the black South Africans during the apartheid regime. I knew that what I was hearing could be challenged, but I didn't have the knowledge or the courage to take him on. Decades later I would be in the audience to greet Nelson Mandela when he visited Boston. What a joyous occasion.

He had been imprisoned by the apartheid government of South Africa for twenty-seven years until his release in 1990. By 1994, Mandela was elected President of South Africa and served until 1999. During his presidency, Mandela enacted social reforms in education, healthcare, housing, pension reform, job training and land reclamation—initiatives that sought to erase the racial inequities of the former

Deeper Roots

government.[1] In 2002, I made my first trip to South Africa where a transformation had taken place. If it had not occurred, I would never have been able—as a black person—to set foot on that country's soil. But I had my problems when I visited the Apartheid Museum in Johannesburg.

I had purchased tickets for the six people I was touring with. Each ticket was one of three colors and I distributed them to our party in no particular order. We were then instructed to walk through the door that corresponded to the color of the ticket. I realized that I was left with the ticket (and door) that led me to the life of a white South African—I froze. I would not go through the entrance not until I was assured that the group would come together again after a brief period. I could see my group members in their respective lines as they watched (as I did) screens that described the lives they would have led had they been black, coloured or, in my case, white. Nothing was more powerful in conveying what it meant to be classified based on the color of your skin. Metaphorically, the tickets directed you to a door that determined your fixed role in life. We did come together after about fifteen minutes but it was a profound experience, especially because we were a racially-mixed group (college-age South Africans among us). We shared our experience in conversation thereafter. This was a country where Africans and coloureds were the majority of the population, yet they had no power or control over their lives.

However, the country was able to move beyond the repressive regime without a revolution. This was possible because of Nelson Mandela who, in my opinion, was the glue that held South Africa together and continues to do so today. Even while he was imprisoned, he was able to keep

---

[1] Unfortunately, the situation of the people at the bottom of the economic ladder has not changed significantly as evidenced by recent strikes and violence to workers inflicted by police.

Chapter Eight: A Lesson in Higher Education

the African National Congress (ANC) alive although it had been banned. He managed to remain in communication with members of the group who had left the country to form an international base of support for the independence of South Africa from apartheid domination. This is not to say that Nelson Mandela stood alone against the regime. White and coloured South Africans stood alongside blacks, academics, writers, artists, religious leaders, etc. and risked their lives as they fought against apartheid.

Nelson Mandela also represents revolutionary patience, and that is what I think allows the statue of Stephanus Johannes Paulus (Paul) Kruger to remain standing in Church Square, Pretoria. Kruger, a Boer of Dutch and/or German descent, believed in the destiny of the Afrikaner in South Africa and the European's civilizing influence on a savage land. However, those Europeans (the Boers and the English) would engage in uncivilized conflicts over land taken from the indigenous population and early immigrants from northern and western Africa. Considered the "father of the Afrikaner nation," he was elected four times as president of the old South African Republic in the late nineteenth century. As a tribute to his influence and leadership, the South African gold coin, Krugerrand, was named for him. "The people who supported him will die...and then we will take it down," I was assured. The sociology professor was one of those people.

My suspicions regarding the professor's ideas about race were proven in a letter of recommendation he wrote for my roommate Vera in which he described her as a "Negrophile." Despite the offensive reference, Vera got the job, researched her file, and discovered her professor's recommendation. Sometimes a letter of recommendation says more about the writer than about the subject of the letter.

Although the subtle (for the most part) racial intolerance on campus and the Supreme Court decision affected me

Deeper Roots

deeply, finances continued to be a priority during my freshman year. During the spring semester I became a tennis instructor for the ten-year- old child of a faculty member, which gave me some spending money.

There were some light moments in that intense first year though. After the spring break of my freshman year I received this humorous letter postmarked April 7, 1954.

Help! Police! Police!

I have been robbed. I mean cleaned out. How could you do this to me. The cold cream in the closet is finished with your help. I went to the cabinet to get the fresh one I thought I had there and behold, that too was gone. Just plain gone. No wonder your bag was so heavy you little rascal you. Strange you didn't forget any of your own stuff. I'll fix you the 8th of May. Just you wait and see.

Was great to hear your voice last night. So glad you arrived safely. What time did you get up this A.M? or did you. How's Anne and Vee. Hope they enjoyed their vacation too.

So alone once more. I shall be counting the days when I get there. Am going to give the whole apt. a good cleaning, that will keep me busy for a few days. Oscar must be gone for real, he didn't show up last night.

O.K. dear, buckle down and study hard now, and make good marks, your life there depends on it. So long until I hear from you,

Much love, Mother

Chapter Eight: A Lesson in Higher Education

I uttered the same complaint when my kids would clean me out when they went back to college after a vacation. "Where are my towels? What happened to the blankets and that nice comforter we had on our bed?" I would ask Hubey.

Just as my mother had predicted, I did receive scholarship aid for my sophomore year and thereafter. Awards from the Jessie Smith Noyes Foundation, the Leopold Schepp Foundation, the National Scholarship Service, the Fund for Negro Students and Mount Holyoke College covered my tuition, room and board. During the rest of my undergraduate years I sold subscriptions for the New York *Times,* worked in the college library and set up and waited tables at lunch and dinner in the dining hall to cover my personal, travel and miscellaneous expenses.

When I returned for my sophomore year, I also found that two Negro girls were in the freshman class, Gloria Johnson and Margaret (Meg) Claytor, and we always spoke when passing each other on campus. Gloria and I first met for tea together, at the invitation of the representative of the National Scholarship Service and Fund for Negro Students when she visited the campus to check on us. At that time Negro students played a predetermined role, which included the pretense that race didn't matter. Our public persona was well described by some lines in Paul Laurence Dunbar's poem, "We Wear the Mask."

We wear the mask that grins and lies,
It hides our cheeks and shades our eyes,--
this debt we pay to human guile;
With torn and bleeding hearts we smile;
and mouth with myriad subtleties.

Deeper Roots

Of course, the 1960s Civil Rights Movement broke that pretense and changed our lives in dramatic ways. Both Gloria and Meg "sat in" to desegregate lunch counters while attending Meharry, a black medical school in Nashville, Tennessee, and I became involved in educational issues regarding desegregation during the 1960s and 1970s.

But we were college students of the 1950s attending a relatively isolated college campus where, overall, the style of living to which we became accustomed was what my mother had envisioned for me: tea and cookies served in the living room Friday afternoon, demitasse after dinner served by Mrs. Knowlton, and on Wednesday evening and Sunday afternoon, dinner served by candlelight. These "gracious living" meals required stockings (seams straight), high-heeled shoes, and a suit or dress. These social graces were assumed to enhance our opportunities for marriage and later career goals. Miss Voorhees advised seniors to wear a dark suit, hat and white gloves for job interviews, and to remain standing until invited to sit. We were never to request a salary—just mention we needed enough money to live.

A secretarial position was a realistic job opportunity for female liberal arts college graduates then. I knew, however, that a secretarial position in a business would not be readily available to me because of racial discrimination.

In addition to social etiquette, academic matters were also taken quite seriously. Through rigorous work and instruction, Mount Holyoke prepared her students to be well rounded women, knowledgeable of the world, and prepared to meet its challenges. Fortunately, Fieldston had given me an excellent preparation for college and I was disciplined enough to spend many hours in the library studying week-nights and weekends. Sometimes groups of us studied together in the dorm.

My interest in social sciences drew me to courses in history, political science, sociology, and psychology. I was

Chapter Eight: A Lesson in Higher Education

deeply disappointed, however, when the psychology course I had chosen turned out to be the psychology of rats. Experimental psychology rather than clinical psychology was the focus of the department.

Letters exchanged between me and my friends from camp and high school—letters I have saved over all these years—reflect how serious we were about our intellectual lives. We wrote to each other about our tests and papers, and about our newest ideas; we engaged in heated discussions about the meaning of life, conferences we attended and the guest lecturers we heard on campus. These friendships, continued through correspondence, helped to bridge the wide gap between the more liberal political perspectives of my New York and former Fieldston friends and the conservative, Republican majority views of Mount Holyoke students.

Dating was also a very important part of campus life and I believed that my choice of a women's college would help ensure a better social life. I knew that at coed institutions, people usually dated students on their own campus; and since there were few black guys on *any* campus, it was advantageous for me to enroll at a female institution where I could meet the few Negro guys attending nearby liberal arts (all male) colleges including Dartmouth, Amherst, Harvard, Wesleyan, Brown, Tufts, Williams and Yale.

At a freshman mixer at Amherst College, Vera and I met two roommates, sophomores Norman Amaker and David Schwartz, whom we began to double date. Norman eventually became a lawyer for the NAACP Legal Defense Fund team, and David pursued a career at Fieldston, working diligently on issues of racial diversity as a teacher and administrator. The social strategy I envisioned worked, and I dated guys at Dartmouth and Wesleyan, in addition to Amherst.

Deeper Roots

On the weekends many students left campus for dates at other colleges. Weekends also brought a deluge of guys to our campus. For two dollars a night dates could sleep on cots at the College Inn, a favorite gathering place with soda fountain service. The proprietor, rightly named Mr. Keyes, played the piano while barber shop quartets serenaded us with hit parade tunes like, *Don't Sit Under The Apple Tree With Anyone Else But Me.*

In the era when the principal goal of most women students, even at elite colleges, was to marry immediately after graduation and begin to raise a family, for many students the ideal was to be adorned with the fraternity pin of your steady boyfriend in junior year (pinned), flash a diamond engagement ring in your senior year and invite friends to a wedding soon after graduation. Women planned to remain at home while their children were growing up. I followed this pattern by "going steady" with Hubey during my junior and senior years while he was a graduate student at Boston University School of Social Work. Hubey and I graduated on the same day and six months later (on December 7, 1957) we got married.

However, this 1950s "ideal" took a different post-nuptials route for some women. My mother (as did many other Negro women) provided a very different role model by combining work, parenting and community involvement. Alice Walker coined the term "womanism" in the 1980s to describe this phenomenon. Frankly, very few black women had the luxury of keeping house, raising children and doing volunteer work as a vocation. I can think of only one Negro woman that I knew in my youth who devoted herself to family at the exclusion of work outside of the home.

The 1960s women's liberation movement to get women back into the labor force did not resonate with many black women of any social or economic group. Black women were already in the work force and were now seeking white-collar jobs. As an example, Ruth Simmonds sought such a course and became a scholar and college administrator, while raising a family of her own. As the first generation of her family to attend college, she broke other barriers when she was selected as President of Smith College in 1997, and in 2001 began her presidency at Brown University as the first African American to head an Ivy League institution. Her leadership in the academy combined responsibilities of work and family typical of the role African American women have always assumed. That was what I considered to be the norm, and I too believed that you could do it all... have a career, raise a family, and do volunteer work at the same time. And I did.

My experience at Mount Holyoke indicates to me that women's colleges have a unique role to play in our society, because they train women exclusively for excellence. A higher percentage of women attending single sex institutions pursue graduate education than their female counterparts at coed institutions. Also, the percentage of women alumnae of color holding graduate degrees surpasses their white peers. There are proportionately more women professors, staff and administrators at women's colleges than at coed institutions, and female students assume all leadership positions within the institution. Women are also able to concentrate on studies without male distraction in the immediate environment.

But there are contradictions. When I attended Mount Holyoke, there were more than twice as many women professors as men, but none of the women on the faculty were married with the exception of a lab instructor. The unwritten rule governing marital status for women professors back then was that they remain single. Male power and control was evident, since the heads of departments in the social sciences were male. The male faculty had wives and children, and many of their families lived in faculty housing often provided by the college. The irony is that between 1937 and 1978, the presidents of this women's college were all men.

Hubey and I often took a Sunday afternoon outing with our young children to Mount Holyoke from our home in Newton. When our daughters got older, I brought them to the campus for mother/daughter recruitment events. Although all of them applied to the college, none chose to attend a women's college. They graduated from Yale, Princeton, Wesleyan and Brown—choices unavailable to me when I attended college, and they hold graduate degrees and post-graduate degrees from Berkeley, Harvard, Princeton, University of Pennsylvania, and Yale. With the acceptance of women at previously male bastions of higher education, the number of women's colleges throughout the country is diminishing, either by attrition or by becoming coeducational institutions. I wonder if I would have chosen a women's college if I had the options that were available to my daughters.

Nevertheless, a women's college offered me a sense of sisterhood that has endured over the elapsed time since our graduation. Anne, Vera, and I were all born in March and celebrated our birthdays over the years by remembering each other with a phone call, a card and/or lunch. I named my daughter Lisa Anne since she was born on my friend's birthday, the 23rd of the month. Anne and her husband, and Hubey and I get together on Cape Cod during annual vacations. Vera Barad, Mary Simmens and Nadja Burns and I have met together bi-monthly in Cambridge over lunch. Our discussions have ranged over many topics as we became grandmothers, divorcees, and wound down our professional careers. Our group listened attentively as my story of discovery of family history unfolded. They attended my

Chapter Eight: A Lesson in Higher Education

museum exhibits, lectures and book signings, and supported me during life crises. Living in a dorm, sharing classes and values had bonded us together. Stephanie Diamond Friedman and I meet annually in either California or Massachusetts. A few years ago Vera moved to California, the first time we've lived in different states since we've known each other. I've visited her in San Francisco, and at the apartment she and her husband kept in New York City. We had a wonderful conversation when Vera called on my birthday in 2010. Vera was happier than she'd been in a long time. After mourning the death of her husband, Edward Marks, she had found love again. When I called her on her birthday later that month, Amelia answered her mother's cellphone at the hospital. My long-time friend had been diagnosed with inoperable brain cancer. Four months after the diagnosis Vera died.

Her vitality had been stilled. I celebrated her life with her family and friends on Cape Cod, a place that had special meaning to Vera. We shared our memories and photographs in an attempt to capture the spirit of this vivacious woman, social worker and fabulous hostess. Vera defiantly stood up for human rights before it was popular to do so—she was my college roommate and the student whom the college professor referred to as a "Negrophile" in his letter of recommendation. Her loss hangs heavy over me.

When I returned to campus for my forty-fifth reunion in June 2002, Clara (Reggie) Ludwig who had interviewed me for admission in 1952 was there to celebrate her sixty-fifth reunion. Fifty years after our first meeting, she was as witty, sharp and kind as ever. The next day nearly 600 alumnae convened in Chapin Hall for a meeting of the Alumnae Association. Despite gray hair, wrinkled skin and increased poundage, we often recognized each other; the voice and person beneath the camouflage of passing years remain familiar. Enveloped in the intimacy of our shared experience,

Deeper Roots

I recalled that I had never missed my five year reunions. My ties to Mount Holyoke run deep.

I began my freshman year at Mount Holyoke, the only African American woman in my class to graduate. I never imagined I would be welcomed back to my forty-fifth reunion by an African American acting President of the college, Beverly Tatum, and by an African American President of the Alumnae Association, Karen Hendricks.

Dr. Tatum, acting President of Mount Holyoke College, addressed the alumnae just before we raised our voices to sing the alma mater at the close of the ceremony. A psychologist and former provost, she began her tenure at the college in 1990. In the summer of 2002, she left Mount Holyoke to assume the presidency of Spelman College, a liberal arts black women's college in Atlanta, Georgia.

As of 2011, Mount Holyoke remains a relatively small women's college of 2,333 with an endowment of over 530 million dollars. Although tuition and fees for the 2011-12 academic year amounted to $41,456, the majority of students who apply for financial aid receive it. The average need per student is well over $30,000 and of the seventy percent of students who receive financial aid, 100% of those students' needs are fully met.

The current president, Lynn Pasquerella ('80), has re-energized the spirit of the college community since taking office in 2010. Her commitment to international programs and diversity within the student body is evident. Her administration has also reached out to alumnae, not only to keep them more informed about the current direction of the institution but to encourage their participation in campus activities.

Clearly, the college thrives as several other single-sex colleges have been subsumed by other institutions or become coed. Mount Holyoke continues to educate women in a comfortable and empowering environment that fosters a

Chapter Eight: A Lesson in Higher Education

certain collegiate devotion. I am not alone in my feeling of sisterhood after all these years. Mount Holyoke's endowment is a reflection of the loyalty among its alumnae — the sisterhood continues.

Kathy and Auntie Maud – 1936

Thede, Kathy and Meme – 1936

Meme Clark Butler – 1936

Catherine Simpson Clark – 1923

Methlin Clark

Phyllis Clark

Clark Family Home, Falmouth Jamaica

View of the George Washington Bridge from my window at
409 Edgecombe Avenue

Kathy and Thede

Kenneth Spottswood

Jane Jackson as George Washington

Mildred Johnson Edwards
1914 – 2007

Midtown Ethical Culture – 6th Grade

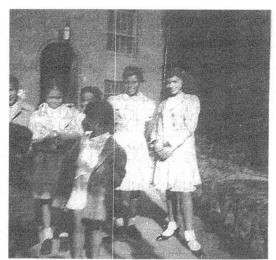

Dunbar Apartments – 1947
To my left is Anne Raven Wilkinson

Ethical Culture School Camp – Summer 1946

Ethical Culture School Camp with my
Bunkmates and Counselor D. Meltzer

Ethical Culture School Camp -1955 Staff Photo
Hubey and Kathy – Middle Second Row

Fieldston Graduation 1953
Kathy and Michael Stone

Fieldston Graduation Day 1953

Mount Holyoke Graduation 1957
Doris and Kathy

Mount Holyoke College – Class of 1957
Forty-Fifth Reunion

New Mexico - 2005
Ann Neuberger Aceves ("Nuey") and Kathy

Chapter Nine:

Young, Gifted and Black

(1957 – 1961)

Ironically, I felt fortunate to have a job in the typing pool immediately following my college graduation and three months prior to my wedding. My work experience at Young and Rubicam (Y&R), one of the largest advertising agencies in the country, had evolved from handling toilet paper and paper towels to handling typing paper. I had worked at Y&R for one week each summer in addition to

Deeper Roots

camp counseling and continued to do so during my first years at college. I knew how lucky I was to have the job with Y&R because a former classmate who worked during her summer vacations at an employment office had described to me the coding system used to ensure that people of color and 'identifiable' Jews were not referred for white-collar 'clean' positions.

I was seventeen at the start of my first week at Y&R in August 1953. I entered the sixteen-story building at 285 Madison Avenue in midtown Manhattan where Y&R had their corporate headquarters. The offices were air-conditioned, a welcome relief from New York City's summer heat. I was to stand in for my mother's customer (and my old Christmas club benefactor), Mrs. Woodland. This would be a dry run for me before Mrs. Woodland went on vacation. She worked in Y&R's experimental kitchen helping develop and test recipes for magazine advertising and food packaging. The "Generals"—General Foods, General Mills, and General Electric—along with Borden, were some of the major clients. The kitchen boasted two complete sets of dazzling white appliances—the very latest models of General Electric refrigerators and ranges plus GE's sparkling new automatic dishwasher. The equipment was astonishing, especially the dishwasher. At that time, the only other dishwasher I had seen was in the model kitchen at the 1939 World's Fair at Lake Success, New York.

Mrs. Woodland's post was in a nook in the corner of the kitchen. On my first day I was shocked to discover that she was outfitted in a black uniform with a white apron and a ruffled white cap. As I stood wondering whether I would be expected to wear this uniform (a request I would have rejected), a statuesque woman wearing a flowered dress came up to greet me. "I'm Miss Fabricant, the nutritionist in charge here. I'm so pleased to meet you, Betty. This is my

202

assistant," she said, gesturing to a petite woman with jet black hair, dressed in a white uniform. "We've heard so much about you from Viola." This was another huge shock to me—it was the first time I had heard Mrs. Woodland referred to by her first name, except when her sister, Mrs. Cokine (who worked in Borden's experimental kitchen) came to our apartment to have her hair done. In our community, last names were always used by adults when addressing each other (except in the case of relatives and very close friends) as a form of respect to counteract the demeaning way in which whites usually referred to colored people of all classes and ages by their first name. Dick Gregory named one of his daughters, "Miss" so that she would never experience such deprecation. From overhearing kitchen conversations, I knew Viola Woodland was a single mother with two grown sons whom she had raised on her meager Y&R salary. For fifty dollars a week, Mrs. Woodland cleaned the pots and pans in the experimental kitchen, put dishes in the dishwasher and stocked the eleven floors of Y&R ladies' lavatories with bathroom tissue and towels. This was the job that I would have for a week.

Mrs. Woodland and I took the service elevator to the supply closet in the basement. We each filled two brown shopping bags with toilet paper and paper towels and took the elevator to the eleventh floor. In the ladies' lavatory, Mrs. Woodland unlocked the paper towel dispenser. "Make sure that the top end of the paper towel in the dispenser folds into the bottom sheet of the new stack of paper towels that you put in," Mrs. Woodland instructed me. "And don't fill the container too full or it will get jammed." We repeated the process until all the lavatories received their daily replenishment. The people we encountered smiled pleasantly when Mrs. Woodland introduced me, "This is Betty. She will be taking my place when I go on vacation next week."

Deeper Roots

The most I can say for filling in for Mrs. Woodland is that it was, in fact, a clean job. There were no floors to scrub, no windows to wash, and no requests to stay a few hours longer at the end of the day. When Mrs. Woodland had first been hired, the matron's job was one of the better positions a Negro high school graduate could obtain. Nevertheless, I felt tremendously sad knowing that Mrs. Woodland was trapped in this job with no hope of doing more interesting work for a better living. I was conscious that my life would be different and I could sense that Mrs. Woodland took enormous pride and satisfaction in the knowledge that wider opportunities awaited me.

My work week went very well. I took the elevator to the top floor and walked down the staircase to each lavatory. Each day I finished distributing the paper products in an hour and read a library book for the rest of the time unless we went to a studio to film food being prepared in the kitchen for magazine advertisements. Elaborate preparations were made for these photo shoots because the food had to look particularly colorful and appetizing. It was an exciting adventure for me. We carefully packed cartons and traveled by taxi to the studio, where we arranged the platters of food on the tablecloths for the cameramen to adjust the artful lighting.

Soon after I began to work at Y&R, I realized that my Harlem neighbor, Roy Eaton, worked on the executive floor of Y&R. We saw each other occasionally, but we did not converse. Although we knew one another from living on Edgecombe Avenue and through our mutual connection with music teacher Irene Chesman, at Y&R we pretended that we were strangers. We knew that we would be conspic-uous if we talked to each other. Maybe no one would pay particular attention to us if we stayed apart, but if we en-

204

Chapter Nine: Young Gifted and Black

gaged in conversation it might be considered conspiratorial. We wanted to fade into the background because the idea that we didn't really belong at Y&R had been conveyed to us because we didn't see other Negroes around, and we didn't want to draw attention to the fact that we were here. I imagined that we were not the only Negroes in the place and that some were "passing" for white. We never discussed the roles we were playing, even when we saw each other in our neighborhood.

When he was a boy and a young man, Roy Eaton used to pass 409 on his way home to his family's apartment farther down Edgecombe Avenue near 150th Street. Roy was a short, studious guy about three years older than me. He wore horn-rimmed glasses and even as a teenager always carried a brown briefcase with stacks of paper spilling over the top. A talented musician, Roy was encouraged to aspire to a career as a concert pianist by his first piano teacher, Miss Chesman, a friend of my mother's. Roy attended the selective Fiorello H. LaGuardia High School for Music and Art and the Performing Arts. Miss Chesman organized solo performances and African American church groups came in droves. I heard Roy play at many of these concerts. One performance stands out in my mind—his repertoire included Bach, Beethoven, Mozart and Debussy. I knew how talented Roy really was when I watched his fingers fly over the keys and heard the marvelous tonality emanating from the piano. Roy looked quite elegant in his tuxedo that afternoon, and got complimentary reviews from the press. I was also taking piano lessons, and appreciated the hard work that went into preparing for these events. Miss Chesman was fiercely proud of her prize student and later presented Roy in several concerts at Town Hall. Members of church delegations who had heard Roy play recitals at their own churches also came to hear him play at Town Hall, and so did I. But the reality of

Deeper Roots

race prejudice interfered with Roy's dream. Even after receiving noteworthy reviews in America, many talented African American artists and performers had to go to Europe to establish themselves as professionals. In Europe they were often well-received, unfettered by the stubborn racial barriers they experienced in the United States. However, financial limitations prevented Roy from that possibility. After graduating from City College, Roy became a commercial jingle writer for Y&R. Roy was the only Negro professional person the agency knowingly employed and probably one of a handful of Negroes in the entire advertising field at the time.

I have often heard white people say that skin color makes no difference. "We're all the same: white, yellow, brown, green or purple." We all may be the same, but we are certainly treated differently. Since there are no green or purple people, this comment minimizes the overt acts of discrimination affecting real people of color and negates these realities.

However, the Chief Executive Officer at Y&R, George Gribbon, was a forward-looking man who apparently wanted to alter the firm's predominantly white environment. During my week at Y&R in the summer of 1957 (I was twenty-one), I learned that a job was available in the print media copy typing pool, and I tried out for it. To qualify I would need to type sixty words a minute with only two errors. I practiced very hard for several weeks to beef up the skills my cousin Edna had taught me years before. The first time I took the test I failed but after my second attempt I was informed that I had passed and the job was mine. My post was now outside the office of George Gribbon who exchanged pleasantries with me when he passed by my desk. One day Mr. Gribbon asked me to consider being his administrative assistant. This was a bold move on his part at

Chapter Nine: Young Gifted and Black

that time. Although it was a token job, the position would have provided an opportunity for a person of color to join the corporate structure and learn about the advertising field. It would have been a significant breakthrough, long before affirmative action was conceived as national policy. As pleased as I was about this, I could not consider Mr. Gribbon's request because I was engaged to marry Hubey and we would be moving to Boston. The position at Y&R was a way to earn enough money to purchase a bedroom set and help pay for the wedding reception. With less than three months before the wedding, my thoughts were focused on the preparations.

My doctor's receptionist kindly offered to make my wedding gown as a gift and my wedding expenses were further reduced because the reception hall at the Ethical Culture Society building, just beneath the auditorium where we were to be married by Henry Herman, was free for use by members. True to form, my mother arranged for the wedding reception of tea sandwiches and punch to be catered by the fabled Schrafft's. Right before I left Y&R to be married, Florence Fabricant, her assistant and my workmates in the experimental kitchen hosted a bridal shower for me. The set of four aluminum canisters they gave me that day, fifty-four years ago, are continually replenished with tea, sugar, flour and rice to this day.

Strange to imagine that I would be marrying Hubey that December in 1957. During the camp years, Hubey and I knew each other because it was a small camp. We became a couple during the summer of 1955 when we were both counselors. We would visit each other on weekends during our university years—he traveling to Mount Holyoke and me traveling to Cambridge.

But here we were—our engagement and wedding were announced in the New York *Times*. I did not include a

Deeper Roots

photograph since I could not recall seeing pictures of people of color on the society page. I did hire photographers who were at our respective apartments on the day of the wedding—our personal paparazzi. Our wedding album shows Hubey adjusting his bow tie in his bedroom, and my mother and me in her bedroom making the last adjustments to my gown before each of us got into the limousines waiting in front of our respective homes. Al Mathew, Hubey's childhood friend (whom I met at camp where we were both counselors) was Hubey's best man and Hubey's brothers-in-law helped out as ushers. My camp friend, Mildred (Millie) Cohen, was my matron of honor and my cousin Alfred (my Dad's nephew) whom I chose to give me away, joined my mother and me for the ride to the Ethical Culture Society building where the wedding took place. The photographer captured Hubey at the front of the auditorium standing alongside Henry Herman whose raised hand signaled me to slow my pace down the aisle. There is no photograph, however, of the huge slice of wedding cake Hubey cut for me at the reception where seventy-five family members, friends, neighbors, and Mom's customers gathered that afternoon.

"Governor Faubus should be here to see this gathering," Mrs. Woodland said to me, referring to the racially diverse wedding guests gathered to celebrate our nuptials. Governor Faubus of Arkansas had opposed the inclusion of Negro students at Little Rock Central High School that September of 1957, and enlisted the National Guard to prevent their entry. Only the federal government-deputized Air Force reserve officers made it possible for the nine teenagers to attend school amid the jeers and racial epithets of the picketing throngs. Hubey and I faced no such racial opposition but the religious differences of Pentecostal and Ethical Culture humanism did present some real challenges for us.

Chapter Nine: Young Gifted and Black

Born and raised on 166th Street between Prospect and Union in the South Bronx, Hubey attended Morris High School (two years ahead of former United States Secretary of State and retired four-star general Colin Powell). Hubey was the fourth child of six (and only son) of a devoted Pentecostal family who worshiped at the Community Full Gospel Church. Hubey's mother, aunt and uncle were the pillars of the church and served on the Trustee Board. The minister of the congregation, William Ellison, was Hubey's uncle. Uncle Billie also served as a father figure since Hubey's dad travelled so much. So in addition to the strong religious commitment, the connection between family and church was also quite strong. I had met his family and all seemed to go well until we decided to get married. Hubey's Aunt Kate became distraught about the wedding and I believe that a combination of factors set her off: I was not Pentecostal and I had no intention of converting and the Ethical Culture hierarchy had declined her suggestion that a Pentecostal minister co-officiate at the ceremony. She refused to attend the wedding and informed us in writing (and told my mother on the telephone) that we were "living in sin" since she did not recognize us as a married couple. As Hubey recalls, "Aunt Kate didn't know she was walking right into a buzzsaw when she called your mother." I think Aunt Kate probably would have suffered a stroke at the ceremony anyway since I had indicated during the pre-marital counseling session with Hank Herman that I would not make a promise to obey my husband-to-be, so that part of the vow was stricken.

Nevertheless, rice was thrown at Hubey and me on that chilly and rainy Saturday afternoon as we left the Ethical Culture Society building to begin our lives together. But first we made a stop at 409, where we changed our clothes for the train ride to Boston. There was to be no honeymoon since Hubey had just been hired as a boy's group worker at Boston

Deeper Roots

Children's Services, a social service agency assisting families with child-related problems.

Hubey and I had discussed this move that would take us away from the city where we were both born and raised. First, he was well-prepared for the position. After his 1951 dishwashing stint at the ECSC, Hubey returned to the camp for several summers as a counselor while he worked toward his bachelor's degree at City University of New York's City College. During the summer of 1956, while he was attending Boston University School of Social Work, he worked at Camp Wediko (part of Wediko Children's Services in New Hampshire) where he worked with emotionally-disturbed boys. (Because of Hubey's affiliation with the organization, one summer the ECSC campers elected to donate the proceeds of the camp's simplified annual dinner to Wediko as a reflection of the organization's work and the ECSC's warm feelings toward Hubey.) He would return to ECSC for the last summer in 1957 (following his graduation from Boston University) to mentor and supervise its camp counselors. Hubey was also familiar with his new employer. He had served his graduate field placement at Boston Children's Services and now they wanted him to work for them permanently.

The move to Boston would also create some space in which to build a new life away from possible interference from family. As things turned out, my mother would always be our greatest advocate—supportive in our decisions especially as it related to our children. Describing her as a "unique human being with a lot to admire" Hubey was impressed that Mom raised no objections at our decision to relocate. He came to the conclusion that Meme's "commitment to her daughter was unbelievable." As a result, Hubey became enamored of Mom early on in our marriage.

Chapter Nine: Young Gifted and Black

Hubey's family, on the other hand, was not as accepting of the way we chose to live our lives over the years. However, despite our differences of opinion we continued to embrace our family ties as we gathered together at weddings in New York City. In the late 1960s we began a bi-annual family reunion tradition first initiated by my younger sister-in-law. This tradition brought us to Boston, Massachusetts, Washington D.C., Chicago, Illinois, and Springfield, Missouri where roots of the Jones-Robinson family were firmly planted. Now the next generation has taken over this endeavor. The extensive organizational planning for these weekends is now administered by our nephew using his extraordinary talent to bring 150 people together to attend these family celebrations. Our nieces and nephews have also shared our home when the need arose. When my youngest sister-in-law and dear friend, Russelle, succumbed to cancer our family asked for her youngest son to live with us and he agreed that it was what he wanted to do. Hubey and I became his legal guardians and he became an integral part of our family. He and our daughter were born two weeks apart and graduated from high school in the same class. After completing college he joined the Air Force and now lives in the south with his wife and two children. Looking back now, we made the right decision to leave New York so many years ago because we were able to establish a strong family foundation, sturdy enough to help other family members when necessary.

Upon our arrival in Boston we stayed at the Sheraton Hotel in Harvard Square for the weekend and then moved into the house where Hubey had lived during his two graduate school years. Hubey and I were surprised to find our bed was filled with rice and had been 'frenched' (a dormitory practical joke where you are unable to get in bed

Deeper Roots

without re-doing the bed linens), by Mamie Easterling, the widowed owner of the redbrick row house where we would live. She had lodged black male Harvard University graduate students who were not welcome in campus housing in the 1930s and 1940s. A mother to her "boys" (who called her Madame), she cooked for them and entertained their friends there as well. This was really their home away from home, and her boys always remembered her by keeping in touch as they pursued distinguished careers in law and the ministry.

My mom was quite satisfied that we were living right across the Charles River from Boston where my father was born. For some reason that made her feel comfortable. Although I know my mother would have been happier to have us live in New York, she never expressed a sense of loss with this permanent separation. Mom was also relieved that we were living with old friends of the Jones family. Even though we knew we were adults (twenty-one and twenty-three years of age), our centenarian landlady, who was born in slavery, made us and our families feel secure. Mrs. Easterling's husband had befriended and mentored Hubey's Dad, Hilma, when they both worked as Pullman porters — shining shoes and making up sleepers — on the trains that were the primary mode of passenger transportation until the airlines took over. Although Hilma Jones was a graduate of Lincoln University, racial discrimination limited job opportunities for the "colored." Yet, my father-in-law found intellectual stimulation and challenge by volunteering with the union of the Brotherhood of Sleeping Car Porters, representing porters in disputes with management. "Hilma, where did you study law?" his beleaguered opponents would ask. Now Mr. Easterling was dead, but Mom continued to provide a safe and nurturing place.

Chapter Nine: Young Gifted and Black

I liked the quaintness of Boston and Cambridge, with its cobblestone streets and strange trolley-like trains that traveled much of their routes above ground. It seemed like a suburb to me and I was content to settle in Mrs. Easterling's home while we looked for a permanent place to live. Our room was on the top floor of the three-floor walkup. Hubey's dad used another room when he was on a layover in Boston, another lodger occupied the third room and we shared a bathroom. A large kitchen (which was used only by us) with a converted wood burning cast iron stove was in the basement with direct access to the back yard and alley. We paid fifty dollars a month rent including gas, electricity and telephone. When the lodger moved out, we decided to rent the entire floor—living room, bedroom and bath—and when our first child, Karen, was born my father-in-law's old room became the nursery.

A group of ten row houses on Broadway and Dana Street in the midst of a white community were owned by black families. I had stayed in the Jones' (no relation) home next to Mrs. Easterling's house free of charge when visiting Hubey on weekends from Mount Holyoke. This was a real community within a community. Hubey and I were often invited over for Saturday breakfast (with homemade grits) and Sunday dinner. Mr. Jones, a postal worker like my dad, subscribed to the Chicago *Defender* and the New York *Amsterdam News* and other popular black newspapers and enjoyed discussing currents events with Hubey. Mrs. Jones' sister, Nan, lived around the corner on Broadway, and she often invited us to watch television with her on Sunday evenings. Next door to the Jones lived a budding real estate entrepreneur, Marvin Eugene Gilmore, whose mother also owned her home at the other end of Dana Street and taught Marvin how to leverage property. Justin Williams, a social worker like Hubey, lived on Broadway with his family and

213

Deeper Roots

we became close friends. I wondered if Harvard University made these properties available for black ownership to house their black graduate students who were not welcome to live on campus.

Many of my friends from high school and college were living in Cambridge while their husbands pursued graduate work at Harvard. Stephanie Diamond Friedman lived within walking distance, Marguerite Mendelsohn Lavin lived in the Brattle Street area, and Vera Barad, my college roommate, also lived near Harvard Square. Hubey's colleagues at work, and graduates of Boston University School of Social Work, introduced us to the greater Boston area by inviting us to their homes in Quincy, Mansfield and Brighton.

A month (January 1958) after Hubey began his new job his supervisor, Miss Warren, suggested that I apply to the Boston Public Schools for a position since there was a grave shortage of teachers in the system. I was hired because I could play the piano and had experience working with children as a camp counselor, in spite of a lack of education courses. I was thrilled to have my first job after college and began work for fifteen dollars a day as a substitute teacher. I was assigned to schools in various sections of Boston (the North End, Dorchester and East Boston) but I was never assigned to any school in Roxbury (where black students went to school). I did not know at the time that my hiring was an exception to the rule—there were only about five tenured African American teachers in the Boston School system in 1958.

For five months I was assigned as a permanent substitute to the Theodore Lyman School in East Boston, located in a predominantly Italian neighborhood. When the principal escorted me to the classroom, I was surprised to meet another teacher in the kindergarten class. I soon realized that the teacher was senile. "Come here with your chairs and

Chapter Nine: Young Gifted and Black

form a circle," she directed the children. When the children followed this direction, she asked, "Why are you sitting here in a circle?" It was a chaotic situation with confused children and a distraught principal. Because of restrictive tenure regulations, the principal was getting no cooperation from the central office to initiate the retirement process on behalf of his kindergarten teacher. I took over the class for the remainder of the year as she sat, watched and appeared to be quite agreeable to this arrangement. She was out of touch with reality and I believe she came to school every day, weekends and holidays included.

Fortunately, the kindergarten teacher in the Dante Alighieri School across the street taught me how to teach. Jan Wilhelm, a Midwesterner, was a recently-married college graduate who had majored in education. Jan lived in Cambridge on Appleton Street, and owned a Volkswagen Bug. She picked me up and dropped me off at my home each day as we traveled back and forth to school. I purchased books on my own and Jan and I did lesson plans together. We became personal friends as we shopped for vegetables and groceries in East Boston and took our students for neighborhood walks together. One day we agreed to pool our resources and bought a rabbit and took turns caring for Pinky on weekends. We spent afternoons at each other's homes and double-dated with our husbands on weekends.

Working with Jan I realized that the materials I was given to work with were outdated and the few visits from the kindergarten supervisor were superficial, but I loved my job, and I adored working with the children. Although reading readiness in kindergarten was preparation for first grade, there were no tests of any kind for us to administer, nor did we have to write commentaries on student achievement. The kindergarten supervisor was right. The songs and games I learned as a child and taught as a camp counselor

215

were useful, and piano playing was an essential asset. I borrowed books for my class from the library a few blocks from my home since there was no school library. The parents were very nice, but were not really welcomed in the school. We met them at the door at dismissal when they came to pick up their children. I was fortunate to be assigned to the kindergarten class at the Lyman School the following September for the 1958-1959 school year—this time without another teacher in attendance.

During the school year, I realized that I was pregnant with my first child and that the Board of Education rules prevented pregnant women from teaching. Because there were so few teachers, I had already managed to circumvent one written rule (my lack of formal teaching credentials) and one unwritten rule (being black) so I was not about to push my luck. I completed the school year without telling anyone that I was having a baby. I knew that by the start of the following school year (1959-1960) I could no longer hide my pregnancy so I did not return to teaching and Karen was born in November of 1959. It is almost impossible to believe in 2012 that pregnancy was once cause for termination (more so than a teacher's senility), but that was the way things were. I became a stay-at-home mom, earned my master's in education and engaged in volunteer activities for the next nine years—volunteer work that evolved into political activism.

We remained with Mrs. Easterling until six months before the birth of our second child, Lauren in 1961. Although we loved where we were, space was getting tight and navigating between our living quarters on the third floor and the kitchen in the basement was difficult, especially during pregnancy. Now that I think of it, difficulty walking up and down stairs during pregnancy was also the reason my parents moved to 409—a nice coincidence. Since Hubey

Chapter Nine: Young Gifted and Black

was now secure in his work, we began looking for a home of our own. It was at this point that the Ethical Culture philosophy went careening (head first) into the philosophy of the real world—again.

An architect who lived close to Mrs. Easterling offered to sell his home to us. However, the three local banks refused to give us a mortgage despite our employment history, income and creditworthiness. We continued our search for a home in Cambridge and contacted the local Fair Housing Committee Chairman who declined to get involved in the matter—perhaps the quota of black home ownership in Cambridge had already been reached. Next, we decided to look outside of Cambridge and settled on a modified cape in the community of Newton but buying that home was problematic as well. The Newton Fair Housing and Equal Rights Committees were formed in the 1950s as an affiliate of the Commonwealth's Committee. The goal of Newton's multi-racial Committee was to assist people of color in the purchase or rental of housing in the city. However, only three realtors were willing to show houses to blacks interesting in buying homes. After we had agreed on a pur-chase price with the seller, members of the local Catholic Church prepared and signed a petition (with the support of the parish priest) that they presented to the owner stating that they did not approve of the sale. One alderman who lived on the street and was a member of the church refused to sign the petition, and we proceeded with the sale, moving into our home in May of 1961. The alderman was not the only resident who was appalled by the petition. Other church members subsequently approached us to lend their support. There was also another black family around the corner who reached out to us, invited us to church and picnics and made us feel welcome—we remain friends to this day. One fireman neighbor, however, immediately sold his property and moved. Apparently, some of the residents had other prejudices as well. At the same time that we moved into our new home, a Jewish family moved next door. Our families became friends and we helped each other feel comfortable in our new homes. We welcomed our second child, Lauren, into the world that September of 1961.

The volunteers at the American Friends Service Committee were instrumental in helping us navigate the racially-charged real estate market and they also introduced us to Newton's Fair Housing and Equal Rights Committee. Hubey and I attended meetings and subsequently joined as committee members. This was the beginning of my grass-roots activism. Sometimes things have to happen, quite literally, close to home to spur a person to effect change. Historians believe that is one of the primary components that differentiate feminism from womanism is that black women agitate for the betterment of their families and community and not just for the betterment of women exclusively. The tool for this agitation is often *in situ* organizations that are in the trenches dealing with the day-to-day issues of a community. The American Friends Service Committee would prove to be one of those vital components of political movements in Massachusetts.

As I began to explore our city, I came to know members of the black population residing mostly in West Newton. This area of several blocks near the Lincoln Park Baptist Church is where the black residents worshipped in the 1800's. It was customary at that time for non-white attendees to be seated in the balcony.

The West Newton group, perhaps in response to this constriction combined with a desire for autonomy, decided to form their own congregation. Led by founder Reverend Edmund Kelley Myrtle Baptist Church was constructed in 1875 on land donated by a deacon of Lincoln Park Baptist

Chapter Nine: Young Gifted and Black

Church. Celebrating more than a century of service to the Newton community, the church has grown in membership and pro-grams, including members from surrounding areas as well as resident Newtonians. Our family welcomed invitations to attend church and to participate in annual church picnics. For many generations, this community served Newton as tradesmen and blue-collar workers and their children were not encouraged to pursue higher educational goals in the local primary and secondary schools. Vocational education, not college education, was encouraged for these students whether or not they remained in Newton. These young people were not likely to be employed in non-service occupations even when we moved to Newton in 1961.

Our family (along with other black homeowners who had moved to Newton) were considered newcomers. We chose not to live within the boundaries of the existing black community and our expectations were somewhat different. In order to learn more about the experiences of black students in Newton, we invited them to our home to have a better understanding of the issues that confronted them. The emerging Civil Rights Movement gave all of us new aware-ness and confidence to challenge the assumptions previously made about the education of our children and the roles they would play in society.

As we began to get to know and understand each other a pivotal incident brought all of the black citizens of Newton together. The Black Citizens of Newton (BCON) was organized after Reverend Ernest Davis, an African American resident of Newton and minister of a Brockton, Massa-chusetts church was arrested on January 4, 1973 while making an early morning phone call at the Newton Centre train station. Davis was also a graduate student at Newton Theological School, the nation's first graduate institution and the oldest seminary school. Davis was returning to the campus when, according to court documents, he refused to identify himself to a police officer, who then called reinforcements of two additional officers. When the minister reached into his pocket to get a cigarette, the arresting officer drew his revolver, pointed it at Davis, patted him down, handcuffed him and took him to police headquarters in a police ambulance. When it became obvious that Davis was not a robber or derelict, he was asked to sign a waiver in order to be released — he refused.

The black community was incensed at the arrest. Led by the minister of Myrtle Baptist Church, members of the church and other Newton black citizens scattered throughout the city galvanized their forces and met with city and police officials. We wanted to know why this incident occurred and we wanted to prevent further actions of this nature. Newton had long prided itself on good relations across racial lines and this arrest caused great consternation in the community. We were an organization of fifty-nine and I was a member of the organization's planning committee. Task forces in human relations, education, economic development and legal procedures were established.

On February 22, 1973, Davis' trial resulted in a "no finding" by Judge Franklin Flaschner. Davis subsequently filed a complaint which led to an official inquiry. The three-hour-long hearing, officiated by Chief William Quinn of the police department, determined that the arresting officer did nothing wrong. Neither Davis nor his attorney were notified or invited to attend — the Newton *Graphic* reported on the inquiry on May 24, 1973.

After the Davis incident, BCON continued its activities within the community. The organization sponsored art fairs, dinners, dances, educational and musical programs.

Chapter Nine: Young Gifted and Black

We also kept citizens aware of civil rights issues confronting the Newton community.

We learned that what made the black citizens of Newton alike was more powerful than the minor things that made us different from each other. This black seminarian exemplified the best in us all. He represented the religious commitment of the first black citizens of Newton who moved away from all that they knew in order to worship as they wished. He pursued that higher calling through higher education— something the new black citizens of Newton valued and were committed to obtaining for themselves and their children.

On a personal level, all that I had learned from Thede, Meme, Harlem, 409, the Modern School through to Mount Holyoke was about to be put to good use, and the overt and entrenched racism I encountered in buying a home provided the spark for my activism. The Civil Rights Movement was in full throttle at this point and I was now in a position and eager to contribute to the discourse and turbulence on behalf of my race.

Chapter Ten: Raising the Stakes/Working Activism

(1961 – Present)

Joining the Fair Housing and Equal Rights Committee in 1961 introduced me to the political workings of Newton, and the education subcommittee supported my goal of changing curriculum to reflect the African American presence as positive contributors to the history of the nation. Integrated texts were coming onto the market but social science texts still represented African Americans in one-dimensional roles—usually as slaves. To drive home the point further, The Newton Fair

Deeper Roots

Housing and Equal Rights Committee sponsored a public lecture where Dr. Kenneth Clark discussed "The Doll Study." The study and the work of African American psychologists Dr. Kenneth Clark and Dr. Mamie Clark contributed to the United States Supreme Court's ruling in *Brown v. Board of Education* that determined de jure racial segregation in public schools was unconstitutional.

In the study, children between the ages of three and seven were shown identical plastic dolls—identical except for their color. After determining that almost all of the children were able to identify the race of the dolls, they were asked a series of questions to determine their racial perception and preference using the dolls as a reference. The questions included which dolls would they like to play with, which dolls were nice, which ones looked good and which ones had a nice color. The majority of the children attributed positive characteristics to the white dolls. The children were then given outline drawings of dolls and asked to color them the same color as themselves. Many of the children, including those with dark complexions, colored the drawings in white or yellow.

The study highlighted an underlying sentiment of self-hatred among black children, especially those who attended segregated schools—schools that were ultimately proven not equal. Apparently, the negative representations found in school texts not only affected the perspective of non-blacks but instilled a negative self-image in black children as well. And those that attended segregated schools were impacted by school texts *and* where they attended school (de facto segregation). I was keenly aware that my children would be attending Newton schools so it was imperative that I advocate for significant change in curriculum and training (as a start).

Chapter Ten: Raising the Stakes

To discuss our concerns, our subcommittee met with the Superintendent of Schools, Dr. Charles Brown. He listened and responded by appointing an elementary school principal to a newly-created administrative position to review books and suggest appropriate materials for classroom use from kindergarten through grade six. I advised Dr. Brown's appointee and subsequently recommended an African American educator who was hired to fill the position.

On the national front, schools were being closed to avoid desegregation. In Prince Edward County, Virginia, African American parents had to devise methods of educating their children without public funding. "Freedom Schools" were held in local churches and staffed by African American teachers who were no longer employed by the County (since the public schools had been closed). These instructors received modest stipends raised from voluntary contributions and church collections. Unfortunately, efforts to provide adequate education under the existing conditions were futile. Through the American Friends Service Committee, Newton families hosted African American children from Prince Edward County in order for them to continue their education.

However, our city of Boston soon became the focus of national attention. Ruth Batson, as Chairperson of the NAACP's Boston Education Committee presented a list of demands to Boston's School Committee. The most important of those demands included: admission of de facto segregation, rectification of said segregation, replacement of inferior neighborhood school buildings and the updating of instructional materials.

There was no response to those demands, and on June 18, 1963 the Massachusetts Freedom Movement

Deeper Roots

called for a one-day boycott of Boston's public schools. Despite Attorney General Brooke's ruling that the *Boston School Dayout* boycott was illegal, 3,000 black students failed to attend public school classes. Organizers then called for another one-day boycott, this time with increased suburban involvement. *Boston School Stay-Out for Freedom* occurred during the public school vacation on February 26, 1964. Churches and community centers reminiscent of those set up in Prince Edward County were comprised of volunteers, including Hubey and I, who organized buses that carried students to freedom schools where African American history and current events were discussed.

Those freedom schools became the model for the Newton/Roxbury Freedom School that I co-founded (with Lillian Ambrosino and Mary Ellen Williams) and administered in 1964. The program began as an after-school program where every month 210 elementary and middle school children of different races came together at alternate sites—Eliot Church in Newton and the Roxbury Neighborhood House in Boston. Field trips, films, classes, guest speakers (including then-Attorney General Edward Brooke) and a lending library of books by and about African Americans comprised the curriculum. Teachers meticulously planned each session which was then followed by a dinner prepared by the parents. Our freedom school was a labor of love and a commitment to the children who were not yet being adequately served by Boston's public school system. The Newton/Roxbury Freedom School operated for two years while we hoped that our concerns would be addressed by the Boston School Committee, but things did not look good.

During those two years (in August of 1965), Governor John A. Volpe proposed the Massachusetts Racial

Chapter Ten: Raising the Stakes

Imbalance Act, which called for the Massachusetts State Board of Education to prohibit racially imbalanced schools or risk losing state educational funding. Moreover, the Act called for local school committees to formulate plans to desegregate those schools where de facto segregation existed. Boston's School Committee challenged the Act in the Massachusetts Supreme Judicial Court and the Court ruled against the School Committee. Although we won in court, protesting in the streets resulted and the substandard education of our children still existed. Hubey and I had three children now, Karen, Lauren and Harlan, and very little had changed in terms of the educational process.

The following September of 1965 *Operation Exodus*, led by Ellen Jackson and Elizabeth Johnson (parents of black children), began a system using taxicabs and private cars to transport 400 students from overcrowded Roxbury schools to available seats in other Boston schools. Fundraising drives to cover the costs lead to the further commitment and the involvement of suburban communities.

In November 1965, the Massachusetts Federation of Fair Housing and Equal Rights held a meeting with suburban school superintendents from more than a dozen communities to discuss their involvement in the Boston public school crisis. Less than ten days later, Leon Trilling, President of the Brookline School Committee, met with suburban school officials, concerned citizens and Chairpersons Paul Parks and Ruth Batson of the NAACP's Education Committee, to develop a plan to transport black students to suburban schools.

Trilling then called together other school superintendents and school committee members (from Brookline, Newton, Lexington, Braintree and Wellesley),

Deeper Roots

a member of the State Department of Education, the League of Women Voters' president, and the Fair Housing and Equal Rights Committee representatives. These series of meetings resulted in the Metropolitan Council for Educational Opportunity (METCO). As required by Massachusetts' Racial Imbalance Act, METCO addressed the de facto segregation that existed in the school districts involved in the meetings. The federal government, under Title III of the Equal Educational Opportunity Act, had also proposed funding for innovative programs that addressed this issue. In December 1965, an extension of the Racial Imbalance Act was filed which would enable students to attend schools outside of their city of residence. That extension was approved.

In January of 1966, Dr. Brown submitted the METCO proposal to the U. S. Office of Education; the notice of approval was received in June 1966. Newton waived tuition and charged only the out-of-pocket costs for books and supplies (about thirty-two dollars per student for fifty children who would attend seven elementary schools in Newton) that would be paid for by the U.S. Office of Education. This made it possible for more students to participate.

During the summers of 1965 and 1966, activists and community leaders formed summer programs in more than twenty communities which brought Boston and suburban children together for cooperative summer camps. This opened up relationships between city and suburban residents, parents and students—relationships that were necessary for the success for the larger METCO program. Finally, the "METCO Bill" passed into law on August 13, 1966 making it possible for 220 students from Boston to attend schools in seven suburban school

Chapter Ten: Raising the Stakes

systems in September. Each School Committee had to vote to participate each year, with the intent to allow the METCO student to complete high school in that school system.

I was elected to the METCO Board of Directors as a community representative with responsibility to organize a base of support for the concept in Newton. These developments also fit right into the focus of my studies at Simmons College where I was working on my master's in Urban Education. The mandate was: to provide an opportunity for an integrated quality education to black students from racially imbalanced schools in Boston, to provide a "new learning experience" and diverse cultural experience to *all* the students of Newton, and to create and foster communication between urban and suburban parents and residents in the Metropolitan Boston area.

However, community leaders and politicians still questioned the program's agenda. Although they understood how the program would benefit the public school students of Boston, they wondered how it would benefit the suburban communities in addition to providing diversity (something they would not be tested on). They wanted to know about the children being bused in and how they were selected. I think most importantly they wanted to know how the suburban communities would be financially impacted: who would pay for busing, who would pay educational expenses and what financial arrangements and contingencies were being made for these new students.

We answered their questions: METCO students represented a cross-section of the black community and the program (not the suburban school) would pay for student costs. There was much to do and a great many folks we had to speak with since the success of the program relied on the grassroots support of parents, school principals and the community residents.

I also chaired a community committee that met with school personnel and Ruth Batson, who was responsible for selecting students for the program. During the summer months prior to the students' arrival at school principals, teachers, school administrators and volunteers met to plan an orientation program for teachers of METCO students. We also had to select host families who served as a home away from home for the children. When the program began in Newton, elementary school children ate lunch at home three days a week and school was dismissed at 1pm on Tuesdays and Thursdays. The METCO students needed a place to each lunch and a place to stay in order to participate in after-school activities—host families would serve that purpose. The lines of communication were kept open between communities, school administrators, psychologists, social workers, teachers, parents and host families through meetings, dinners, concerts, and training and information sessions.

During my years with METCO as a community representative and a director, my experience in teaching in majority-white schools and my children's experience in the majority-white Newton schools gave me a useful and unique perspective. I also brought to the table all of my educational experiences from the Modern School right through to Mount Holyoke—experiences both good and bad—but experiences I had learned from nevertheless. For example, careful planning and placement of students in a receptive environment—where students of color were never placed in a classroom without another student of color—was very important. I wrote guidelines

Chapter Ten: Raising the Stakes

and developed programs for staff training and curriculum which reflected the new diversity in the schools.

In 1968 the Massachusetts Department of Education assumed responsibility for METCO. The program was no longer considered "innovative" by the federal government and more communities could be involved. Dr. Charles Brown asked me to assume directorship for the Newton program as a paid employee of the school system and I continued to serve on the METCO Executive Committee. One of my first requests to the Committee was to waive tuition (as had been done in the past) and to use the money from the State to staff vital positions that had been performed on a voluntary basis up until then. The request was approved and I hired a social worker, psychologist, tutor and program director. How bittersweet that the program came up for its annual approval by the Newton School Committee the week of Dr. Martin Luther King's assassination.

During my years directing Newton's METCO, the program grew from fifty students to 350 students, the number of schools increased from seven to twenty-seven and the African American staff rose from one to ten. The hallmarks of my tenure included ongoing city-wide teacher training in the black experience, involvement of METCO parents and Newton teachers in shared programs held in Roxbury and Newton, reciprocal home visits of METCO students with their suburban counterparts and inclusion of black history in the Newton school curriculum. Originally conceived as a stopgap measure, today the Newton METCO program has the largest number of participants.

Each day, 3,500 Boston students (kindergarten to grade 12) board buses to attend school at 415 sites in Massachusetts. Membership in the program is

Deeper Roots

challenging but well worth the effort. For example, parent participation is mandatory—they must attend at least four of six parent council meetings and parents and students have to be prepared each day for the commute. The waiting list for the program is long, with registration occurring before a prospective student's first birthday. However, the program continues to be energetic, relevant and held in high regard. Ninety-three percent of METCO students graduate on time versus 81.5% statewide and 61% in Boston, and nine out of ten METCO students go on to higher education compared to two-thirds of Boston public school students. The cost per student is $4,900 versus over $12,000 for a traditional Boston public school education—a value on all fronts over forty-five years after its inception. However, we lived under the constant pressure of budget cuts even when our program proved to be a success and expanded as a result of that success.

Ten years into METCO's coordinated and voluntary efforts to bus Boston children to suburban schools, Boston's school system *finally* became legally bound to desegregate *within* its own school system—something detractors termed, "forced busing." The idea of busing students now took on a negative connotation. Legal opposition to busing (as opposed to desegregation) was continually mounted until the 1976 United States Court of Appeals ruling that upheld the integration order of the lower court and accused elected officials of "resistance, defiance and delay" in the desegregating the public schools of Boston. Although there were other destabilizing social issues, the court-ordered busing appeared to blow the lid off of the simmering caldron that was Boston in the 70s. Buses carrying students to school were pelted with rocks and state troopers in riot gear stood sentry in front of school buildings. However,

Chapter Ten: Raising the Stakes

no METCO buses ever came under attack, probably because we were taking the children outside of the Boston system (as opposed to carrying them to schools within the system that were predominately white). Apparently, the thugs who attacked the buses carrying the children knew which buses to target, because all of the buses were alike with the exception of the signage on the side identifying the private operator of the buses. The rioters had no problem attacking children though—children who were overwhelmingly black. That seemed to me, and to others, to be more about race than about busing as their legal representatives argued in court. The definition and intention of busing was turned upside down in an effort to enforce a racist system.

The empirical evidence continues to dispute the legal arguments against busing while the antidotal evidence continues to be uplifting. In Anand Vaishnav's book review of Susan E. Eaton's *The Other Boston Busing Story* (Yale University Press), the most powerful sections of the book are the interviews with METCO students. Some students felt that they had betrayed the students they left behind in order to attend better schools and they were often accused of "acting white" in their community. However, METCO students also felt that they learned to be comfortable around whites—a skill that benefited them once they entered college or began working. I agree with the conclusions of the book. Former METCO students have said the same things to me. Over forty years since those first buses carrying our precious children drove toward a better education.

I still encounter those first METCO students. At the annual events they tell me about their lives now and how the program undoubtedly improved their life. In some instances, there are second- and third-generation METCO students—how gratifying and yet how sad. It is gratifying because of the spectacular results of the program; sad because there is still a need for the program.

I have always felt that it is the exposure to those unlike ourselves and experiences outside our comfort zone have the most positive impact and provide for the most intellectual and spiritual growth. Further, I still believe that busing is one way to accomplish this kind of affirmative growth. I was now the mother of eight children. Lisa, Hamilton, Cheryl and Tanya were born during my years with METCO and I felt more invested than ever in my quest for a quality education for all children.

However, after ten years of administering Newton's METCO program I decided to step down because of reduced funding from the state and loss of a critical base of support from the school committee. But I wasn't about to turn my back on all that I had been committed to all these years. As usual, I had a plan.

Two hundred people gathered at the Knights of Columbus Hall to honor my years of leadership of the Newton METCO Program. School administrators, staff, teachers, some members of the School Committee, Newton parents and Newton METCO parents were seated at the banquet tables listening to tributes from representatives of the Governor of Massachusetts, Mayor of Newton and leaders of civic groups in the city.

A scrapbook of pictures and notes from the children of the Newton Schools had been presented to me, along with a large crayon drawing of the yellow bus marked "METCO" symbolic of the buses that brought 300 children back and forth from Boston each day. Barbara Harrell, chairperson of the Newton METCO Parents

Chapter Ten: Raising the Stakes

Organization, looking elegant with a rose and white silk turban wrapped tightly around her head, addressed me:

> *An atmosphere clock we give to you, Kathy.*
> *...People stand around and watch it in amazement, with curiosity. What makes it go? People stand around you, watch you in amazement, with curiosity, with wonder... What makes her go? Stable consistent, ticking away, touching so many lives. The hands of the clock move, we are unaware of time passing by. Kathy Jones whose time has been available for all of the children now moves on. We have found in you some of the very same qualities as you will find in this clock: integrity, dependability consistency.*

I got up from my seat and walked to the podium to thank all of the people, including my mother, who had come out on that cold and icy November evening in 1976. I was awed by the spirit of love and appreciation that enveloped me. However, the end of my speech caught the audience by surprise:

> *Because I am concerned about what is happening to the Newton schools and to the children who attend those schools, because I am concerned about the present atmosphere of hostility and distrust that exists between the school committee and the school administration and because I care deeply about the future course that the city of Newton will take, I have decided to run for election to the Newton School Committee. As a taxpayer and a parent of eight children, seven of whom attend the*

Deeper Roots

*Newton Schools and as a black citizen, I want
to chart new directions to provide the leadership in education that the city of Newton has
been noted for.*

A burst of applause resounded from the audience.

Things were about to get complicated. I would now
be running for elected office in addition to caring for my
husband and eight children, working in Cambridge as an
elementary staff advisor and beginning my Ed.D. in
Administration and School Policy at Harvard University.

A few weeks later at a meeting in our living room *The
Committee to Elect Kathy Jones to the Newton School
Committee* convened. I opened the session commenting to
the sixteen people, friends and coworkers gathered
around the coffee table. "I want to encourage participation in this process with all of the constituents city-wide.
I can communicate information to lay people without the
jargon usually associated with educators. I know the
schools as a parent and as a school administrator."

Hubey, who had recently been appointed Dean of
Boston University School of Social Work, was the chairperson of the campaign committee and launched the
discussion:

> *Kathy, as the first African American to run for
> this position in a city with a ninety-nine per-
> cent white population, has a tough image to
> counteract. Sure she's an educator, and has
> put in ten years in school administration here
> in Newton, but she's identified with the
> METCO Program. For a decade she's brought
> black students to suburban schools, beginning
> with fifty students that first year. Even though*

Chapter Ten: Raising the Stakes

she has a city-wide base in the community since the program is now in most of the schools, people think that METCO is all that she knows how to do. We have to plan a strategy to change this way of thinking.

We had decided that I would run for election on the "liberal" *Concern* slate against my four male opponents. The Civil Rights and Women's Movements were in full swing and the year-long election campaign electrified the city. I attended 200 fundraiser "coffees" sponsored on my behalf in the homes of Newton residents. I had to campaign harder than other candidates to establish my credibility, despite the fact that I was the sole possessor of a master's degree in education and had twelve years of varied experience in education. We knew it would be a close race.

After a preliminary election (where three of my opponents had been eliminated) and much campaigning, a year later the results were finally in. I had defeated my conservative opponent by a narrow margin. We made history that night. The headlines of the Newton *Times* reported, *Jones Wins Election to the Newton School Committee*. Now *that* was electrifying.

In January of 1978 I assumed my duties as the first African American elected to the Committee. I was elected a total of four times for a maximum of eight consecutive years (1978-1986) as allowed by Newton statute. (We had to wait until November 2011 for the second African American to be elected to the School Committee, running unopposed.)

During my tenure, we provided the means by which girls could have equal access in physical education and varsity teams in accordance with Title IX, and for special

Deeper Roots

education students to be mainstreamed into regular classes when feasible (Special Chapter 766). Mothers were also returning to work in increasing numbers so we arranged for elementary grade students to eat lunch in school on Tuesdays and Thursdays and afterschool programs cared for children until parents returned home from work. Our schools also began offering daycare for preschool children when space was available; and sign language offered at the high school level made communication with deaf students easier.

The School Committee also became more transparent and the public could now participate in the decision-making process regarding school matters. The Massachusetts Open Meeting Law prevented the School Committee from discussing or voting on most issues behind closed doors. Parents were now involved in the hiring of school principals and public hearings were held for the selection of school superintendents. This new law prevented the backroom handshake deals among politicos that often did not serve those most in need.

I am particularly proud of the fact that African Americans employed within the school system increased from less than one percent to ten percent, based on a policy which I convinced the School Committee to adopt—a policy that increased the number of African Americans in administration and teaching positions to more accurately reflect the percentage of the population.

However, I was not always successful in my goal to increase the presence of African Americans in decision-making positions within the system. For example, I was a member of the search committee which selected seven candidates for school superintendent. The candidates were questioned extensively at open school committee meetings. The best qualified candidate was an African

Chapter Ten: Raising the Stakes

American from Shaker Heights, Ohio and the other finalist oversaw the small school system in Pelham, New York. The eight-member committee (in a closed meeting) had to decide between the two candidates, but we were split. Tensions rose in our meeting which lasted well into the night. The Mayor, an ex officio of the Committee who could have been the tie-breaker, refused to vote. I was appalled and disappointed that the city of Newton was not prepared to select an African American as Superintendent of School even though he was the better-qualified candidate. You can't win them all but you have to keep trying.

◆ ◆ ◆ ◆ ◆

Despite all the pressures and responsibilities of modern-day life, it is important to turn around and reach out because you must share what you have learned so far. That is a part of activism—to lead and then teach. Some of the references below may appear dated; however, the messages are not.

On February 14, 1974, shortly after I had become the second African American elected by the alumnae to Mount Holyoke's predominantly male Board of Trustees, I addressed the senior class. The audience listened to my talk from rows of attached brown wooden slatted chairs with seats that made a loud bang when raised or lowered. I described then how individual and institutional growth and change occur independently and yet are interrelated. The college and my life had changed since my graduation, and these soon-to-be alumnae would change too as individuals. I reminded the seniors that Mount Holyoke, as the first women's college in the

Deeper Roots

country, began as a radical institution and our greatest responsibility is to challenge it to enhance its capacity for self-renewal.

I shared my enthusiasm for bearing and raising children as fascinating, rewarding and creative work and warned about the current trend among "liberated" women that deemphasizes and negates this important dimension of womanhood. I suggested that raising children to be cognizant of their responsibility as citizens and knowledgeable of their heritage and culture can change the future. Raising a family, I also suggested, is a political act.

The Civil Rights Movement in the 1960s awakened me to the deep and permeating dimensions of institutional racism which is such an integral part of the fabric of this nation. My suggestion to the senior class to challenge institutions in order for them to continue their evolution was more than that. I would take my own advice and challenge Mount Holyoke.

The Board of Trustees had a Student Affairs subcommittee and had recently formed a Social Responsibility subcommittee regarding investment policy. I served on both subcommittees. My tenure as a trustee began during the years of absolute rule by the white minority apartheid government in South Africa. The government enforced strict separation of races, often by violent removal of blacks and "coloreds" to distant townships where they were relegated to menial and dangerous work at meager pay. I urged the Mount Holyoke Board to divest the portfolio of companies doing business in South Africa as many other colleges in the country were doing by adopting the Sullivan Principles.

In 1971, Dr. Sullivan became the first African American appointed to the Board of Directors of General

Chapter Ten: Raising the Stakes

Motors (one of the largest employers of blacks in South Africa) and he used his position to weaken apartheid in South Africa. The principles he developed was essentially a code of conduct for human rights and equal opportunity for companies operating in South Africa. These principles are:

1. Non-segregation of the races in all eating, comfort, and work facilities.
2. Equal and fair employment practices for all employees.
3. Equal pay for all employees doing equal or comparable work for the same period of time.
4. Initiation of and development of training programs that will prepare, in substantial numbers, blacks and other nonwhites for supervisory, administrative, clerical, and technical jobs.
5. Increasing the number of blacks and other nonwhites in management and supervisory positions.
6. Improving the quality of life for blacks and other nonwhites outside the work environment in such areas as housing, transportation, school, recreation, and health facilities.
7. Working to eliminate laws and customs that impede social, economic, and political justice. *(added in 1984)*

In 1999, United Nations Secretary General Kofi Annan would adopt these principles and bring them before the United Nations. Randall Robinson, the African American founder/director of TransAfrica, also urged economic boycott of South Africa by the international community

241

Deeper Roots

and I joined many others in picketing the Treasury Department Building in Washington D.C..

I also suspended my annual financial contribution to the college that I loved so much. Mount Holyoke did not divest itself of South African holdings until eight years later. My letter published in the *Mount Holyoke Quarterly* stated my position:

> *I wish to congratulate the board of trustees for the decision to terminate investments in companies conducting business in South Africa. As an alumna trustee from 1973 to 1978, I represented a minority perspective (in more ways than one) on this matter.*
>
> *I am pleased to renew my annual financial contribution to the College which I suspended during these years as the institution struggled with the divestment issue. I am pleased also to have a renewed sense of pride in the integrity of Mount Holyoke.*

While on campus for Trustee meetings I also met with African American students to learn of their concerns. In one of these sessions, senior Beverly Scipio described her plan to institute a Black Alumnae Conference. I enthusiastically endorsed this idea which has since become a college tradition. I knew that we could learn a great deal from the many generations of black women who had gone to Mount Holyoke. The first (openly) colored graduate was Hortense Parker, a member of the class of 1873. One and one hundred years later, the first Black Alumnae Conference was held under Beverly's leadership, and women from the earlier classes

242

Chapter Ten: Raising the Stakes

were drawn back to the campus. Frances Williams of '17, Mable Smythe of '37 and Laura Spencer of '36 all came to share their hopes and dreams at Mount Holyoke and recounted their ground breaking careers as educators, government administrators, and social workers.

In the keynote speech that I gave at the Black Alumnae Conference two decades later in October 1994 I described the flickering light from the candles in our hands which illuminated many shades of faces. "We've come a long way, baby," I thought to myself as I looked around the room. I recognized three past and present members of the Board of Trustees and the president of the Alumnae Association among the 150 women of color attending the Black Alumnae Conference. We walked single file into the dining room in a spirit of oneness chanting "I remember" as we took our places around the table for dinner. The names of 677 alumnae identified as African American were called out. Half of us—more than our white counterparts—had gone on to earn advanced degrees. Founder Mary Lyon did not have us in mind when she established her female seminary, but we made Mount Holyoke our own when Hortense graduated in 1883.

I continue to attend these conferences to share my experience and to learn from the younger women. At a recent conference, an undergraduate noted the year ('57) on my name tag. She said with wide-eyed astonishment, "you graduated from here before my parents were born." I could have taken that one of two ways; I decided to take it as a compliment.

The ivory tower has changed significantly over the last few decades for women of color who venture into it to be taught or to teach. On a snowy blustery day in Cambridge, Massachusetts, hundreds of women college

Deeper Roots

professors from across the country convened in 1994 at Massachusetts Institute of Technology's Kresge Auditorium. The topic of the conference, "Black Women in the Academy: Defending our Name: 1894-1994" was coordinated by M.I.T. black faculty/administrators.

The organizers wanted to provide a public forum for black women academics to address research issues and their acceptance (even survival) in the academy. The 80s and 90s in America was a time of challenge for women of color following Anita Hill's 1991 damaging testimony in the Congressional hearings regarding the appointment of Thurgood Marshall's successor to the United States Supreme Court. Clarence Thomas would be confirmed amid controversy as the second African American to hold that position (the first being Judge Marshall, my former neighbor in 409 Edgecombe Avenue).

In 1993 Lani Guinier, a legal scholar, had been withdrawn from consideration as the head of the Civil Rights Division of the Justice Department by President Clinton. Guinier, who became the first woman of color to become a tenured professor at Harvard Law School, was among the keynote speakers. Johnetta Cole, former President of Spelman College (a black women's college in Atlanta), and Angela Davis, scholar, author and former member of the Black Panthers were also keynote speakers. These more experienced academicians offered a healing balm to an enthusiastic audience.

The conference also had a historic component. One hundred years earlier, black women had gathered together in Boston to defend the reputation of black women (in general) and Ida B. Wells (in particular) in the press. A journalist, abolitionist and newspaper editor, Wells had been targeted for her documentation of southern lynchings. Three of my daughters joined me for one of

244

Chapter Ten: Raising the Stakes

the most important series of meetings and panels I have ever attended.

Many junior faculty members attending this conference thought that their credentials would put them on an even footing with their white colleagues. But they were heaped with responsibility for committee work regarding minority affairs and often became distracted from the research and publication necessary to gain and secure positions on the tenure track. In addition, this Lost/Found generation was not prepared for the racial prejudice that their senior counterparts previously experienced and, unlike their senior counterparts, they were often isolated from the support of black communities and institutions. It was our responsibility, as more experienced academics, to support and mentor these new colleagues.

One of the largest African American Mount Holyoke alumnae gatherings occurred in October 2002. Dr. Gloria Johnson Powell (a former fellow board trustee) attended the reunion where poet and social critic, Sonia Sanchez gave the keynote address. We were joined by Gloria's granddaughter, Camilla, a junior at Newton North High School who was making her first visit to Mount Holyoke. Camilla liked the college and the young alumnae that she met there so much that she applied for admission. In February 2004 Gloria telephoned me from Wisconsin. "Camilla is so excited. She just called me and guess what... your daughter Renee was her alumnae interviewer." Camilla proudly informed Renee that her grandmother graduated from Mount Holyoke. Renee replied, "Isn't that a coincidence, so did my mother." Renee knew Gloria and never imagined that Gloria's granddaughter would be old enough to be applying to college. Gloria had even attended Renee's wedding and held a baby shower at her home when Renee and

245

Deeper Roots

Michael were expecting their first child. I was astounded. Renee finally figured out that Camilla's grandmother was my old friend. These traditions and friendships are now stretching over generations.

In the spring of 2007, months before our fiftieth reunion on graduation weekend, my classmate, Carolyn Jobes Kiradjieff asked me to write about my college experiences as the only black person in our class and I was happy to comply with her request. Carolyn's idea was to present a capsule filled with our class memorabilia to the class of 2007 when the alumnae of all classes gather to honor the graduating class and welcome them to the Alumnae Association. This capsule, kept at the college library, will be opened in 2057 when the class of 2007 returns for their fiftieth reunion. The capsule contains our class ring, yearbook, freshman handbook, Junior Show Program, Junior Class jacket along with my chapter and the playbill from my play, *409 Edgecombe Avenue: The House on Sugar Hill*. I hope that my grandchildren will attend this reopening ceremony on the campus.

In 2000 I was involved in forming an African American women's book club, *Sistahs of the Book*, which meets monthly at members' homes to discuss our readings and to support our shared interests and activities. We are an intergenerational group of avid readers ranging in age from the 30s to 70s. What makes this group so special to me is that we enjoy each other's company, share our challenges and victories and care deeply for each other. Our readings cover a wide range of fiction, poetry, history and science fiction, written mostly (but not exclusively) by women of color. My area of knowledge has expanded immeasurably, especially when the authors come to discuss their work with us.

246

Chapter Ten: Raising the Stakes

We are the keepers of the dream, the prophets
of the future and the instruments of change.

Chapter Eleven: Around the

World in Ninety Days

Hubey's request for a semester sabbatical from the deanship of Boston University School of Social Work was warmly granted by President John Silber. Hubey had been working nonstop for a number of years, I was getting ready to embrace the next chapter of my life and the first set of our children had left the nest—it was time for a change of pace. Hubey and I always believed that real knowledge was found outside one's immediate existence and there was no better way to learn that than through travel. Beginning in September 1984, we would use this time for international travel with our children who were at home: fifteen-year-old

Deeper Roots

Hamilton, thirteen-year-old Cheryl and ten-year-old Tanya. We would be traveling without our older children. Karen was living in New York with my mother, Lauren was living and working in Boston and Harlan, Renee and Lisa were enrolled in college. "But who will be my parents when you are away?" Lisa had asked a profound question. She was entering her freshmen year at Yale right before our departure. "Who would you like to take our place?" I asked. Without hesitation she replied, "Aunt Russelle." Hubey's youngest sister lived in Westport, Connecticut with her family, not far from Yale's New Haven campus. Willard and Vivian Johnson, our longstanding family friends who were often judges at the family's annual Black History Contest signed on to be surrogate parents for our Boston area-based children, Harlen and Lauren.

During our travels, Hubey would explore social policy and programs in Scandinavian countries and Europe and I would relinquish my Newton School Committee responsibilities to visit schools in Europe and Kenya in order to meet with policy-making counterparts and teachers in those countries.

I would also be our children's tutor, monitoring their three months of school work while we were abroad. Their teachers developed creative assignments, in part related to the opportunities afforded by our travels and daily events were recorded in a journal. Cheryl was asked to write to her class each week to share her experiences. She would visit and write about government sessions in the capital cities of London, Stockholm, Copenhagen, Paris, Rome, Brussels, Cairo, Athens, Nairobi and Dar es Salaam and take photographs of the government buildings. She was also asked to interview citizens of each country about their civic participation

Chapter Eleven: Around the World in 90 Days

and viewpoints. For her general science course, Cheryl collected rock specimens from the Rift Valley in Kenya and the glacial rocks of Sweden.

My travel agent and I arranged for our family to begin our travels in London where we would meet Tony, my cousin Methlin's son. From London we would travel to Stockholm, Copenhagen, Amsterdam and Brussels and numerous cities in France, Italy, Greece, Tunisia, Egypt, Tanzania and Kenya. In the final stages of preparation for our adventure I discovered the travel guide, *Let's Go Europe* which listed Servas International, an organization founded after World War II to aid travelers and promote peace. Servas arranges for people (called hosts) throughout the world to share their home, free-of-charge, for two (or more) nights with traveling guest members. I found that these interactions (often over the dinner table) formed permanent international friendships. What a wonderful experience for our family to visit homes and get to know people of different nationalities and cultures.

I wrote for applications to Servas' New York office (you can now apply directly and more conveniently online). I was approved for membership and supplied with lists of hosts in the various countries that we were planning to visit. I wrote my letters of introduction to the coordinator of Servas in each prospective city indicating our interest in education and social work. After completing a series of mandatory inoculations, we packed twenty-three bags with clothing suitable for the cold climate of Denmark and the warmth of Kenya. Each of the children would be responsible for his or her bags which also contained their school books and one bag contained medications and gifts for the people we would meet during our travels. Hubey was in charge of transport of luggage from place to place via train, boat or plane. "What will you do about laundry?" my mother-in-law asked. That was a challenge that I had not anticipated.

Nevertheless, undaunted our troupe boarded British Airways from Kennedy Airport for an overnight flight to London. When we arrived the next morning Tanya could not find one of her shoes. We searched the plane but the shoe was never retrieved. That was how we began our journey—minus one shoe. We were a sleepy crew when we arrived at the low-priced boarding house that I had reserved only to discover that because of the change in time zones and my miscalculation the accommodations would not be available until later that afternoon. We left our luggage at the boarding house and started out a bit bleary-eyed to explore the city.

After a few days in the limited boarding house space, we rented lodgings from the London School of Economics. These furnished faculty apartments were not occupied since classes were not yet in session. London would be a two-week stay and this was just the kind of setting to make us feel at home—complete with a kitchen, rooms with desks and ample space for a family of five. My cousin Tony, his partner Carol and her two sons were our first guests. They invited us to their place in London for dinner and Carol delighted in showing us the large platter that my mother had given her when she traveled to New York to meet Tony's mom, Methlin and my mother. We left their home with gifts—a leather folder for travel documents and a laminated tote bag from Harrods Department Store.

Nuey, my friend from high school and college, was also living in London at the time and we spent a wonderful afternoon with her and her husband strolling through the city. We visited many typical tourist sites and rode the double-decker sightseeing bus. I was impressed by the clean efficient tube (subway) which made it easy to travel around the city. We went to see the changing of the guard at Buckingham Palace, Big Ben and the Westminster Abbey. I thought of my mother, who would have loved to sip tea at one of the lovely hotels. For obvious reasons, there would be no pub visits for a pint this time around. Our children got to see Lena Horne perform her hit show, *The Lady and Her Music,* which Hubey and I had seen in New York.

When the time came for us to head to Stockholm, Tony drove us to Heathrow Airport. During the ride, we received our real education in British civics—away from the first-rate marketing efforts of the British tourism industry. Tony explained that his son had been picked up and arrested by the police operating under the 'sus' law that allowed them to stop someone based on 'sus' (short for suspicion) that they might be *intending* to commit a crime. The police were exempt from the Race Relations Act and the targets of the stops and searches were overwhelmingly young black males. Tensions between white Britons, British authorities and Afro-Caribbean Britons had come to a boiling point. Prime Minister Margaret Thatcher's government sought to exclude former colonial subjects (and their descendants) from British citizenship by requiring that a grandfather be born in England. During the early 1980s Brixton (the area in London where the majority of black Londoners lived) had experienced an unemployment rate of fifty percent which lead to an increased crime rate there. Police frequently flooded the community and tensions escalated even further. As a result of these social stressors, Britain experienced the worst race riots in its history and the 'sus' law was done away with. I suddenly felt the damp and chill of the

Deeper Roots

British weather. Race relations in England continue to be unstable. In August of 2011, riots broke out in numerous cities over the police shooting of a local resident.

We flew to Stockholm and lodged in a hostel overlooking the Baltic seaport where "no niggers" graffiti was scribbled on the walls. Now an international traveler, the first thing that Hamilton did when we settled into the hostel was to figure out how the light switches worked, how the toilets flushed and how the street lights functioned so we could cross the streets. In fact, all of our children turned out to be enthusiastic travelers. Theodore Katz, a social worker and teacher, showed us the ropes. He had emigrated from Germany escaping Hitler, but he found prejudice against Jews in Sweden as well. We discovered the International Center with laundry and cooking facilities; it's also a place where the children learn to cook and sew, create pottery, play Ping-Pong and pool, etc. This state-run facility allowed people to stay for six months while they sought employment. Our children played with other children (despite the inability to speak the language) and Hamilton played chess with Mr. Katz. Our children loved the International Center. We took them to visit the Moderna Museet (Museum of Modern Art) and toured the Royal Palace.

I tried to keep part of each morning reserved for helping with homework. We had the most fun dramatizing the prize-winning play, *Raisin in the Sun* by Lorraine Hansberry which Cheryl was assigned. We each took roles written by this young African American woman—roles that addressed conflicts of race, gender, identity and values within a strong matriarchal Negro family living in Chicago in the 1960s. Although we were in Sweden, the universal themes of the play made it

Chapter Eleven: Around the World in 90 Days

topical and relevant—especially with the graffiti at the hostel.

As a social worker and educator, Hubey and I learned about the social problems of living in the northern region of Europe—especially the depression and alcoholism from the long dark winters. We also learned about the social reforms taking place because of Sweden's economic situation.

The second week in Sweden was spent with a young couple on maternity leave with their one-and-a-half-year-old daughter, Sophie. They welcomed us to their four room flat arranged to maximize living space. Our children and Sophie hit it off well and they took good care of the toddler. While living with our hosts, Servas travelers were to vacate the premises during the day, returning to the home for dinner, conversation and sleep. Our hosts extended an invitation for us to stay for a week. We felt very fortunate to have the experience of getting to know people within the intimacy of their home. During our visit, Johan took us to visit his parents' home in the outlying areas. My only frustration was seeing letters in the English alphabet used in configurations that did not spell words in English. Invariably, I would try to make sense of these words when I ventured to the food store with a list to shop. I finally gave up and just tried to find labels that matched the words on my list.

Next it was off to Copenhagen where our host family lived in a commune. Once again, our children and the children in the commune were able to communicate with each other without a common language. Our hosts' parents were both school teachers, who invited me to visit their school and teach some classes for a day. I gladly accepted this exciting challenge. The teachers told me that these junior high students took English, but were not too fluent in the language. On the appointed day I met with the class, careful to speak as slowly and as articulately as possible. I soon discovered that the students were having no difficulty understanding me, much to the amusement of their teachers. Apparently, the students watched a great deal of American television which had trained their ears to our way of speaking. During the class, I mentioned an incident that occurred when Hubey and I and another couple were travelling in the Bahamas. We were driving over a bridge and spotted an unusual array of lights in the sky. We stopped the car and got out to see a spherical shape surrounded by colored lights hanging motionless in the sky. Other cars stopped behind us and all eyes were cast upward for about two minutes. Then as suddenly as it appeared, the object vanished into thin air. My students were astonished. After class my teacher host said, "These students will go home and tell their parents that we had an African American teacher in class today and she told us about seeing an unidentified flying object." The next day the local paper carried a story describing our experience.

During discussions with educators in Stockholm and Copenhagen what became clear was that the teacher unions and school committees were addressing the same issues that the Massachusetts policy makers were facing in 1984 and are still facing in 2012—declining enrollment, school closings and contract negotiations. I guess some things never change, they only evolve.

We used our Eurail passes on the comfortable trains in Europe to get to our next destination, Amsterdam, capital of the Netherlands. Our Servas host had written to me accepting our stay. He unfortunately would be away for the dates of our visit, but would gladly allow us to use his place if only I could assure him that our children would not destroy his apartment.

We got off the train and took the local transit to the appropriate stop, lugging the twenty-three bags in our possession. I soon realized, however, that we would not be able to manage the few blocks to the residence. Luckily some men were working at a construction site and I asked if I could borrow their wheelbarrow for a few minutes to get the bags to our host's apartment. Fortunately for us, they agreed. When we arrived our host took us around to the local shops, showed us where the post office was and left on his way to The Hague for the weekend. We left his place in the same condition as we found it and had a wonderful time getting around Amsterdam on our own.

The Rembrandt Museum, Anne Frank's attic hideaway and the wonderful laundromats were most welcome sights. The public swimming pool with the water slide provided hours of fun for us. The Dutch girls swam topless—a culture shock. When we were traveling on public transportation, I noted the ease of interaction between the recent immigrants of color from former Dutch colonies and the white residents of Amsterdam. The physical space permitted by custom between people of different races is far closer than in similar encounters in the United States.

In Brussels, Belgium our children were enchanted by the lighted area of the Grand Palace, but the most interesting thing to me was the visit to the session of Parliament where issues were debated and translated into Flemish, French and Dutch. How this legislative body can accomplish anything is amazing. Once again, our children were indispensable and quickly figured out the different denominations in the currencies that we had to negotiate in these various countries. The Euro had not come into existence yet, and each nation had its own currency with a different rate of exchange.

Then it was off to France where we stayed in Paris for a few nights with a strange woman with many cats. We ended our visit in that city at the Normandy Hotel, a welcome change in venue from our previous overnights.

In Athens we checked in at an inn where we met other travelers—whom we got to know fairly well during our four-day stay because the inclement weather made it impossible to tour the Mediterranean islands by boat as all of us had planned to do. We were quite fortunate though to meet a woman whose former husband lived in Tanzania, a future stop on our itinerary. She gave us his address and the hotel in Dar es Salaam that her brother owned, the Bahari Beach Hotel outside of the city. Despite the tumultuous activity of the Mediterranean Sea, the weather in Athens did not prevent us from exploring the city, visiting the Parthenon, and touring museums and agoras.

It was on one of these days of sightseeing that Tanya fell while crossing the street and injured her leg. When Hubey took Tanya to the children's hospital for treatment, the doctored examined her, x-rayed her leg and placed it in a cast to heal. "How much do I owe you?" Hubey asked. "There's no charge. Medical services are free here." Our Greek friend also suggested a doctor in Dar es Salaam for Tanya's follow-up treatment.

Our Italian sojourn included Rome, Venice, Florence and Naples where we stayed with our Servas hosts before boarding an overnight ferry for Tunis. There we would stay on the banks of the Mediterranean Sea with a former member of the faculty of the Boston University School of Social Work and his wife and son. Each

Chapter Eleven: Around the World in 90 Days

morning we were awakened by the mullah's call to prayer. From our location we could see the flag fluttering from the offices of the Palestinian Liberation Organization. Tunis would be a place for us to relax after the extensive travel we had just completed. Luckily, our host was proficient in math and was able and willing to work with both Cheryl and Hamilton to get them up to speed with their math assignments. We explored the bazaars, watched the men smoking the water pipes, rode public transportation, but especially enjoyed being with another American family abroad.

"Welcome home brothers and sisters," the travel guide at the Cairo airport called out as we filed through the line from the customs clearance area. "Let me help you to make your stay in Egypt a memorable one by arranging some wonderful tours," he said as we sat down at the table to examine the materials spread out in front of us. It did not take too long to realize that he was going to really "take us for a ride." We declined his offers and hailed a taxi out to the Siag Pyramid Hotel in Giza, a lovely setting many miles away from the frantic and noisy city of Cairo. We awoke the next morning as the rising sun cast this marvelous aura across the nearby pyramids. When we went to the hotel pool, a group of Egyptian children asked my children if they were the Jackson Five. We rode camels by the pyramids and crawled through the narrow passages to view the incredible painted walls that have endured over these many centuries. Tanya read her chapter from the Bible about Moses and the rushes as we stood by the River Nile. We were guided through the Cairo Museum with our Servas host who explained to us the history of the objects that we saw, objects that are part of the permanent collection that never leave the country. At the

Deeper Roots

time in Egypt's history, these streets were safe to walk at night, which was more than I could say for many cities in the United States. We did not know at the time that the United States-supported leader, Hosni Mubarak, controlled the country through military force used against its citizens.

However, one thing Mubarak could not control was the traffic in Cairo. The blaring car horns, taxi drivers wrangling about fares and the heat in the city really pushed me to the limit of my patience as drivers jumped out of their vehicles to argue vociferously about who had the right of way at an intersection. I became tense and anxious in this city. Even the elegant lobby of the Cairo Hilton Hotel where we went to relax could not assuage my uneasiness. While at the hotel we met a well-dressed gentleman who asked us to intervene with the United States government so that he could seek asylum in our country. He was a refugee from Somalia. That was a sobering conversation that quickly made me realize how fortunate we were to be able to travel freely and to return to our home with some assurance that civil strife would not disrupt our lives. As we toured Tunisia and Egypt, we were not allowed to take photographs of government buildings. This regulation also existed in both Kenya and Tanzania where we were not even allowed to sit in on governmental sessions.

Hubey and I replied enthusiastically when Hamilton suggested that we take a train to Luxor to view the tombs of the Pharaohs. Much to my amazement, during that overnight trip Tanya began to decipher some numbers in Arabic. It was on the ride to Luxor that the conductor demanded we turn over our passports to him during the journey—we refused. I threatened to report him to his President. "On this train I am Mubarak," he retorted. We

Chapter Eleven: Around the World in 90 Days

surrendered our passports. It was hot and sticky the morning we finally arrived in Luxor where we stayed at the New Karnak Hotel. When the children questioned the sparse accommodations I responded, "You should see the Old Karnak." The first and only intestinal discomfort any of us encountered during our travels occurred at this stop. Hamilton got sick. Amal, our busboy assured us, "I will bring something that will make your son well again." He soon brought a medicinal concoction to our room and Hamilton was soon feeling fine.

The limited accommodations in Luxor were far superior to the conditions that we faced when we arrived in Dar es Salaam. As predicted by our contact in Athens, the city was indeed barely functioning. Buildings stood in disrepair in this once-beautiful capital city of Tanzania. We summoned a taxi to transport us to our refuge on the banks of the Indian Ocean at the Ideal Hotel suggested by our Athens traveling acquaintance. There were no light bulbs to replace the burned-out one in our room (although the bell desk promised to send one right away), but the place was clean, with tinges of its former elegance, the food was quite good, and we were safe. Swimming in the placid warm Indian Ocean surf in November was beyond anything that I had anticipated. We made contact with the doctor recommended to us in Athens, who took good care of Tanya by removing the cast that allowed her leg to heal. She was now able to move around without restriction.

The ex-husband of our Athens fairy godmother invited us to visit his hemp plantation high in the mountains. There was the spectacular view of the ocean where, on a clear day, you could see the island of Zanzibar. Most of the land that comprised the plantation had been seized by the government after independence

Deeper Roots

from British colonial rule, but the land was lying fallow, and had not been distributed to the indigenous people. We celebrated Thanksgiving at a Greek family restaurant at the invitation of the brother of our Athens contact. We each ordered lobster for the feast away from home. Our family in the States spent Thanksgiving in New York with my mother.

We were checked out by armed border guards when we traveled by private car to cross from Tanzania into Kenya. Our first stop in Kenya was Arusha, where the majestic Mount Kilimanjaro was close at hand. We visited the Kenya Museum to see the work of the Leakey family, which determined through archeological excavations that the origin of man began in African forty million years ago.

Our Newton, Massachusetts friends, Hopkins and Judy Holmberg were living in Nairobi, the capital city of Kenya and we had informed them of our three-week visit to that city. They were kind enough to make reservations for us at the Clearview Hotel, where we had a suite of rooms at our disposal. The Holmbergs had their children, Beth and Danny, with them too and we spent a lot of time together as they guided us through our visit. We traveled to the Rift Valley, toured the Nairobi National Park and walked the streets of the city where Tanya was very concerned about the number of adults and children who were maimed or were missing limbs. They were getting around as best they could by using wheel barrows and clumsy wooden crutches. Perhaps her time spent with an injured leg had made her more sensitive to the plight of the handicapped in Kenya. Tanya, now an adult, works with development programs in Africa. Perhaps her journey, taken so many years ago, had something to do with her career choice.

Chapter Eleven: Around the World in 90 Days

During our trip from Nairobi to Mombasa, (which was the hottest place that we encountered during our travels) I talked with the conductor who invited us to visit his home on our return. We were pleased to accept his hospitality and a lovely meal of chicken stew. His children asked our children, "How many goats and chickens do you own?" Our children responded, "None." Since the answer denotes the wealth of a family, we were considered poor. Our Servas host in Nairobi arranged for us to visit a family outside of the central city. We were sitting in the living room talking when the senior member of the family came to see her granddaughter, who had recently returned home from study at Long Island University in New York. The granddaughter was in the kitchen, busily helping her mother prepare dinner. Much to my surprise the grandmother assumed that we were neighbors in the village, visiting to welcome the granddaughter back from her successful academic pursuit. I wondered how this young woman would adjust to the role of women in this country after four years living in the United States.

Now it was my turn to ponder a very probing question. After we finished our dinner our host asked, "Why do you Americans kill your leaders?" He was, of course, referring to the assassinations of President Kennedy, Attorney General Robert Kennedy, the Reverend Martin Luther King Jr., Malcolm X, etc. I still have not satisfactorily answered that question myself.

Chapter Twelve:

The Brooch

The Connection to the Ancestors

We call her Redie for short. My cousin, Margaret Elizabeth White Winston—my father's niece—sits at the Formica kitchen table facing the west window in her Connecticut apartment. Rays of afternoon sun illuminate the old photographs spread out in front of her.

I have come to the George Beach senior housing complex in Hartford on a balmy April Sunday in 2000 with six tintypes and dozens and dozens of black and white snapshots from the bottom shelf of my father's bookcase.

Deeper Roots

I am hoping Redie will recognize some of these people as family members. I hope especially that she will recognize just one photograph of our grandmother Elizabeth, whom we are both named after, so that I will know what she looked like for sure. Elizabeth died before I was born.

"Follow the signs to Hartford Hospital when you get off Route 84," Redie has told me. The square blue signs with the white letter H lead me down Jefferson Street to the intersection with Washington Street in a neighborhood of striking contrasts. Two men lean up against the side of a boarded-up brick building a few blocks from the gleaming new glass-walled Children's Hospital. Salsa music blares from the radios of repainted sedans while sleek late model convertibles move in and out of the McDonalds and Walmart parking lots. I slow down to make a turn right off Washington Street to 70 Allan Place.

Redie's snowy Afro frames her unlined honey-brown face. Greeting me at the door, my oldest living relative wears her ninety-six years well. Redie is dressed in gray slacks and a pink turtleneck shirt that suits her five foot seven-inch figure. Her sparkling brown eyes and radiant smile express the kind and generous spirit which made her my father's favorite niece.

Now Redie and her youngest half-sister, Mary, are both stooped over the kitchen table poring over the photographs. Mary peers through her thick-lensed glasses, her eyesight dimmed by the ravages of diabetes. The sisters live two floors apart, but Mary spends most of her time in Redie's apartment. They have been together most of their lives, sometimes separated from their other siblings in times of crisis.

When fire destroyed the family farmhouse in Windsor, Connecticut (where Redie and Mary were born seventeen years apart), they moved with Grandmother to

266

Chapter Twelve: The Brooch

my father's Harlem apartment and remained in New York City for many years. Later when Redie's husband died, Mary moved into Redie's suburban home. Eventually they both relocated to this pink brick apartment house for seniors on the edge of Hartford's Trinity University campus, where they share their time together in childless widowhood. Even in her advanced years, when the roles should be reversed, Redie still looks after Mary like a doting mother.

Redie's long fingers remind me of my father's hands. She picks up each picture to examine it closely. In a series of pictures the same group of six tawny brown-skinned people appears in different poses along a shoreline. The three women are dressed in ankle-length skirts, wearing tucked white blouses with high stiff collars. Their tilted wide-brimmed floppy hats sprout plumes arching upward. The single man in the group stands alongside a well-endowed female companion; he wears a three-piece suit with buttoned vest and holds a stylish cane. Only when Redie and I hold the photo up to the living-room wall mirror can we decipher the words on the banner hanging over the ferry dock. The mirror reflection reads "Kingston"—a town on the Hudson River thirty miles from New York City, where this group probably embarked on a day excursion boat.

"I must have been just a little girl when these photos were taken, Betty," Redie says. "I don't know anyone in this group." But the photograph speaks of a time and place long gone; the clothing and setting are historical in nature and worth preserving.

But the faces in another picture are familiar to all of us. Both of our mothers appear in this photo taken nearly seventy years ago at a family gathering in Windsor. Redie's sister-in law, Madeline, is also there dressed in

Deeper Roots

white. She stands slightly separated from the group as though she doesn't belong. Redie's hand is stretched out in back of Meme to touch Madeline's shoulder while Redie's head rests on Meme's shoulder. Meme's slightly narrowed eyes glare defiantly at the camera as though it had imprisoned her, making her an unwilling captive of the moment. Redie's other arm loops around her mother Jessie's neck like the hook of a coat hanger. Redie's eyes are closed, as though she's exhausted from this feat of posing these women all together in one photograph. It is quite a physical and emotional stretch and it is clear that Redie has extended herself in this snapshot as the self-appointed human link between myriad personalities. There has always been tension among these family members though. Jessie resented Meme's existence in her brother Thede's life. (My dad typed a copy of a poem directed to his sister suggesting that he could choose his own friends without her approval.) My mother resented the financial aid my father gave his sister to help raise her children. Standing in front of the three ladies are two wispy girls, their slender bare arms entwined. Mary repeatedly jabs the photo with her forefinger and says, "There I am with Aunt Meme's niece, Edna. We were both about eleven years old." In front of Mary and Edna is a toddler; we cannot see her face and neither Redie nor Mary remembers her name.

This photograph is quite revealing, but it does not include my grandmother Elizabeth. A place inside of me longs to know this woman, my link to my foremothers. Her absence from my life is like a missing piece of a puzzle. I remember that an eight-by-ten framed picture of her always graced the top of my dad's chiffonier, but too many years have passed and I no longer recall what

Chapter Twelve: The Brooch

she looked like. I have searched for that missing picture in 409 in vain.

"But are there no pictures of grandmother among all these photos?" I ask. Redie slowly shakes her head from side to side and silently gazes out of the window as though transporting herself to another place. These pictures have taken her back in time to my father and his first wife's Harlem apartment on 132nd Street, where Redie and Mary went to live after the fire at their Windsor home. Redie turns to face me. Her fingers run over the outer edges of the filigree silver cross dangling from the chain around her neck. "We lost everything in that fire," Redie recalls. "All of the family pictures burned to a crisp. All eight children were scattered to live with family in other places until the home could be rebuilt. Mary was just an infant then." The flames of that fire seared the lives of Redie and Mary, leaving indelible scars. Railroad cars frequently ferried the three generations of the Butler and White families between Harlem and Windsor's Hayden Station. Grandma, Jessie and her four children—Elmer, Alfred, Mary, and Redie—made that journey for many years until the house was rebuilt. My Dad and I also made the trip to the family farm.

Redie recalled that "everyone called Grandma 'Mother B.' She was a quiet, soft-spoken woman. On Sunday mornings she prepared a huge breakfast of bacon and sausage, scrambled eggs and pancakes. The aroma of her cooking drifted through the apartment building from the dumbwaiter shaft on each floor in the hall. When the paper boy dropped off the Sunday paper, he would raise his eyebrows and say, 'You call this *breakfast*, Mother B?' Later I would take Grandmother to Abyssinian Baptist Church, when Adam Clayton Powell, Sr. was the minister. Mother B was one of the first new members of the

269

church when it moved uptown to Harlem. She never missed a Sunday."

"Our oldest brother, Thede, named after your dad, was crazy about Grandma. She would always make something special for him to eat, because he was so sickly," Mary adds. "But all his favorite foods couldn't save him. Both he and Grandma died the same year... 1930. I'll never forget the day of Thede's funeral; I thought my mother was going to jump into the grave herself to be buried with him." The pain of that memory is etched in Mary's face and her eyes fill with tears.

I think about the black leather-covered 1892 Bible that belonged to my grandmother that I found in my father's bookcase. The gilt-edged pages were worn from use and held together by thin white twine since the spine of the book had long disappeared. A firm yet elegant handwriting on the flyleaf read, "A token of remembrance from Cousin Sarah to Elizabeth." In between the tissue thin pages were penciled handwritten copies of Bible verses. I had no words of wisdom or guidance from my grandmother or memories of her, so I scrutinized the copied passages, each initialed "E.A.B.," for advice or some message. Because every generation of my family since 1790 had owned land, the significance of land appealed to me as a portent—and I found it in the following quote: "God appeared to Abram and said, 'Unto thy seed, I give the Land': and there he built an altar unto the Lord. Gen. 12:7." I adopted this scripture about land and its importance to family as the special message my grandmother wanted me to receive.

I am gathering my treasures from the table and preparing to return home. Redie slides her chair away from her place, carefully balancing her weight on her feet before walking across the living room to the small antique

Chapter Twelve: The Brooch

table in the corner. "I've got something for you, Betty. I took this out of the bank safe when I knew you were coming," Redie says. She hands me a small white box. "This is yours."

I remove the lid from the box, and then slowly lift a layer of cotton. Resting on another pad of cotton is an amber caramel-colored cameo of a woman. Ringlets of loose curls frame the profile and a beaded necklace graces the neck above a delicately draped bodice. I remember this piece of jewelry pinned on the lapel of a blouse Redie's mother, Jessie, often wore when she visited us at 409. "This brooch belonged to our great-grandmother, Hannah Weeks," Redie says. "She gave it to her youngest daughter, our grandmother Elizabeth. Your father had a jeweler on Madison Avenue and 125th Street put a safety catch on the clasp before they gave it to me. Now it is yours to wear and pass down to one of your daughters."

How strange that this brooch should belong to Hannah. It was Hannah's marriage certificate that I found in my father's bookcase that started my historical journey. I thought about my trip to Troy, New York when I found Hannah's name in the 1841 Troy City directory. She became real to me then because her address was listed on a page of the red covered booklet—a defined place, in a specific year. She became a person to me although I did not know how tall she was, whether she was plump or thin or whether her complexion was light or dark. She was however my great grandmother, reclaimed and connected to me by a line in the Troy City directory, and now this brooch.

I can feel the blood rushing to my face. I am giddy, light-headed and I feel almost lifted off my feet. Redie and I wrap our arms around each other. The brooch has

Deeper Roots

initiated me into a family tradition I knew nothing about. This cameo was once held in the deft fingers of my tailoress great-grandmother, Hannah Diamond Weeks, who passed it on to her daughter Elizabeth, who gave it to her daughter Jessie, and she in turn to her daughter Margaret Elizabeth. I feel a tangible connection to an invisible chain of four generations of women in our family, each one handing this symbol to the next. My fingers caress the brooch and I know that this is the message I have been searching and waiting for. I become a chosen elder, guardian of a tradition that links generations of daughters.

However, there was one journey left. The journey that would take me . . .

Chapter Thirteen:

Back to Africa

Family

W ould this be a good time to visit?" I asked Stephen Azumah. We were speaking by telephone between Newton, Massachusetts and his home in Accra, Ghana. "Cheryl is teaching English in Gabon and our visit in March would coincide with her spring vacation." There was a slight transatlantic delay, and then Steven said, "This is your home. You are welcome at any time that you decide to come." The retired colonel's immediate generosity was typical of the warm

Deeper Roots

Ghanaian hospitality I had heard so much about from my children and from other visitors to Ghana.

Steven and Mercy Azumah had issued a standing invitation four years earlier when our youngest daughter, Tanya, lived with the family as an exchange student. The Azumahs had made Tanya a part of their family and I was eager to meet the people who so graciously and generously embraced her.

I set out that March day in 1998 from Logan Airport in Boston via Amsterdam and arrived in Kotoka International Airport in Accra one day later. The hot dry night air of Accra felt like a warm cocoon. Stepping outside the airport terminal I scanned the crowd waiting behind security ropes to meet arriving passengers. Dela's eyes lit up when we recognized each other and Akofa's beautiful white smile stretched wide across her square-shaped face as she called out, "Mum, Mum, I'm so glad to see you again. How was your trip? Let me introduce you to my dad." Dela and Akofa had already visited our family in Boston, but this was my first trip to Ghana. I was tingling with excitement about my stay with the family after four years of exchanging photographs, videotapes, letters, card and gifts. "I'm so pleased to finally meet you, Steven," I said as our hands clasped.

Steven had spent twenty-five years in the Ghanaian army during a succession of coups beginning with the overthrow of Kwame Nkrumah, the nation's first president, and I expected him to be a stern, commanding figure. But the only hints of Steven's military life were his trim physique and erect posture. Indeed, what most impressed me at our first meeting was the mischievous expression in Steven's eyes and his disarming humor. "I am so glad that you have come, Tanya's mother."

274

Chapter Thirteen: Back to Africa - Family

Steven and the girls load me into their car and we drive west through the central city to its outskirts. Night has fallen, it is pitch black and there are no street lights to illuminate the way—but Accra is a city that never sleeps. I am sitting on the edge of my seat watching fearfully as cars defiantly move between lanes at high speeds with horns blaring as they pass each other. Pedestrians also risk their lives by dodging through traffic to cross this main highway. I continue to grip my armrest tightly. Although I am exhausted from my travel, my eyes are wide open as I take in my new surroundings. Vendors with makeshift stalls line the side of the road selling their goods by candlelight to throngs of attentive shoppers.

Accra, the capital city of Ghana, is situated on the country's 400-mile strip of the Gulf of Guinea just beneath the Western bulge of the African continent. In the 1400s, Portugal established it as a trading post which was later taken over by the Dutch. Two hundred years later Denmark, Belgium, Italy, France and England used this same trading post to traffic in African slaves. This profitable endeavor diminished the population by hundreds of thousands and provided a source of free labor for the lucrative agricultural development of the Caribbean Islands and the Americas. By 1874 the area, originally called Guinea, was also referred to as the "Gold Coast" by the British because of the abundance of gold discovered there. In 1957, Guinea fought and gained its independence from Great Britain and its citizens renamed their country after the ancient kingdom of Ghana that once prospered in much of the western region of Africa.

The present population of approximately twenty-five million (according to the World Bank) speak 79 languages and belong to numerous ethnic groups, the

275

Deeper Roots

largest being the Akan group. Fante, Ga and Ewe groups dominate the southern region of the country where the results of Christian missionary work is evident in the numerous schools and churches established by the Catholic and Protestant faiths. The northern part of the country, with its prodigious agricultural production, is predominantly Muslim. The central region of Ghana, which the Ashanti group inhabit, is noted for its artisans—weavers, potters, wood sculptors and iron founders.

After a forty-five minute drive, we turn off the main thoroughfare onto a narrow bumpy road in the area called Odoko, where several single-level houses are cramped together on both sides of the street. A Jehovah Witness Temple stands opposite the entrance leading to the Azumahs' home, which is protected by a locked metal gate which Akofa opens after getting out of the car.

"Welcome my sister," Mercy Azumah sings out as I step from the car. We wrap our arms around each other as Mercy says to me, "You have finally come home." Though I am thousands of miles from the United States, I do feel at home, entrusted to the Azumah clan and in their safe hands. Ghana, the place where most Africans were shipped to destinations throughout the diaspora also symbolically represents a homeland for me.

Other members of the family are seated in a spacious yard waiting for us to join them. The Azumah's sons, Mawuli and Kudzo, and two of Mercy's sisters, greet me with my first word in the Twi language, "akwaaba," which means "welcome." We sit in a circle illuminated by a gaslight lantern; drought conditions have reduced the water power needed to generate electricity causing a national emergency and rationed usage. A household helper, wearing cut-off khaki pants awkwardly passes a tray with glasses of water for the traditional libation. As a distant cousin from Steven's village, the helper came to the household to learn skills that would enable him to take up a trade. There are also two female helpers who are receiving their training from Mercy.

As I would learn in time, it is customary for the arriving guest to tell the purpose of their visit and talk about the experience of travel from a distant place. But I was unacquainted with that custom, so I immediately engaged in conversation, asking Mawuli and Kudzo about their academic studies and their choice of careers. The ever-gracious family overlooked my faux pas and adjusted to the conversation easily.

"I will complete my college education this summer, and I want to learn about computers, preferably in the United States, where I would like to take my graduate education," Mawuli responded in a serious, business-like manner. He leans forward, his broad shoulders arch toward each other, "I'm teaching science courses at the nearby high school now for required national service work."

"I want to go to college too," Kudzo said, "but I am not sure what concentration to take. I'll finish high school next year."

Since Dela had received her degree from the University of Ghana the day before my arrival, I then present her with a framed photograph taken in our home of her holding our grandson, Alex, as a graduation gift. Our animated conversation continue into the late hours of the night beneath a canopy of stars that seemed so close I imagined I could reach up and pick one from the sky.

Deeper Roots

After a while the young men bring my luggage from the yard past the verandah where tables and chairs are arranged. We step inside the single-level concrete house to enter the living room furnished with two green upholstered sofas and a wooden framed high back chair. Speckled white, brown and tan tiles cover the floors throughout the house and scatter rugs cover the floors in front of the chairs. The living room is separated from the dining area by an étagère where framed family photographs and awards are displayed. A mahogany phonograph console fronts the living room. We turned right to enter a sitting room furnished with a television, a computer and a couch. Off of this room are the bathroom and three bedrooms: one for Mercy and Steven with its own private bath, the other room shared by Dela and Akofa during my stay (since I was given Akofa's room). The boys will sleep in the living area behind the house. I unpack by the light of a gas lantern at the foot of my bed and the trusty flashlight I had brought with me to cope with the power shortage. After unpacking I fall fast asleep.

Early the next day I am awakened by drumbeats and the jingle of tambourines. I watch from my bed the orange and green salamander that clung motionless against a wire-mesh screen. Outside my window thirty little children, dressed in pastel-colored shorts and dresses, are marching single file in step around the yard, singing songs led by their five teachers. Mercy is an early childhood educator and the director of a school located in a separate building next to her house. Yellow and red swings and a small slide are at one end of the yard near a sand pit where the children play after their lessons. Yellow begonia blossoms and neatly manicured green shrubbery glistened in the early morning sunlight.

Chapter Thirteen: Back to Africa - Family

Stately trees, called Whistling Pines, at the rear of the school/home yard provided a backdrop against the clear blue sky. Steven manages the finances and administrative aspects of the family business, Mother Mary's Private School. The school opened as one preschool class in 1994 and added a grade level each year. By 2002, 230 children (from pre-school through grade six) were attending the school. There is sand and gravel piled high in the adjacent yard to construct a second building in preparation for a middle school program. All of the Azumah children participate in some way in the family business either by working with the children, accepting delivery of supplies and food, running errands, welcoming parents or in the building and repair of the facilities.

I dress quickly in my coolest clothing and join the Azumahs' for a breakfast of oatmeal and tea. How moved I was to find pictures of Tanya and Lisa prominently displayed in the dining area.

By accident, my visit to Ghana coincides with the arrival of then-President Bill Clinton at the beginning of an African tour. Steven had arranged for us to attend the elaborate welcoming festivities for the President at Accra's Black Star Stadium. By 7:30 in the morning we are inching along in the Azumahs' blue Toyota sedan through snarls of traffic. The day has been declared a national holiday and international flags flapped in the wind at every corner. The new white building of the Ford Motor Company is painted with blue letters of greeting: "*Akwaaba* President Clinton."

Swarms of people are walking alongside the road on the way to Independence Square in the center of the city. Young men come up to our car hawking drinks, squares of chocolate candy, designer watches, blue-and-white handkerchiefs, hand tools packaged in cellophane containers, plastic car covers and toothpaste—a virtual supermarket. Since the traffic is at a standstill, there is plenty of time for Akofa to bargain for a fair price. I notice as we inch along that the signs of the business enterprises use religious and international themes: Martin Luther King Automotives, Precious Lord Transport Vehicles, Buckingham Palace Eatery and Everlasting Life Furniture Company.

The air is a hot and dry—100 degrees and there is no wind. By the time we park the car and walk down several streets past rows of government office buildings to the Black Star Stadium, my handkerchief is wringing wet. But thousands of Ghanaians are jammed into the arena unperturbed by the heat. It looks as though all of Accra is here to welcome the President of the United States. It is the first tour of the region ever made by an American president and it is momentous.

When Akofa arrived in Boston on her first visit to the United States the previous October, Tanya and I met her and drove her to what we felt was a rather splendid occasion—a welcoming ceremony for her fellow Ghanaian, newly-elected United Nations Secretary General Kofi Annan. That afternoon we swayed to the beat of the large African drums under a tent on the lawn of the Museum of African American Art in Boston, where the attendees gave a reception to honor the Secretary General. It was a great gathering, but this welcoming is on a different scale altogether.

The African drums, reaching the drummers chest high, beat so loudly that I can actually feel the vibrations inside my body. It is only nine o'clock in the morning and the ceremony won't begin for several hours, but the stands are already full and the special pass for seating that Steven waves before the officials is virtually useless.

Chapter Thirteen: Back to Africa - Family

We decide to stay near the reviewing stand where the breezes from the Atlantic Ocean bring cooling relief. A young man kindly unfolds a metal chair for me to sit down and I take a swig from a bottle of water and lean back to revel in this festive occasion. No crowd of such magnitude has assembled here since Independence Day ended British rule in 1957. *A DREAM COME TRUE* reads the banner headline of Ghana's *Mirror* newspaper. The energy emanating from the crowd makes it feel like we are awaiting nothing less than the second coming of Christ.

Tribal chiefs in full regalia proceed into the Stadium, with their gold-topped staffs held high and their colorful robes dazzling in the sunlight. Some chiefs have ridden from their villages to Accra on horseback under the shade of bright umbrellas with their retinues following closely behind. Countless Ghanaian schoolchildren in brown and tan uniforms are here clutching miniature American flags. When President Clinton appears, an ovation erupts from the elated throng. A few overzealous admirers try to break through the police line to touch President Clinton as he mounts the stage causing security guards and the secret service to swing into action. I climb onto my chair to get a better view and watch as Ghanaian President Jerry Rawlings drapes President Clinton in a ceremonial Ashanti Kente cloth. In the skies, there is the roar of helicopters and American Air Force planes circling overhead. The might, wealth and power of the United States are on display and Ghanaians are engaged in a love affair with America. CDs of popular American vocalists and musicians are sold on the streets, televisions beam in American sitcoms and CNN brings world news each day into Ghanaian homes. The Peace Corps have served in Ghana since the inception of the program in

Deeper Roots

1962 and some Ghanaians, like the first President of the country, Kwame Nkrumah, received their education in the United States. American clothing, appliances and other manufactured items are sought by middle-class Ghanaians.

The purpose of President Clinton's visit is to give the country the recognition it had been denied. In his speech Clinton also promises to deliver foreign aid and to supply generators to help prevent drought from crippling Ghana and neighboring Togo—both of which are dependent on the electricity generated by the Volta Dam to supply them with water. Tumultuous applause from the cheering crowd rocks the Stadium when President Clinton concludes. Ghana will be seen on television around the world because the President of the United States has come to visit and I am here to witness it.

On the drive back to the Azumahs' home I see much that reminds me of Jamaica. The Ghanaian people look very similar to Jamaicans in physical appearance and in the graceful carriage of women who carry baskets and trays on their heads with their arms swinging freely as they walk with babies securely swaddled in colorful cloths on their backs. The various styles of head wraps also remind me of Jamaican wraps and the way my mother tied her head to keep her hair in place before going to bed each night. In a photograph taken of me at Orchard Beach in the Bronx when I was about four years old, my head is tied with a blue polka-dotted scarf in the African tradition in order to protect my plaited hair. Names were also familiar to me here—my mother's name was Meme (Meme in Twi means mother) and my cousin's name is Ouida(h) (which is also a town in Benin).

Chapter Thirteen: Back to Africa - Family

I feel a sense of deja-vu, of having been in these environs before, and in a sense I have. Many of the slave ships traveling from Africa first stopped in Jamaica, where the captives were "seasoned." The plantation system not only determined the worth of each slave and decided who should be kept and who should be shipped off to other parts of the world, but the system also sought to erase African cultural traditions and any personal sense of agency. However successful the European slavers were in controlling the body through brutal force, they ultimately failed to control the minds of their captives. Many African and Ghanaian customs, belief systems, and ways of being and thinking were transported with the bondspeople and have survived the brutality of slavery and the passage of time. My mom, Meme, was the classic example. Herbal medicine, passed on from African cultures, was the choice of cure in my American household. Her holistic belief that the body was designed to function in harmony "as the temple of the living god" minimized dependence on Western medicine—except in special circumstances. My mother also viewed dreams as spiritual manifestations of prophesy upon which resolute decisions could be made. These belief systems are still reflected today in West Indian and African American culture.

Ghana evokes other memories for me when Akofa, Steven and I visit the former home and mausoleum of Dr. W. E. B. Du Bois, located high on a hill on an acre of land lying on the outskirts of the city. In 1961, Dr. Du Bois and his second wife, Shirley Graham, left his American homeland at the invitation of President Kwame Nkrumah, to spend the remainder of his years living in quiet dignity as a Ghanaian citizen.

Deeper Roots

The house and garden, presented by President Nkrumah to Dr. Du Bois, is framed by hedges and trees on once beautifully-manicured grounds. The living room of the home has been converted to a marble mausoleum of honor, surrounded by stools donated by African tribal leaders. Framed photographs hang on the walls, capturing historic events of Du Bois appearing with heads of state of China and the Soviet Union. Tapestries from China and gifts from various countries fill another room. The walls of Du Bois' library are lined floor to ceiling with some of his books. Other valuable papers and documents are archived at the W. E. B. Du Bois Library at the University of Massachusetts' Amherst campus.

Dr. Du Bois and President Nkrumah were drawn together by their shared interest and study of international socialist and communist political movements and philosophy. Kwame Nkrumah received his bachelor's degree in theology at Lincoln University in Pennsylvania in 1939, and earned two master's degrees in education (1942) and philosophy (1943) from the University of Pennsylvania. (Du Bois had also done extensive sociological research at the University years before.) Nkrumah lived in London briefly while studying at the London School of Economics. During his time in the United States and England, Nkrumah became involved in pro-Africa movements and organizations deemed "left wing radical" and studied the writings of Dr. Du Bois, among others. He returned home (then referred to as Gold Coast) in 1947 and became the President at the age of forty-six in 1951. President Nkrumah led Ghana until 1966 and oversaw Ghana's independence in 1957. As Ghana was the first colony to gain independence from foreign rule in sub-Saharan Africa, Nkrumah also led the newly invigorated Pan-African Movement—a concept

that Dr. Du Bois had begun to actualize in the previous
century.

But while Nkrumah was nation-building in Africa,
Du Bois' support of radical movements and communism
stigmatized him as a supporter of the United States'
enemy, the Soviet Union. On February 16 of 1951, Dr. Du
Bois was summoned to Washington to be indicted by a
federal grand jury for his role as President of the Peace
and Information Center. He was charged with failing to
register the organization (which the Justice Department
considered to be a "subversive" group controlled by foreign communist governments). Although the organization was subsequently dissolved, Dr. Du Bois (then an
elderly gentleman of eighty-two years) was subjected to a
grueling trial. I was enraged at the time when I saw a
news photograph of Dr. Du Bois wearing handcuffs.

The NAACP and other Negro leadership groups
distanced themselves from Du Bois, as did anthropolo-
gist Margaret Mead and diplomat Ralph Bunch who
rescinded their acceptances of invitations to attend Du
Bois' eighty-third birthday scheduled to be held at New
York's exclusive Essex House on Central Park South. The
hotel management cancelled the contract, so the
remaining sponsors moved the celebration to Small's
Paradise in Harlem where seven hundred people joined
in toasting the octogenarian with sociologist Franklin
Frazier presiding. Paul Robeson made a stirring speech
and tributes were read from poet Langston Hughes and
musician Leonard Bernstein. Du Bois and his new bride
toured the country for several months during the spring
of 1951, successfully filling speaking engagements to
drum up a broad spectrum of support for Du Bois'
pending trial.

Deeper Roots

The trial date, after many postponements, was set for November 13, 1951. Judge Matthew McGuire ultimately dismissed the case, and although Du Bois was not convicted his passport was withheld for eight years. Both the State Department and Justice Department believed by now that further harassment of Dr. Du Bois would reflect poorly on the image of the United States in the international community. The whole episode was a tragic miscarriage of justice.

A decade later, Du Bois and Graham accepted the invitation of President Nkrumah to relocate in Ghana. Du Bois continued his scholarship in his newly adopted country, using his library to work on a long standing vision—organizing the Africana Encyclopedia which Henry Louis Gates, Director of the Du Bois Institute at Harvard University subsequently completed and published. As Director of Television, Graham set up Ghana's first television studio, produced educational programming and provided technical training. Graham also became a trusted advisor to President Nkrumah. International visitors, including African Americans, sought audiences with these prominent expatriates. Despite Du Bois' failing health and advancing age, he survived for two years in Ghana, dying on August 27, 1963 at the age of ninety-five. How fitting that the announcement of Du Bois' death was made to a worldwide audience at the historic Great March on Washington on August 28, 1963. The traditional Ghanaian funeral, with all the fanfare and ceremony accorded a head of state, was a well-deserved tribute to a brilliant, prolific and outspoken world citizen.

Dr. Du Bois was not only my neighbor at 409, he was also a personal hero and a man who devoted his life to both national and international racial, economic and

Chapter Thirteen: Back to Africa - Family

social justice. My visit to his last home was to pay tribute to him.

I was elated with my visit because the Azumahs allowed me to see the country and its citizens in a way that I could not if I had been a tourist just out and about taking pictures. I truly felt part of the family.

Chapter Fourteen:

Back to Africa

Business and Tradition

Mercy's sister, Henrietta Appiah invited me to spend a weekend at her home on the northern outskirts of the city. Henrietta is a medium-sized woman with ebony skin and her eyes and hands move rapidly as she speaks in breathless animation. Her home, surrounded by potted plants, is a large, two-storied white concrete structure with a balcony. From her rooftop, we enjoy the cool evening breeze and observe planes taking off from nearby Kotoka International Airport as we ate delicious Ghanaian seafood. Henrietta shares her home with her niece, Vera, who is learning to manage a household and is also being trained in the retail business Henrietta owns.

Deeper Roots

The following morning we visit Henrietta's shop in Accra. As we drive through the gate I notice an elderly man sitting in a chair dozing. He is the guardsman, although I didn't think that he is capable of protecting the home or Henrietta's two Mercedes-Benz cars from theft. But he is a deterrent in a country where the disparity in income and poverty make theft and corruption major social issues.

We arrive in the city just after dawn, but the streets are already bustling. People jostle for space, going in every direction—it reminds me of the streets in Bangkok. Automobiles toot their horns, bicycle riders weave in and out of traffic and women pass us bearing woven baskets on their heads containing cassava, yams, tomatoes, plantain and other vegetables unfamiliar to me. Already the heat is sultry and enervating. The equatorial heat makes the air suffocating, almost as though it would burn my lungs if I inhaled too deeply and I feel almost overwhelmed by the welter of rich, unfamiliar smells. We are on our way to Makola Market—a six block area containing stalls standing shoulder-to-shoulder where everything imaginable can be purchased. Pavilions shade the shoppers, giving some shelter from the blistering sun. The vendors are all women, some of whom display their goods on ground cloths spread out in front of the stalls. The women wear plastic flip-flops to keep their feet cool, short-sleeved or sleeveless cotton tops and multicolored printed skirts of geometric and floral designs. Some have their heads wrapped with turbans and some are bare-headed other than the padding for the basket they carry with regal grace like a crown.

We arrive at Henrietta's shop, which keen business-lady Akofa and two of her male cousins have already opened for the day. A glass case contains costume jewelry while another case atop the counter displays nail polishes of various colors and small bottles of perfume. The shelves behind the counter are stacked high with pomades, home permanents, shampoos, conditioners, dyes and body lotions. During school vacations, the younger members of the family help operate the shop. As a senior market woman, Henrietta teaches the younger people the intricacies of banking, accounting, marketing, and sales. Henrietta's sons, Nasi and Paggi, are already adept enough to manage the business whenever Henrietta travels to New York City's lower Manhattan wholesale district to replenish her inventory and arrange for the products to be shipped to Ghana by container vessels.

At a stool at the front of the shop, I can observe the street activity and watch Henrietta conduct her business. I am surrounded by colorful piles of American-brand shirts from Adidas and Polo Ralph Lauren. Ghanaians want goods that have American designer labels purchased in New York although, ironically, they are often manufactured by cheap labor abroad.

Henrietta bargains with her customers over prices of the shirts hanging on a rack. A shrewd negotiator, Henrietta always gains the upper hand in both sales and purchases. Business in good today because Easter Sunday is only two weeks away and mothers are flocking to this shop to make selections from the racks of pastel yellow, pink and blue dresses detailed with fancy embroidery for their daughters and to select a dress for themselves.

"How much?" Henrietta asks a vendor passing her stall with a straw basket of large plantains balanced on her head.

"100 ccs a hand, ma'am," she responds.

Deeper Roots

"That is too much. See, these plantains are beginning to turn brown, but I'll take the whole bunch for 50ccs to help you out."

"Oh, ma'am. You must be joking. I might as well give them to you for that price. I'll come down to 75ccs."

"Never mind. You can move on," Henrietta says, waving her hand dismissively.

Toward the end of the afternoon the banana vendor returns and agrees to accept Henrietta's first offer.

"Oh," Henrietta says, "you are too late. I've made other arrangements." Other vendors bring fresh vegetables and Henrietta purchases a coconut for me. The vendor hacks off the top with a machete; the milk is cool and sweet and surprisingly quenches my thirst. Some market women gather and place their baskets of vegetables in front of Henrietta's stall. They trade amongst themselves, selecting from each other's wares — the conversation and laughter exchanged in this social interaction is infectious and a smile creeps across my face even though I cannot understand what they are saying.

Market women like Henrietta who import from abroad must master the complexity of constantly fluctuating foreign exchange rates, devaluations of the Ghanaian currency, international trade practices, marketing, as well as managing their lines of credit. Changes in import regulations may require Henrietta to purchase products from countries other than America to complete her inventory.

A tall young woman, well dressed in a crisply-starched white cotton blouse and a navy cotton short-sleeved business suit stops by the shop with a bevy of papers on a clipboard. She identifies herself as a representative of the United Nations and invites Henrietta to interview as part of a study to determine how market women run their businesses. Henrietta declines. "Why should I waste my time participating in this inquiry?" she says to me. "I don't want them to know my business."

A buxom tradeswoman from Nigeria arrives at the stall with a beautiful delicate blue fabric woven with silver rectangles. She drapes it over me and wraps my head with a turban of the same fabric. "Lovely, Miss. It is so becoming to you. Don't you want to take this back to America?" Then she unfolds a maroon crocheted piece, drapes it on herself and poses so Akofa can snap a picture of her modeling this gorgeous ensemble.

I am an African American woman linked to Africa, yet in Africa I am an American woman. I feel comfortable here because I am a daughter of the continent from which my ancestors were taken, yet this is not my country or my place anymore. Some Ghanaians refer to me as a "white lady" because white, wealth, power and America are synonymous. The United States media have spread that image. I am from America, therefore, I am a white lady despite my brown complexion that indicates my African descent.

The parade of vendors and customers continue all through the morning. A manicurist hailed by Henrietta carries her specially-arranged tray on her head with fifty bottles of nail polish in a variety of colors. She enters the shop and in one swirling motion places the tray on the floor for me to select a shade of polish. Henrietta is treating me to a manicure and pedicure. I have chosen a brilliant red shade for both my fingernails and toenails. Although I am a bit apprehensive about the instrument to be used for this pedicure, I must admit that the manicurist wields her razor blade on my toenails with adroit skill.

Deeper Roots

Well into the afternoon, pedestrians continue to carefully step around the women selling their wares in front of the stalls. A huge live tortoise is sold for soup. A black-and-white goat with a rope tied around its neck is led down the road be sold for the Easter dinner feast. I learn that it is customary to present a goat to the member of the family preparing the Easter banquet.

As evening approaches, we hear the wail of a siren approaching. The police van stops in front of Henrietta's stall and two policemen emerge with nightsticks drawn to chase a vendor from the sidewalk where she is illegally trading. Henrietta's helper intercedes and argues with the police and a scuffle ensues. Sharp voices exchange angry words that I cannot understand. Not knowing what caused the furor, nor understanding the scene, I climb on a stool to snap a picture of the tumult. As I do, I see Henrietta's helper being dragged into the police van. Immediately Henrietta leaves the shop in order to be at the station when her worker arrives there. Shaken, Akofa and I go to the entrance of the market where Steven picks us up at the appointed time. Soon after we arrive home, we are relieved to hear from Henrietta. She has been able to negotiate her employee's release by making a small payment to the police. I was visibly shaken from the experience, but Henrietta is capable and in-charge because this, too, is a part of doing business in Ghana.

I am having a wonderful and exciting time, but I am starting to miss my family a bit so I am happy when, over a period of several days and a flurry of dropped phone calls, Cheryl's faintly-audible voice comes through the phone line in the Azumahs' living room. "Mom, I will arrive in Accra in five days. I have to get a visa in Togo before I can cross the border to Ghana. That may take a day or so. I can't wait to see you."

Chapter 14: Back to Africa – Business/Tradition

"Steven suggests that we meet at the Golden Tulip Hotel downtown, I shout, "It will be easier to find you there."

On the day of Cheryl's expected arrival, Mercy, Steven and I pile into the car for the ride into the center of town to meet her at the five-star Golden Tulip Hotel. For the occasion, Steven is wearing one of the Boston Red Sox caps that I brought as gifts for the men in the family. With his royal blue "NYDK" shirt and denim dungarees, he looks quite American. Mercy, in contrast, resembles an African queen in a flowing royal blue long dress with the embroidered yoke stitched in light yellow and deep purple.

Steven finds Cheryl seated in a deep-cushioned brown leather chair in the lobby. "Miss Jones, I presume? It's a good thing that you didn't cut off your dreadlocks—I recognized you from the pictures that you sent to us." Mercy and I are browsing through some pamphlets at the Ghana Tourist Board Desk when Steven brings Cheryl to us. "Do you know this lady from Koulamoutou [the capital of Gabon] that I have found?" Steven asks.

I throw my arms around Cheryl, feeling overjoyed and relieved. We haven't seen each other since she returned home for a brief visit at Christmas. Despite three hours of travel, often over nearly impassable roads, Cheryl's radiant smile illuminates her glowing copper complexioned face—and tears roll down her cheeks.

"Mom, I can't believe that we are really here."

"Well, my third American Jones daughter has come to Ghana," Mercy says greeting Cheryl with a hug.

A week after Cheryl's arrival, we pay a visit to Steven's family in Chian, a small village four hours from Accra by car. Steven is a member of the Ewe group, which dominates this Eastern region of Ghana. On a clear night, Steven, Mercy, Akofa, Cheryl, and I slowly drive into Chian. We pass through many villages on good roadways but as we get closer to Chian, the roads become smaller and dustier. The last portion of the trip we bump along on twisting rocky dirt roads full of people walking and goats that occasionally block our way. Chian lies near the border with Togo. Togo was a German colony until Germany was defeated by Britain, France, and the United States in WWI. The area was subsequently divided, arbitrarily separating families by geographical lines into separate protectorates ruled by different colonial powers.

The flicker of a few lanterns scattered on the flat land are the only illumination as our car makes its way slowly through the darkness. But the beams from our headlights act like a magnet drawing children to witness our arrival. This is Steven's birth village and he has built a home here. When he visits, Steven brings a gas generator because electricity has not yet been brought to the village.

"I come here at least once a month to visit my brothers and other relatives. They live in the compound where I was raised. You will meet my family tomorrow," Steven says.

Early the next morning church bells call us to worship service at the Catholic Church. Communicants parade from the village center bearing palms for the Palm Sunday service. Within the large high-vaulted stone edifice, we are escorted to our seats of honor near the altar where the church dignitaries sit. "I want you to meet my two brothers; they are the elders of the church," Steven says. We shake hands and seat ourselves in this special section. That afternoon we visit the ancestral compound where the Azumah family members have lived for many generations. As we tour the village,

296

Chapter 14: Back to Africa – Business/Tradition

Steven points to a cement-block house. "There's the house my brother built. This is where he will come when he and his wife, who is also from this village, retire from their life in Worcester, Massachusetts. We all must return as elders to the place where our placenta is buried to share our wisdom and to help our village."

Similarly, when we arrive in the village of Aseto to meet Mercy's family, we take libation and exchange gifts in the ancestral home. Since Mercy and Steven belong to different tribal groups and speak different languages, they communicate with each other in English—although their children speak all three languages. Cheryl, Mercy, Steven and I visit the school nearby where Tanya taught for a few weeks during her stay in the village while living with Mercy's sister's family and Mercy's mother, the Queen Mother of Aseto.

The Akan group is matrilineal. In their belief system woman is the God of creation and women are, therefore, revered and honored as descendants of God—the direct link with the universe. "Meme" is the word in Twi (the language spoken by this Akan group) for "mother" and since is no word for "aunt" in Twi, all senior women are called Meme. This is an excellent example of the contrast in gender roles found in Africa versus most European countries, because the concept of a "Queen Mother" in Africa is different from the term used to describe the Queen Mother in the British Royal Family.

During our visit, Mercy's mother complied with my request to see the ceremonial drums that are used only for special occasions. They are kept in storage nearby and locked up for safe keeping—only the Queen Mother and the Chief have the key. Afterwards, the principal of the village school gathered the faculty in an informal ceremony and gave me a letter of appreciation for Tanya's work with the school and a wooden engraving made by a student. "I'll give this to Tanya when I get home," I said, thanking the principal. "No," he said, "you misunderstand. This gift is for you because you are Tanya's mother." I was overwhelmed by the appreciation of Tanya's contribution and the respect for elders and mothers evidenced in this culture.

It is now up to Mercy to decide whether to return to Aseto to assume the responsibility of Queen Mother when her own mother can no longer continue to serve in that capacity. It is customary for the oldest daughter, in this matriarchal Akan group, to assume the role of Queen Mother; but Mercy may recant because of her administrative responsibilities at her school twenty miles away. It is a huge decision and she must weigh carefully which duty holds the higher priority.

Several days after our visit to Aseto, I had the privilege of returning to Steven's village of Chian to participate in the wedding ceremony of Jerome Azumah, Steven's nephew. Because Jerome's father is deceased, Steven is responsible for arranging and directing the wedding. "This will be a traditional wedding of the Chian clan," Steven declared; Steven will meet with his nephew to discuss the responsibilities of matrimony. Steven elaborated, "no one except the elders of our family will be present at the official ceremony; and unless the bride's family accepts our gifts, there will be no wedding. Even though the wedding arrangement has already been agreed upon between the families, we must observe this custom."

Jerome protested, "Oh Uncle, don't be so old-fashioned." Jerome wanted all of the guests to witness the ceremony. But Colonel Azumah was the senior person and his wishes prevailed.

Chapter 14: Back to Africa — Business/Tradition

"I will also have my former commanding officer serve as interpreter since he and your fiancée's family are from the same region and speak the same language," Steven said.

Jerome drove up to the Azumahs' home on the day before the wedding, a bit later than the appointed time, and walked in carrying a large aluminum tub filled with various items. We all sat in the living room—Dela, Mercy, Cheryl, Jerome, and I. Steven stood by the doorway, taking the items from the tub, inspecting them, and checking off each item on his list before they were carefully wrapped in shiny red foil paper by Mercy and Dela and packed in a decorated Samsonite suitcase which would be presented the next day. These were the gifts requested by the bride's family. In addition to the gifts, the brother of the bride receives a small sum of money: a token from the groom in exchange for the brother's loss of the domestic services of his sister.

On the wedding day, Mercy surprises me with the gift of a royal blue traditional dress and matching head wrap made especially for me. Dressed in these regal garments, I feel like an African queen. We are waiting for other members of the family to arrive for the automobile procession to the home of the bride's uncle, where the wedding will take place. "Punctuality is important. It is an insult to keep the family waiting for us," Steven frets while looking at his watch. But at last we arrive at the uncle's home and I am honored to be invited to accompany the elders of the family upstairs to observe the official ceremony.   We introduce ourselves and shake hands with the bride's family, who are seated in folding chairs to receive our greetings. After libations there is conversation, the family accepts the gifts and then surrender the waiting bride to her new family. All eyes focus on a closed door that the bride's grandmother knocks on to inform the bride that an agreement has been reached. The door opens and the bride appears to present herself to the groom. She is elegantly dressed in a lavishly-embroidered gown with a matching five-inch-high headpiece. Her ebony skin glows but her eyes and her countenance appear to be anxious and uncertain. Now other guests, including Cheryl and the younger family members, cram into the room to see the Catholic priest administer the vows as the couple exchange rings. At a later date a Catholic ceremony will be held in a church, but this traditional wedding is fully recognized by the community. After the senior women offer their marital advice to the young couple, we join the guests in a court-yard reception.

Several days after the ceremony, Mercy, Cheryl, Steven and I walk down the road to the home of Steven's friend and former commanding officer, who served as interpreter to the bride's family during the wedding cere-mony. We sit under a large shady tree in the yard and enjoy a libation. I am interested in Jerome's bride, who has only recently completed high school (where Jerome was one of her teachers). I asked Steven's friend, "What will happen to a young woman who has no advanced education and has no particular skills? From what I have seen in this brief visit, many women have businesses of their own. I've seen bakers, seamstresses, factory work-ers, merchants and these women not only produce, but market and distribute their products." The officer responds that without special skills or further education, Jerome's young wife will be relegated to the role of the "traditional" wife who cares for the home and the chil-dren exclusively.

Chapter 14: Back to Africa — Business/Tradition

Before ending our visit, we tour a concrete building on the property where the retired officer's wife designs and makes beautiful batik, which she sells both domestically and abroad. I receive a gift of fabric, enough to make a dress and I purchase several other designs in shades of blue and fuchsia. It has been an interesting and informative day.

Chapter Fifteen:

Back to Africa

Exploring the Past and Future

The temperature has already reached 92 degrees the following morning when Steven drops Akofa, Cheryl, Mercy, and me at the bus depot. We are setting out to make a pilgrimage to visit the Slave Castles at Elmina and Cape Coast, from which Africans were shipped after capture. Akofa has visited the castles once before on a class trip from Cape Coast University and I had visited Goree Island in Senegal on a previous trip to Africa. I was moved by the enormity of the inhuman acts that made this slave trade possible. I felt so small and deeply saddened when I stood at the dungeon's

Deeper Roots

"door of no return," but I also felt a bond with ancestors taken from this place. Now I was going to the largest slave trading post in Africa. I needed time to emotionally prepare myself for this trip, so I focused on the scene developing before me.

A refugee boy from war-ravaged Chad, his tawny brown face aged beyond his years, comes over to where we are seated. On his skinny four-foot frame he wears baggy yellow shorts, an oversized black T shirt and his bare feet are thrust into blue rubber thongs. With a tattered cloth he wipes the pocketbooks of the women and rapidly polishes their shoes for a tip. He bows for each coin he is given, placing his five fingers to his lips indicating that he is hungry. The women chatter with each other. One lady ignores him completely, but the woman seated next to her smiles at his ingenuity in collecting so many bills and a few pieces of change, which he places in a small bag tied to his waist. He stands nearby when we board the bus and waves farewell with his cloth as we begin our journey to the Slave Castles.

The bus is air-conditioned and I sink down into a comfortable cushioned seat next to Mercy. The Ghana radio station broadcasts American music and the female disc jockey relates the local news and events of the day in a clipped English-accented sing-song voice. I am grateful for the three-hour ride to prepare myself for what can only be a grueling and emotional trip.

Chapter 15: Back to Africa – Exploring ...

Our motor trip ends by the azure coastal waters of sandy beachfront where palm trees sway in the gentle breeze. We arrive at the imposing white structure of Elmina Castle—a fort built on the edge of the Atlantic Ocean in 1482 by Portuguese gold traders. When the Dutch captured the fort, they converted its use to the more lucrative slave trade. We traverse a moat covered by a small bridge to enter a passageway into the huge courtyard where captives were brought to wait for days, weeks or even months until there were enough bodies to fill the galleys of the slave ships. Because so many people died in the horrific journey known as the Middle Passage, a full load was necessary to make a trip profitable. From the balcony above the courtyard, traders and crew would review their "stock" and select those who appeared hardy enough to survive the journey. The ones who did not measure up were abandoned—they were the fortunate souls. If African women selected for the sexual pleasure of the European traders became pregnant before departure time they were also kept ashore. Many of the descendants of the African-European offspring still inhabit Cape Coast.

The guide signals us to gather at the mouth of the passageway that will take us to the loading place—the place of no return. There is no electricity because of the power shortage; only the low beam of the guide's flashlight helps us navigate the unfamiliar footing in this cavernous dungeon. Mercy and Akofa, Cheryl and I, mothers and daughters, African and African American—we are two generations, two families and two continents—linked in this symbolic experience. Slowly, carefully we retrace the steps that our ancestors made in the darkness. Akofa cups her hand under my elbow, leading me while Cheryl guides Mercy, their arms entwined. We descend the seemingly endless cobblestone incline curving into the dark emptiness. I feel my way along the cool walls like a child playing blind man's bluff. One thousand people, our guide intones, were jammed into this place at one time. There was no room to move and many died at this place, shackled with iron rings—a few of which remain in place bearing silent and cruel testimony.

Standing by the rocks at the loading area we gaze on the sparkling waters of the Gulf of Guinea. White soapy foam splashes up from the waves crashing against the massive rocks. The beauty of the blue water belies the barbarity and inhumanity of the acts performed here. The incessant roar of the ocean must have drowned out the screams of the people. I try to imagine being loaded onto a boat for an unknown destiny. Cheryl and Mercy, Akofa and I stand together to bear witness. We have come together, transcending time and place, because our children have ventured beyond the confines of their birthplaces to know and care for one another.

Five months after my return from Ghana, I receive an unexpected call from Jerome. "Where are you?" I ask, pleased and surprised to hear from him. I assume that he is calling from Ghana.

"At school, Mama Jones," he replies. "I'm preparing for my master's degree. I'll be up to see you as soon as I get settled."

Again I ask, "Where are you?"

"At Morgan State University in Maryland."

"Where is your wife?"

"She's at home in Ghana. Perhaps she will join me later."

Jerome did come to visit us, as promised, during a vacation visit to Azumah family members in Worcester, Massachusetts. Jerome continues the long established tradition of Africans who study abroad in the United States, other former European colonial countries, and especially the United Kingdom. Eventually Jerome's wife did come to join him and they remained in Maryland where he now teaches.

In December, 1998 Mawuli Azumah made his Boston visit and explored the universities in the area where he might study computer technology. The freezing New England weather was a new experience—as was the magic of gently falling flakes of snow and the resulting hard packed and slippery substance. However, Mawuli quickly acquired adroit balancing skills. He helped Hubey and I select our tree that year: a tall, full fir that reached to the ceiling. It was Mawuli's first Christmas away from home and he missed his family. After the gifts were opened, we called Ghana and passed the phone around the living room so that all of the Joneses could talk with the Azumahs.

Hubey and Steven finally met each other when the Azumahs came to the United States. "When will you come to visit us in the United States, Steven?" I asked during one of our telephone conversations. "When one of your daughters marries," Steven promised me. And so it was a moment of magic and inexpressible joy for me when in June 2000, I spotted Steven pushing a luggage cart through the gate at JFK International Airport with a beaming Mercy walking a few paces behind him. "The original Jones," Steven said on meeting Hubey for the first time. Fulfilling their promise, Steven and Mercy arrived in ample time for Cheryl and Noland's July 1st wedding. Now it was our turn to welcome the Azumahs as family. They stayed with us in New York at 409, but the towering buildings, busy traffic and crowded streets were a bit much for the Azumahs—they were anxious to be in quieter surroundings in Massachusetts. Back in Newton, the Azumahs met with their family and finally met our other Boston-based children, our grandson Alex and our newborn twin granddaughters, Renee and Michael's Julia and Shannon.

On my second trip to the Slave Castles, Steven and Hubey were with Mercy, Akofa, and me. We also visited the castle at Cape Coast which overlooks the fishing village of the same name where Kofi Annan, the first African President of the United Nations was born. Fortunately, we were there when the Fanti fishermen stowed their multi-colored fishing nets and guided their brightly decorated boats to shore to unload the silvery-glimmering, squirming catch. The women fish mongers make their pick, arrange their selections near the shore in plastic tubs placed on ground cloth and call out in loud voices what they have to offer for sale. Mercy makes her selection for our evening meal and I once again get caught up in the frenzy as crowds of shoppers gather round jostling for position to bargain.

When I was leaving to return to the United States, Mercy's mother, the respected elder Queen Mother looked at me intently with her dark eyes sparkling with mischief. "You have all those children in America" she said. "Tanya is *mine.*" It was an endearing and protective message and conveyed to me how precious my daughter was to all the generations of this family. To this day, Mercy and Steven always know where Tanya is assigned during her travels to Ghana. The house that Tanya found as her base when she moved to Accra as a permanent resident had to be checked out by Mercy and Steven to determine the security of the premises. "I am retired Army Colonel Azumah and I will be looking out for Tanya's welfare," Steven warned the building supervisor.

Our families, spanning distance, and generations are joined together. Despite the obstacles imposed to interfere with the continuity of relationships between Africans and African of the diaspora, we have endured, we have prevailed and we have triumphed.

◆ ◆ ◆ ◆ ◆

Family Update

All four of Mercy and Steven Azumah's children have visited our families in Newton on many occasions. Mauwi was with us when terrorists attacked on September 11, 2001. After making sure that our nephew, Kenric, (whose office was on the 64th floor of the first tower to fall) was safe, we called the Azumahs to let them know that their son was safe and sound with us. Mauwi entertained us in South Africa when we visited there, and we went to London to see him receive his master's degree. He now lives in Accra with his wife, Beatrice, and their five children.

Hubey and I attended Dela's wedding. (That was Hubey's first visit to Ghana.) Dela and her husband, Alex, were married at Christ the King Catholic Church in Accra. Tanya also attended the wedding, since her work assignment was in Accra. It was a joyous occasion with the infusion of African dance in the usually sedate formalities that I associate with Catholic religious observances. Following the ceremony, the dancing continued at the lavish banquet held on the expansive grounds of the Army Officers' Club. Alex, Dela and their children still live in Ghana as does Mawuli's family. Dela came to

Chapter 15: Back to Africa – Exploring ...

Boston for a conference in 2007 where she met Tanya's recently-born son, Malik Ibrahim. (Tanya met Malik's dad, Ibrahim, in Ghana and they married in California while Tanya studied for her PhD in sociology at the University of California.)

The following year Steven came to stay with us in Newton for several weeks, making a side trip to Worcester to visit his brother and family there. (Vera also lives in Worcester with her husband and children.) His first stop in the United States, however, was in Charlotte, North Carolina to visit his daughter Akofa, her husband, Ciaus, and their two boys. I knew from Akofa's first visit that she liked the United States so much that she would eventually end up living here, and so it has come to pass. Of course, Hubey and I were in Ghana for Akofa's wedding which was held at the same church where her sister married, Christ the King Catholic Church in Accra. I often think of the Queen Mother, dancing with her granddaughter's new husband, swaying to the beat of the drums in the heat of the afternoon sun as beads of perspiration sprouted on her forehead. A grand lady full of spirit and determination! Queen Mother now lives with, and is cared for, by Mercy who decided to remain in Accra at the family homestead. Mercy's sister is now "acting" Queen Mother.

Mercy was in Newton with us when our daughter, Lauren, married John in Washington, D.C.. We all flew down for the ceremony. Mercy also joined us when our daughter Lisa received her master's degree from the Kennedy School at Harvard University and carried her infant daughter, Sophia, with her to the podium to receive her degree. Lisa's husband, Ken, snapped a photo to commemorate the event.

Akofa called one afternoon to tell me that she had introduced her brother, Kudjo, to her former college roommate and they were communicating via email on a regular basis. Kudjo is now married to Abigale and the father of a baby daughter. They live in Richmond, Virginia—only a three-hour drive from Akofa and her family.

When Akofa told me that another friend of hers from school was coming to Boston from Accra to do part of her medical residency at Brigham and Women's Hospital, I offered to have her stay at our home during those cold winter months. How Cordelia (who is Abigale's older sister) suffered with her first experience with snow. But she survived, and she and her husband, Andrew, and their three children live in Bridgeport, Connecticut where they both serve as physicians on the medical staff of the local hospital.

It is traditional that when a new member comes to the family, one of the female relatives (usually a sister or mother) comes to the home and assists in taking care of the newborn and other children in the family. When Akofa delivered their daughter, Mercy came to help out. Her visit coincided with the marriage of our youngest son, Hamilton to Abim in June 2012. Abim's background extends over two continents and two worlds as well; her father is from Nigeria and her mother was born in the United States. Most of the members of the Azumah family on the east coast attended the wedding. The bonds across the ocean that began with Tanya's stay with the Azumahs have benefitted us all. Our families have shared culture, foods, history and politics spanning several generations.

Kathy with mother, Meme
December, 1957

Left to Right: Best Man Al Mathew, Matron
of Honor Mildred Cohen, Kathy's Mother
Meme Butler, Kathy, Hubey, Hubey's Mother
Dorcus Jones, Hubey's Father Hilma Jones

Kathy, Hubey, Kathy's Aunt Jessie
and cousin Alfred White

The Jones Girls 1982
First Row: Russelle, Mama Dorcus, and Hilda
Second Row: Katherine, Francine, Jane and Kathy

Top Row: Gwendolyn, Meme, Redie, Jessie
Bottom Row: Edna and Mary

2000
Mary and Redie

1978
Newton School Committee

March through Roxbury -1976
Kimberly and Karen Johnson, Lisa and Cheryl
Jones, Tanya Jones on Alice Carew's shoulders,
Hamilton Jones

Giza 1984
Tanya, Cheryl, Hamilton and Kathy on Camels

London 1984
Hubey, Kathy and Ann Neuberger (Nuey)

Kenya 1984
Hair Braider, Cheryl, Kathy and Tanya

London 1984
Cheryl, Hamilton, Kathy and Tanya

Ghana
Azumah School

Ghana
Easter Sunday at Christ the King Church
Kathy and Hubey Jones with
Mercy and Steven Azumah

Ghana 2004
Queen Mother Dancing with
Dela's husband,Alex, at Akofa's Wedding

Ghana 2000
Mercy, Cheryl and Steven

Ghana 2004
Henrietta at Akofa's Wedding

Ghana
Market Women at Henrietta's Shop

Newton 2010
Grandson Malik with his father, Ibrahim

Boston 2012
Daughter-in-law Abim and
Kathy's grandson, Nicholas

Boston 2012
Kathy's Grandsons Nicholas and Malik

Boston 2012 Family Photo
Abim's and Hamilton's Wedding

Epilogue

"Dem Bones Dem Bones Will

Rise Again"

In October of 1991, workers at the construction site on Broadway and Reade Street, in lower Manhattan, were digging the foundation for a 39-story federal building near City Hall. Suddenly, a construction worker stopped his crane. An odd crunching sound caught his ear and he descended from the cab to investigate. Kneeling down to examine the earth, he saw that the sound had come from the metal shovel of his crane scraping against a cluster of bones. Looking closely, the workman recognized the bones as human. Christopher Moore, a reporter who had reviewed old city maps knew what was beneath the site and conferred with the workman. "Yes," the crane operator said, "human skeletal remains have been uncovered—hundreds of them." This was the

Deeper Roots

site, Moore knew, of the eighteenth-century African Burial Ground which was located a mile outside of the city wall, a fortification built to protect the city during the French Indian War. A few days later, Moore called fellow reporters from the New York *Daily News* and the local television program, Fox News. Crews came to the site that night with lights blazing and television cameras rolling in time for a live broadcast on the evening news.

The fact is, the Federal government would have gone ahead with this project had it not been for the fast action of Christopher Moore, a man I can only call a national hero. In response to media reports of this poignant discovery, letters, faxes, and columns from individuals and organizations emphasized the historic significance of the find and called for scientific research on the uncovered evidence. However, it was not easy to stop the building construction. Despite promises made by the General Services Administration to preserve the burial ground, the digging continued. In February 1992 Daniel Pagano, New York City's official archeologist, reported in the New York *Times* that he saw jawbones and arm bones among remains scooped up by a backhoe and twenty skeletons covered by newly-poured concrete. The General Services Administration responded by saying that they had been accidently misinformed about the dimensions of the African Burial Ground.

New York State officials, led by Congressman David Patterson, formed a task force to monitor the area and report any violations of the agreement that ceased excavation at the African Burial Ground site. Mayor David Dinkins, the first black mayor of New York City, also assured protection of the site. After a ceremonial event at the grounds that included traditional African drumming and prayer, forty of the skeletons were exhumed, later

Epilogue

followed by 350 additional remains. Urban archeologists were called in to begin formal excavation and examination of the Africans and African Americans buried there from 1626 through 1794. Since the cemetery was closed in 1794, we know that the remains are some of the earlier Africans brought to New York. In 2003, after DNA analysis and study, the bones were reburied in the same area with the remains facing east, in keeping with Muslim ritual. The African Burial Ground National Monument located on the site was established in 2006.

Some of the findings of the archeologists were disturbing, some were uplifting and all were fascinating. One skeleton was found with a musket ball in her side indicating she had died a violent death. Teeth found at the site had been filed into an hourglass shape—a status symbol indicating people born and raised in Africa. A woman was buried with African beads around her waist and shroud pins fashioned from metal forged in the West African tradition, while others were buried with beads made by a special process originating in the Gold Coast region. Some of the bodies were wrapped in newspaper with hands folded over the chest, conforming to the belief that the spirit would thereby be trapped for the next life.

The most controversial finding, however, concerned one of the wooden caskets marked with an image resembling a heart, similar to the Sankofa of the Ashanti of West Africa. While some historians deduced that the symbol was indeed the Sankofa, other historians argued that the burials actually *predated* the Sankofa symbol since there is no evidence of its existence before a 1927 R.S. Raattray catalog of adinkra symbols. Adinkra art, they posit, is not static; it continues to grow and now includes modern images and commercial logos for soft

317

Deeper Roots

drinks and cars (apparently alongside Akan burial symbols). They further argue that white slave owners could have purchased the coffins, so the image on the coffin lid may have represented the Anglo belief that the heart holds the soul and its ascension to a Christian heaven. Finally, these Africans, the historians suggests, drew on remembered African practices and white American culture to create something new to believe in.

There are, of course, problems with the arguments. First, in Africa the Sankofa symbol would have been displayed on an adinkra cloth and the stamps used to mark the fabric would have been made of wood—two materials that disintegrate over time leaving no evidence centuries later—especially considering that no one was looking for the symbol in the first place. Further, Africans in the diaspora prepared their own for burial (including building and decorating the coffins)—slave owners were rarely involved in the process as indicated by documents. Records found indicating an owner's purchase of a coffin for a slave represent a fraction of a percent of the number of slaves who died in New York. Finally, not all of those buried at the African Burial Ground were born in the New World, some were brought from Africa. If these Africans of the diaspora did indeed fashion something new from remembered African practices, who is to say that the Sankofa symbol was not something that they had actually seen, remembered and made a part of something new? These arguments appeared to me to be more of the same—this time an attempt to "season" the descendants of Africans. It didn't work in the 1600s and it still doesn't work. That straw dog wasn't hunting and it could not detract from the importance of the African Burial Ground.

Epilogue

I thought this to be one of the most important archeological finds relating to Africa/African American life which called upon historians, archeologists, bone specialists, anthropologists and sociologists to pool their knowledge regarding this historic discovery. I was so excited about the work that I went down to Washington D.C. where analysis of the remains was being conducted at Howard University by a team of experts led by Dr. Michael Blakey. I went to visit the lab along with members of the African American Genealogy Association at its Annual Conference in 1995. I already had an idea of how some of those interred at the site died and how they were buried. However, during the visit, I learned about how they lived.

Dr. Blakey told us that his team examined the skeletal remains of over 400 men, women and children of all ages, whose bones and teeth revealed, among other facts, the effects of overwork and poor diet. Deep indentations on large bones could be attributed to excessive muscle strain, which tore the ligaments away from bone. Forty percent of the skeletons were children under fifteen years of age and had rickets, scurvy, and anemia—most of them died of malnutrition. I watched in awe on that autumn afternoon as researchers in lab coats bent over small particles of white weathered bone, using tiny brushes to remove the brownish powdery soil. Each piece of bone was labeled and placed in a protective sleeve. How ironic that the deceased would receive the kind of care that they did not receive while they lived.

This territory near the tip of Manhattan is hallowed ground. These remains are a tangible connection between captured Africans and their descendants in the New World. The captives who left via the Slave Castles of West Africa are connected to these skeletal remains and

319

Deeper Roots

the remains bear testimony to their dismal fate. We know that many stories and bodies remain buried in the foundations of Lower Manhattan (estimated to be between 10,000 and 20,000). Just as we can no longer see the brands or the lash marks on the skin of these people, so too their stories have vanished. Many stories were not passed down, just as the story of my ancestors was not passed down to me. Now black Americans must piece our stories, our history, together—even as archeologists piece the fragments of bone together—to illuminate history for all of us.

"Them bones, them bones" did rise again at a fortuitous time—when scientific inquiry can offer good information about the life of these people, our people.

I share the story of the African Burial Ground because it is the perfect encapsulation of two very important points I have been making throughout this book. First, whatever the meaning or intention of the symbol found on that coffin lid, the Sankofa is unmistakably represented at the memorial site, standing the test of time in a way that fabric and wood cannot. The Sankofa is symbolic of the past and its relevance to the present and future and it urges us to look into our collective past (the bodies *and* the history) in order to chart our future. But the symbol also directs us to respect our living elders, who carry the past and its lessons within their hearts as they continue to do in Ghana.

The second point is borne of the diaspora—unlike the Sankofa. The information we seek does not come easily; often it is a result of unceasing activism. Our history will rarely come to us and if it does, there will be those who wish to subsume it either in the interest of expediency (to build an office building) or keep history static and safe (even as new evidence surfaces). There will be those who

Epilogue

will disparage the accomplishments of our forefathers because their forefathers enslaved them. Just as activists fought to preserve the African Burial Ground and erect a memorial to honor those buried there, family members must search out the truth and lend a voice to those who were not able to speak for themselves—we owe that to our ancestors.

My husband and I have lived a life of activism, and I imagine that we will continue to do so until we draw our last breath.

71240957R00223

Made in the USA
Columbia, SC
23 May 2017